THE IRISH TIMES

Nealon's Guide
to the 30th Dáil & 23rd Seanad

Edited by
Stephen Collins

Gill & Macmillan

Gill & Macmillan Ltd
Hume Avenue
Park West
Dublin 12
with associated companies throughout the world
www.gillmacmillan.ie

© The Irish Times/Gill & Macmillan 2007
978 7171 4272 9
Original design concept by Elizabeth Fitz-Simon
Print origination by Carole Lynch
Index compiled by Cover to Cover
Printed by Butler & Tanner, Frome, Somerset

*The paper used in this book is made from the wood pulp of managed forests.
For every tree felled, at least one tree is planted, thereby renewing natural resources.*

A catalogue record is available for this book
from the British Library.

1 3 5 4 2

Contents

Acknowledgments

This *Nealon's Guide to the Dáil and Seanad* is the 11th in the series started by Ted Nealon after the 1973 general election. It is now produced by *The Irish Times* in conjunction with Gill & Macmillan. The Guide to the 30th Dáil contains more information than ever, with the inclusion of the Northern Ireland Assembly results and the membership of the Northern Executive.

As before, the key elements of the *Nealon's Guide* are the full counts in all 43 Dáil constituencies and the biographies and contact details of all 166 deputies. Biographies of all 60 members of Seanad Éireann are also included.

First of all, I would like to thank Joe Joyce and acknowledge his huge contribution to the production of this *Nealon's Guide*. He contributed to all aspects of the publication and remained calm when at times it appeared that the task would overwhelm us. I would also like to thank Kieran Fagan for his considerable contribution to the Guide and his sense of humour which helped to lighten the task.

Thanks also to Mick Maguire in the systems department of *The Irish Times*, who processed the figures without fuss, and to Peter Thursfield, the Picture Editor, and the Photographic Department of *The Irish Times* for supplying the photographs.

Thanks to the press offices of all the political parties, particularly Sinead McGovern of Fianna Fáil, Joanne Lonergan and Anne Talbot of Fine Gael, Dermot O'Gara of the Labour Party, Gerry Mullins of the Green Party, Shaun Tracey of Sinn Féin, and Paul McAuliffe of the Progressive Democrats for their assistance. Thanks also to Kieran Coughlan, Clerk of the Dáil, and his staff, the Franchise Section and press office in the Department of the Environment, the offices of the European Parliament and European Commission and the First Minister and Deputy First Minister of Northern Ireland, for their help.

Special thanks are due to Dermot Quinn who suggested improvements in one of the most important tables in the book, General Elections 1923 to 2007. The new table is designed to show the rise and fall in the fortunes of smaller parties as well as those of the big parties who have survived for the whole period.

A particular word of thanks to Aoileann O'Donnell of Gill & Macmillan, for her active involvement in the project and her diligence in ensuring that deadlines were met. Thanks also to Fergal Tobin, Nicki Howard and Emer Ryan.

Thanks also to all those members of the Dáil and Seanad who cooperated with this project and supplied their biographical details and photographs, thus helping to ensure that the *Nealon Guide* continues to be the standard reference work on Irish election results.

STEPHEN COLLINS
August 2007

Foreword

An Taoiseach, Mr Bertie Ahern TD

I congratulate the publishers, Gill & Macmillan, and the *Irish Times* team for publishing the 11th in the series of *Nealon's Guide to the Dáil and Seanad*. For many years now *The Irish Times* has been regarded as the newspaper of record; their insistence on accuracy continues in this publication and the guide makes another valuable contribution to the annals of Ireland's reference and record. This new collaboration ensures that the long-established and essential Irish political directory will live on for many years to come. Of course we owe a special tribute to its originator, Ted Nealon, for its inception over thirty years ago. This year's edition, which is wonderfully compiled, will, I am sure, continue to be compulsory reading for politicians, party strategists, political journalists and all those studying the political system today, and in the future.

Election 2007 has delivered a new and exciting political landscape. It reflects a desire for stability, reform, and greater appreciation of the world we live in today, and suggests an awareness of responsibility in relation to a desire for continued political priority in the area of environmental protection and planning.

In dealing with the result of the election, the overriding consideration in my mind was to try and bring together a government that would truly reflect this new determination. I wanted to establish a government of ideas, energy and experience. A government that would have both a sense of purpose and the capacity to take Ireland forward. In bringing together this coalition I believe that, collectively, we can provide the stable government that is required to implement the strong and ambitious Programme for Government that we have agreed.

Ireland stands as a strong economy in a global marketplace. We enjoy the full employment, the good wages and the promising opportunities of which the generations that secured our independence, and who built our democracy, could only dream. But it is clear that we are entering a period of more challenging economic conditions. Now our duty is to secure our prosperity and to use it to build a better Ireland. Success cannot be assumed, and together with our new partners in government, we will continue to build upon the foundations already laid, for a stronger and fairer Ireland.

In doing so, we look forward to achieving with the social partners the challenging goals we agreed in *Towards 2016*. I also look forward to leading the public service into a new phase of modernisation and change for the benefit of all our people. A sound economy is the essential bedrock of social progress. It is the foundation for all our ambitions — in health, enterprise, welfare and education.

During the past number of months, attention has understandably been focused on the course of the general election. In the future, I believe, a far greater regard will be given by history to the new and glad departure in the relations between unionist and nationalist and between North and South on this island. We have recently witnessed political collaborations which only a few years ago would have seemed not just improbable, but impossible.

Today, we live in an Ireland of unprecedented peace and prosperity. This has not happened by chance. Through every single day of the past decade many people have worked hard for the cause of peace. There now exists between British and Irish, nationalist and unionist, an agreed consensus on our shared future. It is not an end of history, but it is a new beginning. Much work lies ahead to shape and to strengthen that shared and better future. In doing so, we can begin to put the divisions of the past permanently behind us. All of the island of Ireland can be a place of peace and of promise.

The election campaign was certainly an exciting one for journalists and spectators alike. Whilst Ireland is a country of success and achievement, it is also a country facing new challenges, and emerging issues. Some of these issues were debated in the election campaign, many were not. Notwithstanding that fact, the Irish electorate has established, beyond doubt, that it is not prepared to take long-term decisions based on short-term election campaigns. Rather, this election proved that the substantial changes that have occurred in this country over the last ten years have not been lost on the individual.

Progress and development are something that people have come to expect and they want it to continue into the future. Politics is about the individual. Irish people greatly value their vote and recognise that it has real implications for every aspect of their lives. I believe that political stability was a key determinant in this election. Re-election to government is not the winning prize for achievement, but it is an acknowledgement of capability, and the capacity to deliver on commitments. We intend to work hard over the next five years to address the existing, as well as the new, issues on our agenda.

In total there are 49 new TDs, which means that almost a third (29.5%) of the Deputies today were not in the previous Dáil. This is particularly significant when benchmarked against recent previous elections. Many observe that politics is a profession, which holds little appeal to those who have not been born into a political party or come from a particular party tradition. It is a welcome fact that this is no longer the case. It is necessary for the body politic to attract new people with new ideas and new vision. In this election many talented people were willing to see beyond the negative manner in which this profession is sometimes portrayed, and were prepared to put themselves forward to make a contribution to Irish public life.

In addition to the many new faces in the Dáil, the Houses of the Oireachtas are currently engaged in educating the public about the role of the legislature generally. This is a worthwhile and necessary exercise, and I believe everyone who is involved in politics can and should play a role. It is our responsibility to earn respect as legislators, and to do all that we can to ensure that we are generating a transparent accessible legislature that the public is confident will debate and deliver the foundations to deal with the ever-changing society that we live in today.

As I said in my acceptance speech in Dáil Éireann, I am privileged and honoured to have been voted Taoiseach by the Oireachtas for a third successive term. I have many ambitions for the development of this country. I intend to put all my energies into building on the progress we have made in recent years, to deliver the services and society that modern Ireland is entitled to expect. The public expects its politicians and political parties to work as hard as they do, to give the commitment they give, day in and day out, to listen to its concerns, and to take the necessary steps to deliver change. As politicians we will continue to campaign for people's confidence, and as parties in government we will continue to deliver the changes Ireland expects and needs.

Bertie Ahern

The Election Background

Stephen Collins

The election of 2007 was one of the most exciting and unpredictable contests for decades. It was full of drama and controversy, and the fortunes of all the parties fluctuated through the campaign. In the end, Bertie Ahern won the Taoiseach's office for the third successive time. It was a hugely impressive achievement but the contest was, in the words of the Duke of Wellington after Waterloo, 'a damn close-run thing'.

Mr Ahern made it clear from the very beginning of the 29th Dáil, in June 2002, that he intended to run a full five-year term, and he did exactly that. Nobody was under any illusion that he would cut and run to the country before May 2007, but that understanding turned it into the longest election campaign in the history of the state. All of the parties and the candidates were in full campaign mode for months before the election was actually called.

The long run-in gave all the parties plenty of time to prepare their strategy and, unlike the previous election, there was a clear alternative on offer in 2007. Fine Gael and Labour had decided early in the life of the 29th Dáil that the only chance they had of breaking Fianna Fáil's near monopoly on power was to fight a joint campaign offering the voters an alternative government.

The big ace up the sleeve of the incumbent Fianna Fáil–Progressive Democrat coalition was that the Celtic Tiger economy continued to boom for most of the 2002–07 period,

even if it became increasingly reliant on the domestic construction sector rather than manufacturing exports. The Opposition was always going to face an uphill battle trying to persuade voters to change horses as long as the boom continued, but the Opposition parties felt that there was a genuine mood for change among a significant segment of the electorate.

The election of 2002 saw Fianna Fáil winning 81 seats and the PDs doubling their Dáil representation to eight. That gave the two parties a comfortable majority between them. One source of hope for the Opposition was that the election victory of 2002 had been bought at a price. During the campaign, the Taoiseach and his Minister for Finance, Charlie McCreevy, pledged that 'no cutbacks, secret or otherwise' were being planned to deal with the economic slowdown that gripped the world economy in late 2001.

Once Fianna Fáil and the PDs were back in government, however, curbs on public spending were immediately introduced. While this prompt action helped to keep the economy on track, it damaged Fianna Fáil's credibility to such an extent that in 2004 the party suffered the worst European and local election results in its history. It was a remarkable turnaround in two years, particularly as the economy continued to surge ahead.

After the humiliating loss of more than 20 seats in 2002, Fine Gael elected a new leader, Enda Kenny, and he set about rebuilding the party in a deliberate fashion. Pat Rabbitte was elected as the new Labour leader on the basis of his declared hostility to doing any kind of deal with Fianna Fáil. The 2004 local and European election results persuaded both men that they would have a real chance of winning power if they came together to offer the country an alternative. In 2005, Mr Rabbitte got the backing of a Labour conference for such a strategy, and it became clear that there was going to be a real contest.

Mr Ahern's reaction to the mid-term reverse was to send his flamboyant, controversial

Minister for Finance, Charlie McCreevy, to Brussels as Ireland's EU Commissioner, and to replace him with Brian Cowen, who had been in Foreign Affairs for the previous five years. Mr Ahern also retired some senior Ministers and promoted Mary Hanafin and Willie O'Dea to the cabinet. On the PD side of the coalition, Mary Harney moved from Enterprise and Employment, after seven years, to take over the enormously difficult portfolio of Health. Michael McDowell remained in Justice where he had taken on a range of reform projects, as well as proving a combative opponent to Sinn Féin in the Northern talks process.

A shift in emphasis in budgetary strategy emerged in Mr Cowen's first budget, with a greater focus on the lower paid and the elderly. Mr Ahern publicly described himself as a socialist and invited Fr Seán Healy, campaigner for the underprivileged, to address the Fianna Fáil parliamentary party.

When, in early 2005, the opinion polls showed the party recovering most of its lost ground, it appeared that the corner had been turned and that Fianna Fáil would be able to power its way to the following election. However, the loss of two by-elections, in Meath and Kildare North, in 2005, was another warning to Mr Ahern that Fianna Fáil still had a lot of ground to make up. To prove the point, the party's poll ratings began to slip again.

The Taoiseach's persistence in his quest for a settlement in the North, despite a series of setbacks, paid off in the end with the decision of Ian Paisley and the DUP in early 2007 to enter a power-sharing executive with Sinn Féin. To cap this triumph, the date for the establishment of the executive was fixed for May of 2007, which was clearly going to coincide with the timing of the election campaign. Mr Ahern had shown the same dogged persistence in his pursuit of agreement among the twenty-five nations of the EU on a new constitutional treaty, during the Irish presidency of 2004.

Mr Ahern's personal finances became a critical issue for himself and his party in September 2006, with the disclosure in *The*

Irish Times that he had received between €50,000 and €100,000 from business people for his personal use while he was Minister for Finance in 1993/1994. The issue was being investigated by the Mahon Tribunal and there was a huge controversy when the information came into the public domain. In a television interview, Mr Ahern maintained that the money had been provided by friends as a 'dig-out' for him following his marriage separation.

The astonishing feature of the controversy was that after weeks of intense media focus and debates in the Dáil on the issue of standards in public office, the first measurement of public opinion in an *Irish Times*/TNS MRBI opinion poll showed a dramatic increase in support for Fianna Fáil. It was an ominous signal for the Opposition parties who were unnerved for the remainder of the year.

By early 2007, the Government had staked out its ground for the contest. The 2007 budget was followed by the €84 billion National Development Plan, with a series of announcements about individual projects due to be rolled out by individual Ministers. While Fianna Fáil was in confident mode, the junior coalition partner, the Progressive Democrats, were in a very different state.

There was dissent within the PDs during the summer of 2006 over whether the Tánaiste, Mary Harney, should continue as party leader until the election. She had been party leader for thirteen years and had given indications that she intended to step down. The Minister for Justice, Michael McDowell, had indicated his desire to take over but there was confusion about what would happen. Ms Harney did call it a day as party leader in September and was succeeded by Mr McDowell.

He was immediately landed with the task of trying to cope with the fall-out from the Ahern payments controversy. Having initially supported the Taoiseach and then called on him to answer questions, Mr McDowell ultimately backed Mr Ahern on condition that new legislation to cover similar incidents would be produced by the coalition.

The PDs were in obvious difficulty in advance of the election because of the simple fact that a rise in the Fine Gael vote, which by then appeared inevitable, would put the squeeze on them. The outlook for the other smaller parties looked much rosier. With the issue of global warming dominating the international news from the beginning of 2007 and opinion polls showing its vote rising, it appeared that the Green Party's hour had finally come round. The party expressed a preference for joining a rainbow coalition of Fine Gael and Labour, but pointedly refused to rule out coalition with Fianna Fáil, although the party leader, Trevor Sargent, said that he would resign rather than lead his party into such a coalition.

The outlook for Sinn Féin also appeared good. The party had done well in the local elections of 2004 and even better in the European elections, with Mary Lou McDonald winning a seat in Dublin and Bairbre de Brún winning a seat in Northern Ireland. While polls showed the party vote dropping in the Republic, after the failure to reach agreement on power sharing in 2005, it appeared to be rising again in the first months of 2007 as a power-sharing agreement began to look likely.

All the parties had national conferences in the spring of 2007. Labour kicked off the season with the surprise commitment by party leader Pat Rabbitte to cut the lower rate of income tax to 18 per cent. The PDs followed with a range of tax-cutting commitments, including a big reform of stamp duty. Fine Gael leader Enda Kenny announced a contract with the Irish people and gave five specific commitments, including 2,400 new hospital beds. He promised that, if elected Taoiseach, he would step down if he failed to deliver.

At the Fianna Fáil Ard-Fheis, the Taoiseach capped all the promises made by the other parties with a range of proposed tax cuts and spending commitments under the theme 'Now, The Next Steps'. As well as cutting the higher and lower rates of tax, Mr Ahern also announced a halving of the PRSI rate to 2 per cent and the abolition of the ceiling on earnings. By the end of the party conference

season at Easter, all the parties had effectively announced their election manifestos and the only thing left was the announcement of the date itself.

The manner in which the election was called caught almost everybody by surprise and generated the first big controversy of the campaign. The Taoiseach travelled to Áras an Uachtaráin very early on the morning of Sunday, 29 April, and asked President McAleese for a dissolution, before she flew off to the United States on an official visit. At his press conference later in the day to launch the Fianna Fáil campaign, Mr Ahern made a short statement and refused to take any questions.

The timing of the dissolution of the 29th Dáil generated a political and media frenzy. The Mahon Tribunal was due to resume the following day with an opening statement about Mr Ahern's personal finances. The newspapers that same weekend carried detailed reports about the complex financial dealings surrounding his decision first to rent and then to buy the house at Beresford Road, Drumcondra, where he still lives, from a Manchester-based businessman, Micheál Wall.

One of the details revealed in the media was that Mr Wall had handed Mr Ahern a briefcase containing stg£30,000 in cash which was first stored in a safe in Mr Ahern's constituency office and then lodged in a bank in O'Connell Street in Dublin. When the Mahon Tribunal met the following day, proceedings were adjourned until immediately after the election. The Taoiseach's financial affairs dominated the first week of the campaign and all of the parties found it impossible to get the media to focus on their manifestos.

At the daily media campaign briefing, Fianna Fáil Ministers vainly tried to get the focus on to the economy. The Minister for Finance, Brian Cowen, made a tongue-in-cheek remark about 'slowly roasting the Opposition on the barbie', but he found it impossible to get an economic debate going during that first week. The launch of the Fianna Fáil manifesto was again dominated by the

The Election Background

Taoiseach's personal finances. Most of the key manifesto pledges had already been announced and the only significant addition was a pledge to abolish stamp duty on houses for first-time buyers.

By contrast, Fine Gael got off to a good start, promoting its 'Contract for a Better Ireland'. The party mounted a fast-moving campaign with a series of publicity stunts designed to focus attention on the party's core issue in the campaign — the state of the public services and, particularly, the health service. The Fine Gael strategy was to keep the debate on health, where it felt it could score, and away from the economy on which the Government was strong.

Enda Kenny toured the country with an upbeat, confident campaign that gave his party organisation the confidence that victory was at least possible. It represented a big change from the previous campaign in 2002. For the first half of the campaign, it also marked a contrast to Bertie Ahern's more muted performance. With his personal finances dominating the headlines, the Taoiseach appeared to be in real trouble at the end of the first week.

Two things then happened which had a profound influence on the final outcome. The first was that the PDs, unnerved by the Taoiseach's problems, threatened to pull out of office in the middle of the campaign. Mr McDowell pulled back from the brink but insisted that, before the election, Mr Ahern would have to make a full statement about his finances.

On the same day that this drama came to a head, the three most powerful Fianna Fáil Ministers, Brian Cowen, Micheál Martin and Dermot Ahern, postponed a scheduled press conference and devised a strategy to deal with the problem. At the delayed press conference, Mr Cowen announced that, at some stage in the campaign, Mr Ahern would make a statement about his finances.

The decision to confront the issue gradually turned the campaign around for Fianna Fáil. With the ending of the media saturation coverage of Mr Ahern's finances, economic issues gradually came to the fore. The party's campaign was also helped by the Taoiseach's high-profile involvement in three major events that reinforced his image as a statesman. The first was the formal establishment of a power-sharing executive at Stormont; the second was a meeting between Mr Ahern and the North's new First Minister, Ian Paisley, at the Battle of the Boyne site; and the third was an address by Mr Ahern to MPs and members of the House of Lords at Westminster.

The public backing for Mr Ahern by the British Prime Minister, Tony Blair, in a Fianna Fáil party political broadcast, reinforced the Taoiseach's image. The Opposition parties were furious at what they regarded as direct interference in the politics of the Irish Republic by the British Prime Minister, but they declined to make an issue out of it for fear of appearing petty.

With his three big events behind him and the economy beginning to feature as a big issue, the Taoiseach went into his television debate with Enda Kenny in a confident mood, a week before the election. While the Fine Gael leader performed reasonably well in the debate, Mr Ahern proved the master of detail and he effectively threw doubt on his opponent's mastery of his brief. The performance buoyed up Fianna Fáil for the final weekend of the campaign, and the party pulled out all the stops in the final days.

The television debate between the four smaller party leaders had an equally dramatic impact. The PD leader, Michael McDowell, took on the Sinn Féin president, Gerry Adams, tackling him about the Northern Bank robbery and republican involvement in Colombia. Mr McDowell also needled Labour leader Pat Rabbitte and Green Party leader Trevor Sargent, warning that any rainbow coalition in which they would be involved would represent 'the left, the hard left and the leftovers'.

A TNS MRBI poll conducted for *The Irish Times* after the two debates showed the momentum shifting to Fianna Fáil in the final days of the campaign. While the gains made by Fine Gael since the beginning of the year appeared to be holding, Labour remained becalmed, the Greens and Sinn Féin were in reasonable shape, but the PDs were headed for disaster.

When the votes were counted on 25 May, the message of the poll was borne out in remarkable fashion. The Fianna Fáil vote was slightly up on 2002 and, while the party's seat total dropped back to 78, it was still in pole position to form a government. The PDs were almost wiped out, losing six of their eight seats, with one of the fallen being the party leader, Michael McDowell. Paradoxically, the two parties targeted by Mr McDowell in the course of the campaign, the Greens and Sinn Féin, also suffered badly. The Greens managed to hold their six seats, but only just, and the party vote was considerably lower than the polls had been predicting.

For Sinn Féin, the result was worse. Instead of doubling its number of seats to ten, as had been widely predicted, the party actually came back with one seat fewer than it had in the 29th Dáil. It was a stunning reverse, particularly as expected seat gains in the two Donegal constituencies and in Dublin were regarded as vital to give the parliamentary party an infusion of young talented new TDs.

The main Opposition party, Fine Gael, had a very good election, gaining 20 seats to come back with 51 TDs. It was the biggest-ever seat gain in a Dáil where the total number of seats had not been increased. The problem was that Labour failed to make any gains and came back with 20 seats, exactly the same number as it had won in 2002 when the Ceann Comhairle's position was excluded. The alternative government of Fine Gael, Labour and the Greens had 77 seats, just three less than the 80 won by the outgoing coalition of Fianna Fáil and the PDs. Those three seats were the difference between Government and Opposition.

The turnout in the election, at 68 per cent, up 5 per cent on 2002, showed a welcome reversal of the downward trend that had been in evidence at every successive election since 1987. The long-overdue attempt to clean up the electoral register certainly had something to do with it, but the keenness of the contest promoted a renewed interest in politics.

While Enda Kenny maintained that a Fine Gael-led government was possible, the combination of parties and Independents required to win office never looked likely. Bertie Ahern was in a strong position to form his third government in a row, but he went about it in a remarkable way. Initially he said that he would favour a deal with the PDs and like-minded Independents, which would give him a bare Dáil majority, similar to that which he had achieved in 1997. Contacts were made and negotiations begun in the days after the election.

With everything falling into place for a third term, Mr Ahern then made the surprise move of offering to negotiate with the Greens as well. After a week of talks, a breakdown, and a resumption, the Greens signed up to a Programme for Government with Fianna Fáil and the PDs. The Green negotiators freely accepted that they got very little in policy terms, beyond the commitments already made on Green issues in the Fianna Fáil manifesto. They also had to accept the continuation of the PD policy on hospital co-location, which was that party's bottom line in the talks.

What the Greens did get was two cabinet positions and one junior ministry. The offer of serious jobs in government swung the deal, which was accepted by an overwhelming vote of a special party conference. Mr Sargent resigned as party leader but made it clear that he would be accepting a junior ministry.

When the Dáil resumed on 24 June, Bertie Ahern was elected Taoiseach by 89 votes to 75. He was supported by the Greens, the PDs and four Independents, Jackie Healy Rae, Finian McGrath, Michael Lowry and Beverley Flynn, all of whom announced that they had deals with him.

It was the first time that Fianna Fáil had entered a three-party coalition and the first time that the Greens had participated in government. They got two powerful Departments, with John Gormley becoming Minister for the Environment, Heritage and Local Government, and Eamon Ryan Minister for Energy and Communications.

By underpinning the Government with four legs, Mr Ahern ensured a remarkable degree of security for himself. He put himself in the position of having a secure majority, even if either of his coalition partners decides to withdraw during the lifetime of the 30th Dáil. By bringing in a party not strictly necessary for the numbers, he has conducted a new experiment in Irish politics.

HOUSES OF THE OIREACHTAS
Address
Leinster House, Kildare Street, Dublin 2

Switchboard
Dáil Éireann (01) 618 3333; From outside Dublin 1890 337 889
Seanad Éireann (01) 618 3111. From outside Dublin 1890 732 623

Email: The email address for deputies and senators follows the convention: firstname.surname@oireachtas.ie. Ministers and Ministers of State have individual email addresses, but some deputies and senators use their own email address and some may opt not to use the address provided for them by the Houses of the Oireachtas.

KEY TO ABBREVIATIONS
FF	Fianna Fáil
FG	Fine Gael
Lab	Labour
PD	Progressive Democrats
GP	Green Party
SF	Sinn Féin
SWP	Socialist Workers' Party
CSP	Christian Solidarity Party
WP	Workers' Party
Ind	Independent
*	Outgoing

The Campaign

Miriam Lord

Bertie Ahern always said he wouldn't call a snap election. From the time he took office in 2002, he insisted that his administration would run its full term and go to the country sometime in the summer of 2007.

The Taoiseach was true to his word. He fixed the date for late May but, in typical fashion, still managed to pull off a surprise in the process.

As Ireland slept on the morning of 29 April, contact was made with selected media outlets, advising them that it would be worth their while to get to Áras an Uachtaráin before breakfast. Drowsy journalists and camera crews raced to the Phoenix Park, where they recorded an uncommunicative Taoiseach scuttling into the Áras in order to catch the President before she left for a flight to America. Mrs McAleese duly dissolved the 29th Dáil, whereupon a sheepish looking Bertie Ahern ducked back into his Mercedes and shot off at speed.

It seemed an oddly furtive way to end his second successful term in power, and a most peculiar beginning to his campaign to achieve a third.

Strong rumours that the long, phoney war was about to end had hit political circles late on Saturday night. When Mrs McAleese signed the order just after 8 a.m., Opposition parties were already at full throttle in their campaign headquarters.

In contrast, Fianna Fáil's reaction to the news was curiously low-key and sluggish.

If Bertie held the advantage of firing the opening shots at a time of his choosing, it wasn't in the game plan that he should aim at his foot.

The rather frantic manner of his early-morning flit to the Park was followed by a disastrous first day. The atmosphere in Fianna Fáil Mission Control was subdued and edgy. Across the city, as the main Opposition leaders got stuck into the fight, the Taoiseach marked his campaign launch by mumbling a dull statement to the media and refusing to take questions.
Despite the lame excuses he would trot out in the following weeks, most observers fathomed that there was only one reason for the strange events of that Sunday: The Mahon Tribunal.

Had Bertie Ahern not sought a last-gasp Dáil dissolution from the President before she left the country, a Tribunal enquiring into certain planning matters and payments to politicians would have reconvened for business the following day. On the second morning of his election campaign, unusual aspects of his personal financial dealings when he was Minister for Finance in the early 1990s would have been put on the public record.

There would have been questions raised about large bank deposits seemingly inconsistent with his income. He would have been required to expand on his explanations that some of this money came from unsolicited cash 'dig-outs' from friends in Dublin, and a surprise 'whip-around' for him by businessmen in a Manchester hotel where he had given an after-dinner speech on the Irish economy.

These embarrassing questions had first arisen after *The Irish Times* published a story in September of 2006, revealing that the Tribunal was investigating a number of payments to Mr Ahern. Under intense pressure to explain, and conscious that his PD coalition partners needed reassurance, the Taoiseach went on the six o'clock news

and bared his soul to the nation. Voice cracking with emotion, he told how his friends had rallied around him financially following the break-up of his marriage, when he had found it difficult to make ends meet. The public reaction was largely one of compassion and understanding.

For a brief period, after more detail emerged and his PD coalition partners began to wobble, it looked like Bertie's long hold on the reins of power might loosen earlier than planned. But after much soul searching the PDs backed off, Fianna Fáil rowed in behind its leader, the public decided that the payments affair was not a resigning matter, the Opposition's popularity went down in the opinion polls and Bertie Ahern's personal rating rose. Having learned that it was neither popular nor profitable for them to make a fuss about the Taoiseach's puzzling financial history, the Opposition steered clear of further involvement in the controversy.

The episode would become known nationally as Bertiegate, and introduced a gleeful public to two of the Taoiseach's generous whip-around friends — Paddy the Plasterer and Micheál 'didn't eat the dinner' Wall.

And so the long build-up resumed. Pre-election think-ins and conferences were organised to keep the troops motivated. Fine Gael leader Enda Kenny and Labour leader Pat Rabbitte pushed their 'Alliance for Change'. Trevor Sargent resolutely refused to be drawn on the Green Party's intentions, other than to say that the party was keeping its options open. The two main parties said that they wouldn't do business with Sinn Féin.

As the countdown dragged on, Deputy Kenny embarked on a series of pre-election rallies around the country. He had taken on a party in shock after its severe mauling at the polls in 2002, and, to no small amount of derision, he promised to 'electrify it'. While his Dáil performances were often unimpressive, his energetic commitment to rebuilding a shattered Fine Gael began to pay dividends. From a no-hope situation five years earlier, the party grew in confidence under his leadership. An increasingly bullish membership suddenly began to believe they were contenders.

Another worrying aspect for Bertie Ahern — until then, the unchallenged Man of the People when it came to electioneering — was the fact that Enda Kenny liked campaigning, and was every bit as shameless as his illustrious rival when it came to kissing babies and pressing the flesh.

Fianna Fáil wasn't doing well in the opinion polls. At a party think-in as far back as September 2006, deputy leader Brian Cowen admitted that the Government had 'failed to articulate' its achievements to the voters. Meanwhile, the Opposition pounded away at the state of the health service, the problem of traffic gridlock and inadequate public transport and the increase in violent gangland crime. Overspend embarrassments such as the PPARS computer system and the useless e-voting machines were mentioned at every opportunity.

The Dáil was not a happy place for Bertie. However, once he got over his Tuesday and Wednesday appearances, he had the rest of the week to travel around the country, cutting ribbons, unveiling plaques and laying the foundations for 'The Next Step'.

The polls gave heart to the Alliance for Change, and panic attacks to coalition deputies. Jittery Government backbenchers became increasingly disconsolate as the figures showed the alternative coalition nudging ahead. But the Taoiseach insisted that he would not cut and run, while Finance Minister Cowen steadied the ship and stressed that prudent management of the economy was the only way to go.

Labour was first out of the blocks at its pre-election conference, with a promise to cut the standard rate of tax by 2 per cent as part of a series of five election pledges. Fine Gael talked about reforming stamp duty on house purchases. Bertie dismissed the moves as an attempt to buy votes. The Opposition dangled more promises and policy documents before an interested electorate. The Government rolled out Séamus Brennan.

At a special press conference, the Minister for Social Welfare was dispatched to underline the Government's commitment to prudence. His colleagues would not be indulging either in 'alarming auction politics' which would 'bankrupt' the country or in a 'vast splurge' of promises. This approach was 'debasing politics'.

Four days later, the Taoiseach was on his feet delivering the keynote address at Fianna Fáil's pre-election Ard-Fheis. With the campaign looming, prudence was suddenly and shamelessly sidelined. In a giveaway speech, he made a total of 53 promises. Fine Gael's turn came the following week. Instead of trying to trump the Taoiseach's impressive list, Enda Kenny came armed with his Contract for Ireland. If the people bought into it, he would implement all the pledges set out in his contract. If he didn't, he would fall on his sword. A novel idea in Irish politics, where resignation sets in only when the barman refuses to pull any more pints.

At this stage, all the parties were ready to roll. All that remained was for Bertie to pull the plug. Tensions rose in Leinster House as deputies from all sides speculated on a possible date. Many contributing factors were discussed — including a big rugby match one weekend, an international golf tournament on another and the date President McAleese was due to leave the country.

Finally, and with politicians in a state of nervous collapse and barely able to function, the Taoiseach embarked on his Sunday-morning surprise trip to the Park and put them out of their misery.

The Progressive Democrats, with new leader and Tánaiste Michael McDowell, launched their campaign later that morning. Their slogan was an optimistic 'from good to great'. Little did they know that, at the end of the election, they would be neither good nor great, but almost gone.

Enda Kenny caught the first flight from Knock to make his party's midday launch, punching the air as he stepped from his car. From then until polling day, whenever he saw an open door with a camera or a crowd

on the other side, he jumped through it with his fist aloft. This was to bolster the image he wanted to project of a vigorous and dynamic young leader.

A rather miffed Bertie Ahern was not averse to pointing out, when reminded of Enda's exploits in climbing Mount Kilimanjaro or cycling around the Ring of Kerry, that he was actually a few months younger than the Fine Gael leader.

Sinn Féin and the Greens also held launches on Super Sunday, but they got scant attention. The start of the campaign was dominated by fresh revelations in the Bertiegate saga. There followed a torrid couple of weeks for the Taoiseach on the campaign trail, where he was dogged by reporters demanding answers as he refused to give them. Fianna Fáil's carefully planned manifesto launch was hijacked by veteran journalist Vincent Browne, who used the event to fire relentless questions at Bertie on the inconsistencies in his explanations about his financial dealings. To make matters worse, when director of elections, P.J. Mara, tried discreetly to bring the interrogation to a close, Browne reminded him how his former boss, Charlie Haughey, had once tried to stop him from asking awkward questions too.

Suddenly the Progressive Democrats remembered that they traded on the image of being the coalition's moral watchdog. During a fraught weekend, the party top brass held secret meetings and debated whether or not to withdraw support from Fianna Fáil. After much farcical huffing and puffing, Michael McDowell announced at a shambolic press conference that his party was staying put.

Once bitten, the main Opposition parties largely ignored the controversy and tried to concentrate on 'the issues'. Pat Rabbitte spoke at length on them, as did the Fine Gael election team at daily briefings, while Enda Kenny continued around the country kissing babies and punching the air like a man possessed. He got a lot of favourable coverage.

There was a diverting sideshow when the other party leaders had their TV debate. It was a lively spectacle, enlivened by Pat

Rabbite's description of Michael McDowell as 'a menopausal Paris Hilton'. But that's all it was: a sideshow.

In the end, photogenic Enda had to stop grandstanding and return to Dublin to face Taoiseach Ahern in a live debate. In the closing weeks of the campaign, issues had begun to fade into the background as the battle between Fianna Fáil and Fine Gael, and more specifically, Bertie Ahern and Enda Kenny, came to the fore.

Enda traded on his energy. Bertie played the statesman. The Fine Gael leader outpaced him and out-kissed him on the hustings, notching up the feel-good photo ops. But the Taoiseach welcomed Ian Paisley to Dublin on an historic morning at Farmleigh House; he addressed the joint houses of Parliament in Westminster in another historic milestone; then he accepted the gift of a musket from Dr Paisley at the Battle of the Boyne site in Meath, to complete his hat-trick of history.

The two leaders squared up to each other on TV in what was seen as a make-or-break encounter. With the economy the main battleground, Deputy Kenny held his own, but he was outclassed by the Taoiseach, who came across to voters as more competent and authoritative. At this point, public opinion began to shift back towards the Government. Led by Finance Minister Cowen, team Fianna Fáil pointed to the success of the national economy, and then played the stability card.

They pointed to Bertie — ten years of prosperity under his stewardship, and they pointed to Enda — very nice chap, but untried and tested. Would you be willing to take a chance on him?

Fine Gael fell in the polls. Fianna Fáil rallied. 'Ten more years!' shouted Bertie's supporters. 'Dream on, baby!' scoffed Enda.

By election day, the pundits were falling back on the old reliable 'too close to call' gambit. But next morning, exit-poll results pointed to another Fianna Fáil win. And so it was, tribunal travails and Government fatigue notwithstanding, that Bertie Ahern headed for a third term.

He says he slept through results day, waking only at teatime. With another successful campaign to add to his achievements, he posed for pictures with his newborn twin grandsons, Rocco and Jay. Out on the hustings, he had fielded more questions about the tiny twins than he had about running the country.

After an excellent performance, Enda Kenny clung to the mathematical possibility that he might still become Taoiseach, but the sums were never going to add up. 'I expect people were concerned about the fragilities of the economy,' mused Pat Rabbitte. On the night of the count, Michael McDowell resigned as leader of the PDs and left politics, having lost his seat. Sinn Féin failed to make the gains it had been hoping for, saying that its candidates were 'victims of the squeeze' between Fianna Fáil and Fine Gael.

And the Greens continued to keep their options open until Fianna Fáil wooed them into power with two cabinet seats, a junior minister and a brace of senators.

Bertie Ahern returned to his familiar seat in the chamber, ten years behind him, with a possible five to go.

Like nothing had ever changed.

The Opinion Polls

Damian Loscher

The important role of opinion polling in revealing the public mood was never more obvious, and the task never more challenging, than in the weeks and months preceding the 2007 General Election. The public mood seemed to change so fast that it was often difficult to catch a glance let alone take a long, hard look. Almost every opinion poll seemed to hold a surprise.

Put simply, voters were asked if they wanted a change of government and were presented with a clear alternative coalition. The idea behind this proposal from the main opposition parties was to create a counterbalance to the dominance of Fianna Fáil. The see-sawing of opinion that followed suggests that Fine Gael and Labour, initially at least, succeeded in creating a real alternative. But voters were never convinced that change for change's sake was a sufficiently compelling proposition.

From a polling perspective, the first clue that voters were in two minds about a change of government came in the *Irish Times*/TNS MRBI opinion poll conducted in October 2006 when the controversy surrounding Bertie Ahern's personal finances served only to boost support for Fianna Fáil to 39%, up by a staggering eight percentage points. Movements from poll to poll of one or two points, up or down, are to be expected. Shifts of eight points are exceptional. Only the existence of a substantial and highly volatile group of voters could explain such a dramatic swing.

In many ways, the 2007 General Election campaign kicked off in January with Fianna Fáil launching its National Development Plan and Pat Rabbitte refusing to be drawn on whether or not Labour would go into government with Fianna Fáil. But despite the best efforts of the various political parties to dictate the media agenda, concerns over the health of the economy and the state of our public services dominated the headlines. Slowly the desire for change resurfaced: by April, Fianna Fáil had dropped six points (from October 2006) to 34%, while the Alternative Government of Fine Gael and Labour was up four points to 41%. The momentum was with Enda Kenny. If only it could be maintained.

The first in the official series of *Irish Times*/TNS MRBI Election 2007 polls, conducted in early May, held good news for the Alliance for Change. Fine Gael and Labour together attracted 41% of first-preference votes, compared to 36% for Fianna Fáil. With the PDs on just 2%, the current Government did not look like being returned.

Then came the leaders' debate, a seminal moment in the campaign.

There can be no doubt that Bertie Ahern won the debate, by a margin of almost three to one according to the *Irish Times*/TNS MRBI poll conducted immediately following the debate. Perhaps more critical to the outcome of this election was how Ahern won the debate. Remember that voters felt nervous, so the objective was to win their confidence. On the night, Ahern came across the more competent, the more informed, the more controlled. Kenny scored points with his composure and his enthusiasm, but did not succeed in convincing voters that he had all the answers.

It could be argued that the Alternative Government parties underestimated how discerning and discriminating voters were. When you ask voters why satisfactory public services are not being delivered, the answer is not a lack of resources. Instead, bureaucracy and vested interests are cited

as the main barriers to delivery. Yet the focus of the campaign was on *what* would be delivered, not *how*. Addressing the question of how was always likely to put some noses out of joint, but the failure to grasp this nettle did not give floating voters the reassurance they needed.

The final *Irish Times*/TNS MRBI poll showed a post-debate surge in support for Fianna Fáil, up five points to 41%, opening up a significant gap on Fine Gael and Labour with 27% and 10% of first-preference votes respectively. Yet another surprising opinion poll result. The truth was, Fianna Fáil and Bertie Ahern had managed to convince the undecideds that the risk of an Alternative Government was not worth the reward. Thursday 24 May was a great day for Fianna Fáil who emerged with 41.6% support. It was also a good day for Fine Gael who, on 27.3%, managed to add five points to its 2002 performance. For the smaller parties, the result was far less satisfying. With 10.1% of first-preference votes, Labour was disappointed, while the PDs were rocked by their 2.7% showing on election day. Similarly, the Greens (on 4.7%) and Sinn Féin (6.9%) failed to realise the full potential indicated by earlier polls.

The post-election consensus was that the two larger parties had squeezed out the smaller ones. Certainly the public had been presented with a choice, not a continuum. However, this may be too simplistic an analysis. It can be no coincidence that the smaller parties were also more radical with their economic policies. Michael McDowell's 'left, hard left and leftovers' sound bite potentially had more impact than Ahern's debate success, in that it reminded the electorate that every choice has consequences.

Why was the momentum for an alternative, as indicated by the polls, not maintained? Was it the economy? For decades, researchers have cultivated techniques to uncover the real motivations behind party choice, because simply asking voters to name the issues that are most important to them will not reveal the full picture. In particular, the importance of economic success and personal financial well-being are

The Opinion Polls

often understated on the doorstep. If actions speak louder than words, we can safely conclude that Ireland voted for prosperity and against change.

Hopefully the 2007 *Irish Times*/TNS MRBI series of opinion polls will go some way towards confirming the important role played by opinion polls. As the insert table shows, the final *Irish Times*/TNS MRBI opinion poll provided a remarkably accurate measure of voting intentions. In addition, opinion polls remain the only source of information on the journey voters took on their way to polling day. The 2007 series of polls will prove a valuable resource in this regard.

The volatility in polling data which characterised the 2007 series has also brought two unforeseen benefits. Firstly, our understanding of the motivations of the electorate is greatly enhanced by the significant movements in party support as measured from one poll to the next, as these changes cannot be written off as mere statistical variance. And secondly, the suggestion that opinion poll findings can influence voting patterns is not supported by the 2007 series which frequently produced poll findings that confounded the media, the politicians and the public.

Damian Loscher is Managing Director of TNS MRBI

PRE-ELECTION POLL FINDINGS VS. ELECTION OUTCOME

	20 May Opinion Poll	24 May Election Outcome	Variation
Fianna Fáil	40.5	41.6	-1.1
Fine Gael	26.9	27.3	-0.4
Labour	10.3	10.1	+0.2
Sinn Féin	9.5	6.9	+2.6
Progressive Democrats	1.6	2.7	-1.1
Green Party	5.9	4.7	+1.2
Independents/Others	5.3	6.6	-1.3

Dublin City Council
Comhairle Cathrach Bhaile Átha Cliath

HELPING TO BUILD COMMUNITIES

Dublin City Council is fostering an environmentally
sustainable Capital City in partnership with its citizens

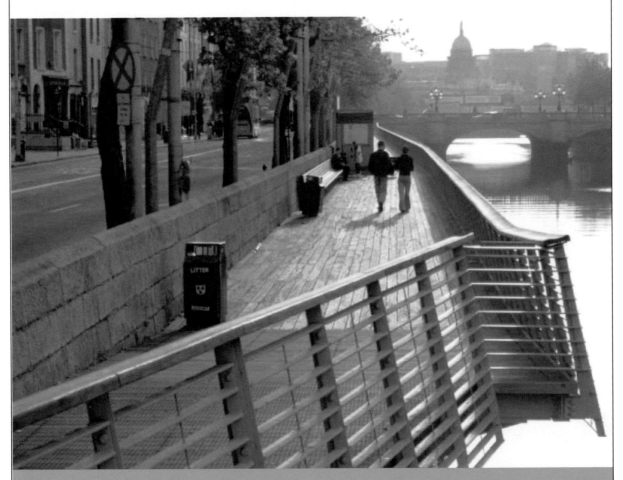

A Better Environment for Better Living

Civic Offices, Wood Quay Dublin 8.   Tel: (01) 222 2222.   e-mail: customerservices@dublincity.ie

The 30th Dáil (elected 24 May 2007)

The 30th Dáil was returned by 43 constituencies, one more than the 29th Dáil. Number of members of parties returned in the general election:

Fianna Fáil	78
Fine Gael	51
Labour	20
Green Party	6
Sinn Féin	4
Progressive Democrats	2
Others	5

Deputy	Party	Constituency
Ahern, Bertie	FF	Dublin Central
Ahern, Dermot	FF	Louth
Ahern, Michael	FF	Cork East
Ahern, Noel	FF	Dublin North-West
Allen Bernard	FG	Kildare North
• Andrews, Chris	FF	Dublin South-East
Andrews, Barry	FF	Dún Laoghaire
Ardagh, Seán	FF	Dublin South-Central
• Aylward, Bobby	FF	Carlow–Kilkenny
• Bannon, James	FG	Longford–Westmeath
† Barrett, Seán	FG	Dún Laoghaire
• Behan, Joe	FF	Wicklow
Blaney, Niall	FF	Donegal North-East
• Brady, Áine	FF	Kildare North
• Brady, Cyprian	FF	Dublin Central
Brady, Johnny	FF	Meath West
Breen, Pat	FG	Clare
Brennan, Seamus	FF	Dublin South
Broughan, Tommy	Lab	Dublin North-East
Browne, John	FF	Wexford
Bruton, Richard	FG	Dublin North-Central
† Burke, Ulick	FG	Galway East
Burton, Joan	Lab	Dublin West
• Byrne, Catherine	FG	Dublin South-Central
• Byrne, Thomas	FF	Meath East
• Calleary Dara	FF	Mayo
Carey, Pat	FF	Dublin North-West
• Carey, Joe	FG	Clare
† Clune, Deirdre	FG	Cork South-Central
• Collins, Niall	FF	Limerick West
• Conlon, Margaret	FF	Cavan–Monaghan
Connaughton, Paul	FG	Galway East
• Connick, Seán	FF	Wexford
• Coonan, Noel	FG	Tipperary North
Costello, Joe	Lab	Dublin Central
Coughlan, Mary	FF	Donegal South-West
Coveney, Simon	FG	Cork South-Central
Cowen, Brian	FF	Laois–Offaly
Crawford, Seymour	FG	Cavan–Monaghan
† Creed, Michael	FG	Cork North-West
Cregan, John	FF	Limerick West
• Creighton, Lucinda	FG	Dublin South-East
Cuffe, Ciaran	GP	Dún Laoghaire
Cullen, Martin	FF	Waterford
Curran, John	FF	Dublin Mid-West
• D'Arcy, Michael W.	FG	Wexford
Deasy, John	FG	Waterford
Deenihan, Jimmy	FG	Kerry North
Dempsey, Noel	FF	Meath West
Devins, Jimmy	FF	Sligo–North Leitrim
• Dooley, Timmy	FF	Clare
• Doyle, Andrew	FG	Wicklow
Durkan, Bernard	FG	Kildare North
English, Damien	FG	Meath West
Enright, Olwyn	FG	Laois–Offaly
Fahey, Frank	FF	Galway West
• Feighan, Frank	FG	Roscommon–South Leitrim
Ferris, Martin	SF	Kerry North
Finneran, Michael	FF	Roscommon–South Leitrim
• Fitzpatrick, Michael	FF	Kildare North
† Flanagan, Charles	FG	Laois–Offaly
• Flanagan, Terence	FG	Dublin North-East
Fleming, Seán	FF	Laois–Offaly
Flynn, Beverley	Ind	Mayo
Gallagher, Pat (The Cope)	FF	Donegal South-West
Gilmore, Eamon	Lab	Dún Laoghaire
Gogarty, Paul	GP	Dublin Mid-West
Gormley, John	GP	Dublin South-East
Grealish, Noel	PD	Galway West
Gregory, Tony	Ind	Dublin Central
Hanafin, Mary	FF	Dún Laoghaire
Harney, Mary	PD	Dublin Mid-West
Haughey, Seán	FF	Dublin North-Central
† Hayes, Brian	FG	Dublin South-West
Hayes, Tom	FG	Tipperary South
Healy-Rae, Jackie	Ind	Kerry South
Higgins, Michael D.	Lab	Galway West
Hoctor, Máire	FF	Tipperary North
Hogan, Phil	FG	Carlow–Kilkenny
Howlin, Brendan	Lab	Wexford

Kehoe, Paul	FG	Wexford
Kelleher, Billy	FF	Cork North-Central
Kelly, Peter	FF	Longford–Westmeath
† Kenneally, Brendan	FF	Waterford
• Kennedy, Michael	FF	Dublin North
Kenny, Enda	FG	Mayo
Killeen, Tony	FF	Clare
Kirk, Séamus	FF	Louth
† Kitt, Michael P.	FF	Galway East
Kitt, Tom	FF	Dublin South
Lenihan, Brian	FF	Dublin West
Lenihan, Conor	FF	Dublin South-West
Lowry, Michael	Ind	Tipperary North
Lynch, Kathleen	Lab	Cork North-Central
• Lynch, Ciarán	Lab	Cork South-Central
• Mansergh, Martin	FF	Tipperary South
Martin, Micheál	FF	Cork South-Central
McCormack, Padraic	FG	Galway West
McDaid, James	FF	Donegal North-East
McEllistrim, Thomas	FF	Kerry North
McEntee, Shane	FG	Meath East
McGinley, Dinny	FG	Donegal South-West
• McGrath, Mattie	FF	Tipperary South
• McGrath, Michael	FF	Cork South-Central
McGrath, Finian	Ind	Dublin North Central
McGuinness, John	FF	Carlow–Kilkenny
• McHugh, Joe	FG	Donegal North-East
McManus, Liz	Lab	Wicklow
Mitchell, Olivia	FG	Dublin South
Moloney, John Anthony	FF	Laois–Offaly
Morgan, Arthur	SF	Louth
Moynihan, Michael	FF	Cork North-West
Mulcahy, Michael	FF	Dublin South-Central
Naughten, Denis	FG	Roscommon–South Leitrim
Neville, Dan	FG	Limerick West
Nolan, M.J.	FF	Carlow–Kilkenny
Noonan, Michael	FG	Limerick East
• O'Brien, Darragh	FF	Dublin North
Ó Caoláin, Caoimhghín	SF	Cavan–Monaghan
O'Connor, Charlie	FF	Dublin South-West
Ó Cuív, Éamon	FF	Galway West
O'Dea, Willie	FF	Limerick East
• O'Donnell, Kieran	FG	Limerick East
O'Donoghue, John	FF	Kerry South
O'Dowd, Fergus	FG	Louth
Ó Fearghaíl, Seán	FF	Kildare South
O'Flynn, Noel	FF	Cork North-Central

O'Hanlon, Rory	FF	Cavan–Monaghan
(outgoing Ceann Comhairle)		
O'Keeffe, Batt	FF	Cork North-West
O'Keeffe, Jim	FG	Cork South-West
O'Keeffe, Ned	FF	Cork East
• O'Mahony, John	FG	Mayo
† O'Rourke, Mary	FF	Longford–Westmeath
O'Shea, Brian	Lab	Waterford
Ó Snodaigh, Aengus	SF	Dublin South-Central
• O'Sullivan, Christy	FF	Cork South-West
O'Sullivan, Jan	Lab	Limerick East
Penrose, Willie	Lab	Longford–Westmeath
Perry, John	FG	Sligo–North Leitrim
Power, Peter	FF	Limerick East
Power, Seán	FF	Kildare South
Quinn, Ruairí	Lab,	Dublin South-East
Rabbitte, Pat	Lab	Dublin South-West
• Reilly, James	FG	Dublin North
Ring, Michael	FG	Mayo
Roche, Dick	FF	Wicklow
Ryan, Eamon	GP	Dublin South
Sargent, Trevor	GP	Dublin North
• Scanlon, Eamon	FF	Sligo–North Leitrim
† Shatter, Alan	FG	Dublin South
• Sheahan, Tom	FG	Kerry South
† Sheehan, P.J.	FG	Cork South-West
• Sherlock, Seán	Lab	Cork East
Shortall, Róisín	Lab	Dublin North-West
Smith, Brendan	FF	Cavan–Monaghan
Stagg, Emmet	Lab	Kildare North
Stanton, David	FG	Cork East
Timmins, Billy	FG	Wicklow
Treacy, Noel	FF	Galway East
• Tuffy, Joanna	Lab	Dublin Mid-West
Upton, Mary	Lab	Dublin South-Central
• Varadkar, Leo	FG	Dublin West
Wall, Jack	Lab	Kildare South
Wallace, Mary	FF	Meath East
• White, Mary	GP	Carlow–Kilkenny
Woods, Michael J.	FF	Dublin North-East

The 30th Dáil has 166 deputies, the same number as the previous Dáil. Of these, 117 were members of the 29th Dáil, 11 were previously members (denoted by †) but not of the 29th Dáil, and 38 are new deputies (denoted by •).

Green Party leader Trevor Sargent, deputy leader Mary White and other candidates at the launch of the Green Party's election manifesto in Dublin on 4 May 2007.

The 2007 general election was called on 29 April 2007. Voting took place on 24 May 2007. A total of 466 candidates were nominated for the 166 constituencies. However, as one candidate contested four constituencies and another contested two, 470 candidates were listed.

The outgoing Ceann Comhairle, Dr Rory O'Hanlon, was returned automatically for his constituency of Cavan–Monaghan. Fianna Fáil, Fine Gael, the Labour Party, the Green Party, the Progressive Democrats, Sinn Féin, the Socialist Party, the Workers' Party and the Christian Solidarity Party nominated candidates. There were 90 Independent candidacies, though many described as Independent were members of political parties which were not formally registered as such for electoral purposes.

State of the Parties

Election	FF	FG	Lab	PD	DL	GP	SF	SP	Others
2007	**78**	**51**	**20**	**2**	**—**	**6**	**4**	**—**	**5**
2002	81	31	21	8	—	6	5	1	13
1997	77	54	17	4	4	1	1	1	7
1992	68	45	33	10	4	—	—	—	6
1989	77	55	15	6	—	—	—	—	13
1987	81	51	12	14	—	—	—	—	8
Nov. 1982	75	70	16	—	—	—	—	—	5

Line-up

Election	Electorate	Candidates	Seats
2007	**3,066,517**	**466**	**166**
2002	2,994,642	463	166
1997	2,741,262	484	166
1992	2,557,036	481	166
1989	2,448,813	370	166
1987	2,445,515	466	166
Nov. 1982	2,335,153	364	166

First-Preference Votes

Election	FF		FG		Lab		PD		GP		SF		DL		Others	
2007	**858,593**	**41.56%**	**564,438**	**27.32%**	**209,175**	**10.13%**	**56,396**	**2.73%**	**96,936**	**4.69%**	**143,410**	**6.94%**	**—**		**136,912**	**6.63%**
2002	770,846	41.49%	417,653	22.48%	200,138	10.77%	73,628	3.96%	71,480	3.85%	121,039	6.51%			203,329	10.94%
1997	703,682	39.33%	499,936	27.95%	186,044	10.40%	83,765	4.68%	—	2.8%	—	—	44,901	2.51%	270,657	15.13%
1992	674,650	39.11%	422,106	24.47%	333,013	19.31%	80,787	4.68%	—	1.4%	—	—	47,945	2.78%	166,352	9.64%
1989	731,472	44.15%	485,307	29.29%	156,989	9.48%	91,013	5.49%	—	1.5%	—	—	—		192,032	11.59%
1987	784,547	44.15%	481,127	27.07%	114,551	6.44%	210,583	11.85%	—	—	—	—	—		186,357	10.49%
Nov. 1982	763,313	45.20%	662,284	39.22%	158,115	9.36%	—	—	—	—	—	—	—		105,008	6.22%

Turnout

Election	Total Poll		Spoiled Votes		Valid Poll	
2007	**2,065,320**	**67.35%**	**19,491**	**0.95%**	**2,045,829**	**66.71%**
2002	1,878,393	62.73%	20,280	1.08%	1,858,113	62.05%
1997	1,807,016	65.92%	18,031	1.00%	1,789,985	65.26%
1992	1,751,351	68.49%	26,498	1.51%	1,724,853	67.46%
1989	1,677,592	68.51%	20,779	1.24%	1,656,813	67.66%
1987	1,793,406	73.33%	16,241	0.91%	1,777,165	72.69%
Nov. 1982	1,701,393	72.86%	12,673	0.74%	1,688,720	72.32%

Regional First-Preference Percentages by Euro Constituencies

Constituency	FF		FG		Lab		PD		GP		SF		Others	
Ireland North-West (Connacht–Ulster)	158,862	38.47%	143,614	34.82%	13,661	3.31%	12,485	3.03%	10,199	2.47%	43,943	10.65%	29,888	7.25%
Dublin	196,057	38.75%	94,789	18.47%	73,490	14.53%	20,919	4.13%	41,813	8.27%	35,256	6.97%	43,569	8.61%
Ireland East (Leinster)	246,899	45.23%	147,843	27.08%	62,317	11.42%	14,122	2.59%	23,614	4.33%	32,301	5.92%	18,773	3.44%
Ireland South (Munster)	256,955	42.17%	178,183	29.62%	59,707	9.92%	8,870	1.47%	21,310	3.54%	31,910	5.30%	44,682	7.43%

Taoiseach Bertie Ahern and President McAleese with newly appointed members of the Cabinet at Áras an Uachtaráin after presentation of their seals of office, on 14 June 2007.

FROM LEFT TO RIGHT
Front:
Mr Micheál Martin TD, Minister for Enterprise, Trade and Employment; Mr Noel Dempsey TD, Minister for Transport and Marine; Mr Brian Cowen, Tánaiste and Minister for Finance; President Mary McAleese; Mr Bertie Ahern, Taoiseach; Ms Mary Harney TD, Minister for Health and Children; Mr Dermot Ahern TD, Minister for Foreign Affairs

Back:
Mr Tom Kitt TD, Chief Whip and Minister of State at the Department of Defence; Ms Mary Coughlan TD, Minister for Agriculture, Fisheries and Food; Mr Martin Cullen TD, Minister for Social and Family Affairs; Mr Éamon Ó Cuív TD, Minister for Community, Rural and Gaeltacht Affairs; Mr John Gormley TD, Minister for the Environment, Heritage and Local Government; Mr Seamus Brennan TD, Minister for Arts, Sport and Tourism; Mr Eamon Ryan TD, Minister for Communications, Energy and Natural Resources; Mr Brian Lenihan TD, Minister for Justice, Equality and Law Reform; Ms Mary Hanafin TD, Minister for Education and Science; Mr Willie O'Dea TD, Minister for Defence; Mr Paul Gallagher SC, Attorney General

Taoiseach	Bertie Ahern
Tánaiste and Minister for Finance	Brian Cowen
Minister for Health and Children	Mary Harney
Minister for Transport and the Marine	Noel Dempsey
Minister for Foreign Affairs	Dermot Ahern
Minister for Enterprise, Trade and Employment	Micheál Martin
Minister for Arts, Sport and Tourism	Séamus Brennan
Minister for Social and Family Affairs	Martin Cullen
Minister for Community, Rural and Gaeltacht Affairs	Éamon Ó Cuív
Minister for Agriculture, Fisheries and Food	Mary Coughlan
Minister for Education and Science	Mary Hanafin
Minister for Defence	Willie O'Dea
Minister for Justice, Equality and Law Reform	Brian Lenihan
Minister for the Environment, Heritage and Local Government	John Gormley
Minister for Communications, Energy and Natural Resources	Eamon Ryan
Attorney General	Paul Gallagher

Ministers of State (appointed 20 June 2007)

Department	Special Responsibilities	Name
Taoiseach and Defence	Government Chief Whip and Information Society	Tom Kitt
Health and Children	Children	Brendan Smith
Taoiseach and Foreign Affairs	European Affairs	Dick Roche
Health and Children	Health Promotion and Food Safety	Pat 'the Cope' Gallagher
Agriculture, Fisheries and Food	Fisheries	John Browne
Enterprise, Trade and Employment, and Education and Science	Innovation Policy	Michael Ahern
Finance	Office of Public Works	Noel Ahern
Justice, Equality and Law Reform	Equality	Seán Power
Environment, Heritage and Local Government	Housing, Urban Renewal and Developing Areas	Batt O'Keeffe
Community, Rural and Gaeltacht Affairs; Education and Science, and Justice, Equality and Law Reform	Integration Policy	Conor Lenihan
Agriculture, Fisheries and Food	Forestry	Mary Wallace
Environment, Heritage and Local Government, and Communications, Energy and Natural Resources	Environment and Energy	Tony Killeen
Education and Science, and Enterprise, Trade and Employment	Lifelong Learning, Youth Work and School Transport	Seán Haughey
Agriculture, Fisheries and Food	Food and Horticulture	Trevor Sargent
Enterprise, Trade and Employment	Labour Affairs	Billy Kelleher
Health and Children	Children	Brendan Smith
Community, Rural, and Gaeltacht Affairs	Drugs Strategy and Community Affairs	Pat Carey
Foreign Affairs	Overseas Development	Micheál Kitt
Health and Children	Disability and Mental Health	Jimmy Devins
Health and Children	Older People	Máire Hoctor
Enterprise, Trade and Employment	Trade and Commerce	John McGuinness

The general election of 24 May 2007 resulted in the return of Bertie Ahern as Taoiseach for his third successive term. His new Government was a three-party coalition composed of Fianna Fáil, the Green Party and the Progressive Democrats. Three Independent TDs also negotiated formal deals to support the Government for its full term.

When the 30th Dáil assembled on 14 June, Mr Ahern was nominated for appointment to the Taoiseach's office by 89 votes to 75. In addition to the votes of 77 Fianna Fáil TDs, after the election of John O'Donoghue as Ceann Comhairle, he was supported by the six Green Party deputies, the two PDs and four Independents, Jackie Healy-Rae, Finian McGrath, Michael Lowry and Beverley Flynn. It was the first time that Fianna Fáil had entered a three-party coalition and the first time that the Greens had participated in Government.

Mr Ahern's nomination was opposed by Fine Gael, Labour, Sinn Féin and one Independent, Tony Gregory.

The motion approving the nomination by the Taoiseach of the other members of the Government was carried by 87 votes to 73. The Cabinet was composed of 12 Fianna Fáil Ministers, two Greens and one PD.

A week later, Mr Ahern announced the appointment of 20 Ministers of State, including one Green Party TD. New legislation was required to provide for an increase of three in the number of junior ministers.

Carlow–Kilkenny

Elected

Party Share of Vote

1st Preferences	Number	%	Gain/Loss
Fianna Fáil	32,272	47.70	-2.50%
Fine Gael	20,031	29.61	7.73%
Labour	6,324	9.35	-3.81%
Prog Democrats	1,073	1.59	1.59%
Green Party	5,386	7.96	-0.19%
Sinn Féin	2,568	3.80	0.38%
Others	0	0.00	-3.20%

Statistics

Electorate	102,686	
Total Poll	68,359	66.57
Spoiled	705	0.69
Total Valid Poll	67,654	65.88
Seats	5	
Quota	11,276	
Candidates	11	

	Quotas	Seats
FF	2.86	3
FG	1.78	1
GP	0.48	1
GP gain from Lab		

John McGuinness (FF)

Home Address
Windsmoor, Brooklawn, Ballyfoyle Road, Kilkenny
Constituency Office
11 O'Loughlin Road, Kilkenny
Telephone
Mobile 087 285 5834; *Fax* (056) 777 0674; *Office* (056) 777 0672/3;
Email johnmcg@eircom.net
Website www.johnmcguinness.com
Birth Place/Date
Kilkenny. 15 March 1955
Married
Margaret Redmond. 3 sons, 1 daughter
Education
Kilkenny CBS. Diploma in Business Management
Occupation
Full-time public representative

John McGuinness was appointed Minister of State at the Department of Enterprise, Trade and Employment, with responsibility for Trade and Commerce, in June 2007.

He was first elected to the Dáil in 1997. Vice-Chairperson of Public Accounts Committee in last Dáil. Member, Joint Oireachtas Committees for European Affairs, Enterprise and Small Business (Government Whip), Justice, Equality and Women's Rights in 28th Dáil.

Member, Kilkenny Corporation 1979–2003. Mayor of Kilkenny, 1996–97 (third generation of family to serve as Mayor of the Borough). Member, Kilkenny County Council 1991–2003.

Bobby Aylward (FF)

Home Address
Knockmoylan, Mullinavat, Co Kilkenny
Constituency Office
22 Upper Patrick Street, Kilkenny
Telephone
Home (051) 898 118; *Office* (056) 779 4570; *Mobile* 086 810 5847.
Birth Place/Date
Knockmoylan, Mullinavat, Co Kilkenny.
1 April 1955
Married
Helena. 1 daughter, 2 sons
Education
Castlegannon NS; Vocational School, Ballyhale; Kildalton College (Green Cert)
Occupation
Farmer and public representative

Bobby Aylward is a new deputy.

Member, Kilkenny County Council 1992 until his election to the Dáil. Chairperson of the council 2003–04.

Chairman of Southern and Eastern Regional Authority 2000–01 and 2003. Chairman, Shamrocks GAA club 1992–95.

Bobby Aylward is a brother of Liam Aylward, TD for Carlow–Kilkenny 1977–2007, who was elected MEP for Leinster in the European elections in 2004 and did not contest the 2007 general election. Liam Aylward was also a Minister of State at the Departments of Energy and Education between 1998 and 1994 and at the Department of Agriculture and Food from 2002 until his election to the European Parliament.

Philip Hogan (FG)

Home Address
Grovine, Kilkenny
Business Address
1 High Street, Kilkenny
Telephone
Constituency office (056) 777 1490;
Fax (056) 777 1491;
Website www.philhogan.ie
Birth Place/Date
Kilkenny. 4 July 1960
Married
Kathleen Murphy. 1 son
Education
St Joseph's College, Freshford; St Kieran's College, Kilkenny; University College, Cork (BA, HDipEd)
Occupation
Public representative.

Phil Hogan was appointed party spokesperson on Environment, Heritage and Local Government in September 2007.

He was first elected to the Dáil in 1989. He was appointed Minister of State at the Department of Finance, with special responsibility for Public Expenditure and the Office of Public Works, in December 1994. He resigned in February 1995. Since 1997, he has been Political Director of the Fine Gael Organisation and a member of the Fine Gael front bench. Chairman of the Parliamentary Party, 1995–2001. He was Fine Gael Director of Organisation from 2002 until June 2007.

He was a Senator, Industrial and Commercial panel, 1987–89.

Member of Kilkenny County Council, 1982–2003 (Chairman, 1985–86 and 1998–99); South-Eastern Health Board 1991–99.

Member, Gaelic Athletic Association; Kilkenny Archaeological Society; Castlecomer Golf Club.

M.J. Nolan (FF)

Home Address
Shandon House, Strawhall, Carlow
Telephone
Home (0503) 30800; *Mobile* 087 224 1967
Birth Place/Date
Bagenalstown, Co Carlow. 25 January 1951
Married
Mary Forde. 2 daughters, 2 sons
Education
De La Salle, Bagenalstown; Mount St Joseph's, Roscrea
Occupation
Public representative

M.J. Nolan was elected for the Carlow–Kilkenny constituency at his first attempt in November 1982 and re-elected at subsequent general elections until he lost his seat in 1997. He ran unsuccessfully for election to the Administrative panel of the Seanad in 1997 and was re-elected to the Dáil in 2002.

He began his national political career when the then Taoiseach, Mr Charles Haughey, nominated him as a Senator in May 1982. M.J. Nolan was later to criticise Mr Haughey, as one of the 'Gang of Four' in the autumn of 1991.

Member, Carlow County Council 1979–2003.

He is a son of former Fianna Fáil minister, Tom Nolan, who was a TD for Carlow–Kilkenny 1965–82, Minister for Labour December 1980–81 and Minister of State at the Department of Health and Social Welfare in 1980.

Mary White (GP)

Home Address
Old Rectory, Killedmond, Borris, Carlow
Telephone
(059) 977 3184; *Mobile* (087) 270 7189;
Email marywhite@oceanfree.net
Website www.carlowkilkennygreens.com
Birth Place/Date
Co Wicklow. Date not supplied
Married
Robert White. 1 daughter
Education
Ursuline Convent, Waterford; Trinity College Dublin
Occupation
Public representative

Mary White is a new deputy. She stood unsuccessfully in the 1997 and 2002 general elections and for the Industrial and Commercial panel in the Seanad in 2002.

She was appointed Deputy Leader of the Green Party in 2001. Member of Carlow County Council since 1999 local elections, topping the poll in Borris, and re-elected in 2004.

Founder member of the English Society at TCD and awarded a 'Pink' for sporting excellence. Author of a walking guide to the Blackstairs mountains (with Joss Lynam) and of *Environment, Mining and Politics*, an account of an anti-mining campaign.

She is an organic grower and a keen hill-walker.

Carlow–Kilkenny

Seats 5
Quota 11,276

	1st Count	2nd Count	3rd Count	4th Count
		Transfer of **Lacey** Votes	Transfer of **McGuinness** Surplus	Transfer of **Aylward** Surplus
AYLWARD, Bobby (FF)	11,600			
BROWNE, Fergal (FG)	4,948	*(+136)* 5,084	*(+3)* 5,087	*(+5)* 5,092
FUNCHION, Kathleen (SF)	2,568	*(+29)* 2,597	*(+22)* 2,619	*(+19)* 2,638
HOGAN, Phil* (FG)	8,589	*(+84)* 8,673	*(+52)* 8,725	*(+26)* 8,751
LACEY, Walter (PD)	1,073			
McGUINNESS, John* (FF)	11,635			
NOLAN, M.J.* (FF)	9,037	*(+444)* 9,481	*(+212)* 9,693	*(+208)* 9,901
O'BRIEN, Michael (Lab)	2,923	*(+16)* 2,939	*(+18)* 2,957	*(+15)* 2,972
PHELAN, John Paul (FG)	6,494	*(+54)* 6,548	*(+20)* 6,568	*(+36)* 6,604
TOWNSEND, Jim (Lab)	3,401	*(+128)* 3,529	*(+5)* 3,534	*(+2)* 3,536
WHITE, Mary (GP)	5,386	*(+147)* 5,533	*(+27)* 5,560	*(+13)* 5,573
NON-TRANSFERABLE		35		

5th Count	6th Count	7th Count	8th Count	9th Count
Transfer of **Funchion** Votes	Transfer of **O'Brien** Votes	Transfer of **Browne** Votes	Transfer of **Townsend** Votes	Transfer of **Nolan** Surplus
(+98) 5,190	*(+36)* 5,226			
(+305) 9,056	*(+487)* 9,543	*(+1,817)* 11,360		
(+449) 10,350	*(+107)* 10,457	*(+679)* 11,136	*(+1,457)* 12,593	
(+332) 3,304				
(+237) 6,841	*(+520)* 7,361	*(+809)* 8,170	*(+1,329)* 9,499	*(+316)* 9,815
(+196) 3,732	*(+1,553)* 5,285	*(+1,104)* 6,389		
(+693) 6,266	*(+429)* 6,695	*(+710)* 7,405	*(+2,478)* 9,883	*(+581)* 10,464
328	172	107	1,125	420

Cavan–Monaghan

Elected

Brendan Smith (FF)*	1st Count
Caoimhghín Ó Caoláin (SF)*	1st Count
Seymour Crawford (FG)*	4th Count
Margaret Conlon (FF)	4th Count

Party Share of Vote

1st Preferences	Number	%	Gain/Loss
Fianna Fáil	24,851	37.77	2.83%
Fine Gael	20,528	31.20	6.03%
Labour	796	1.21	0.32%
Prog Democrats	0	0.00	-1.83%
Green Party	2,382	3.62	1.84%
Sinn Féin	13,162	20.01	2.49%
Others	4,068	6.18	-11.68%

Statistics

Electorate	92,248	
Total Poll	66,547	72.14
Spoiled	760	0.82
Total Valid Poll	65,787	71.32
Seats	5	
Quota	13,158	
Candidates	9	

	Quotas	Seats
FF	1.89	2
FG	1.56	1
SF	1.00	1

The 5th seat was filled by Dr Rory O'Hanlon (FF), Ceann Comhairle of the 29th Dáil, who was returned automatically: FF gain from Ind

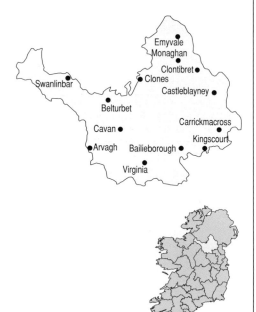

Rory O'Hanlon (FF)

Home Address
Mullinarry, Carrickmacross, Co Monaghan
Constituency Office
Carrickmacross
Telephone
Home (042) 966 1530; *Fax* (042) 966 3220; *Office* (042) 966 1530; *Fax* (042) 966 1530; *Website* www.roryohanlon.ie
Birth Place/Date
Dublin. 7 February 1934
Married
Teresa Ward. 4 sons, 2 daughters
Education
Mullaghbawn NS, Co Armagh; St Mary's College, Dundalk; Blackrock College; University College, Dublin (MB, BCh, BAO, DCh, LM)
Occupation
Public representative. Medical doctor

Rory O'Hanlon was Ceann Comhairle of the 29th Dáil and returned automatically to the 30th Dáil.

He was first elected a Dáil deputy in 1977. Leas-Cheann Comhairle 1997–2002. Chairman of the Fianna Fáil Parliamentary Party 1995–2002. Minister for the Environment November 1991 to February 1992; Minister for Health 1987–91; Minister of State, Department of Health and Social Welfare October–December 1982. Party spokesperson on Health 1983–87.

Member and Vice-Chairperson, British–Irish Inter-Parliamentary Body. Member of National Forum on Europe. Member, New Ireland Forum. Former Chairman of Cross-Border Development Committee, Eastern Region.

Member of Monaghan County Council 1979–87. Medical representative on North-Eastern Health Board 1970–87.

Brendan Smith (FF)

Home Address
3 Carrickfern, Cavan
Business Address
Department of Health and Children, Hawkins House, Dublin 2
Constituency Office
75 Church Street, Paddy Smiths, Cavan
Telephone
Constituency office (049) 436 2366; *Fax* (049) 436 2367; *Ministerial office* (01) 671 8142/8985
Birth Place/Date
Cavan. June 1956
Married
Anne McGarry
Education
St Camillus's College, Killucan, Co Westmeath; University College, Dublin (BA)
Occupation
Full-time public representative.

Brendan Smith was appointed Minister of State at the Department of Health and Children, with special responsibility for Children, on 20 June 2007. He has 'super' junior ministerial status that allows him to attend Cabinet meetings.

He was Minister of State at the Department of Agriculture and Food, with special responsibility for Food and Horticulture, from 2004 to 14 June 2007.

First elected to the Dáil in 1992, replacing former Tánaiste John Wilson to whom he had been political adviser for the previous 15 years. Government Whip on Oireachtas Joint Committee on Foreign Affairs in 28th Dáil. Former Co-Chairman of British-Irish Inter-Parliamentary Body. Member, Dáil Committee on Procedure and Privileges 2002–04.

Caoimhghín Ó Caoláin (SF)

Home Address
14 Mullaghdun, Monaghan
Constituency Office
21 Dublin Street, Monaghan
Telephone
Constituency office (047) 82917;
Fax (047) 71849
Birth Place/Date
Monaghan. 18 September 1953
Married
Briege McGinn. 4 daughters, 1 son
Education
St Mary's CBS, Monaghan
Occupation
Full-time public representative. Formerly bank official

Caoimhghín Ó Caoláin was first elected a Dáil deputy in 1997, the first Sinn Féin representative to be elected after the party abandoned the policy of abstentionism. Parliamentary Leader of the Sinn Féin deputies in the Dáil since the 2002 election. Candidate in the general elections of 1987, 1989 and 1992.

Party spokesperson on the Peace Process and the Six Counties in the 29th Dáil. He also had responsibility for Finance and Health and Children. Member of British–Irish Inter-Parliamentary Body.

Member of Monaghan County Council 1985–2003. Member, Sinn Féin Ard-Chomhairle since 1983; Sinn Féin delegation to the Forum for Peace and Reconciliation. Member of Sinn Féin delegation in direct talks with British Government representatives.

Director of elections for Kieran Doherty who was elected TD for Cavan–Monaghan in 1981 and died on hunger strike in Long Kesh. General manager *An Phoblacht/Republican News* 1982–85.

Seymour Crawford (FG)

Home Address
Drumkeen, Aghabog, Co Monaghan
Constituency Office
18 The Diamond, Monaghan
Telephone
Office (047) 71911; *Fax* (047) 71912;
Mobile 087 254 4886
Birth Place/Date
Monaghan. 1 June 1944
Marital Status
Single
Education
Mullagreenan National School; High School, Clones
Occupation
Public representative. Farmer

Seymour Crawford was first elected to the Dáil in 1992.

Vice-Chairperson, British–Irish Inter-Parliamentary Body 2004 and member, 1993–2007. Fine Gael deputy spokesperson for Agriculture and Food 2004–2007; deputy spokesperson, Community, Rural and Gaeltacht Affairs 2002–2004.

Member of Monaghan County Council 1991–2003.

Member of the Irish Farmers' Association since 1965 (Vice-President, 1984–88). Chairperson of the National Livestock Committee 1979–84. Chairperson of the EU Beef and Veal Committee (1981–86) and a member of the CBF (Irish Livestock and Meat Board) 1979–86. Received Bastow Award for service in meat and livestock in 1986.

Margaret Conlon (FF)

Home Address
Tullynanegish, Loughmourne, Castleblayney, Co Monaghan
Constituency Office
Thomas Street, Monaghan
Telephone
(047) 82524; *Fax* (047) 83793;
Mobile 086 300 1047
Birth Place/Date
Drogheda. 17 September 1967
Married
Seamus. 2 sons, 1 daughter
Education
St Oliver Plunkett's NS, Loughmourne;
Our Lady's Secondary School, Castleblaney;
NUI Maynooth.
Occupation
Deputy school principal and public representative

Margaret Conlon is a new deputy.

Chairperson of Monaghan Comhairle Dáil Ceanntair of Fianna Fáil and secretary of South Monaghan Comhairle Ceanntair. Deputy principal of St Louis Secondary School in Monaghan Town.

Founding member of the Fianna Fáil Cumann in NUI Maynooth and was a member of party's national executive from 1986 to 1988. Member, Fianna Fáil National Youth Committee 1986–88.

Cavan–Monaghan

Seats 5 Quota 13,158	1st Count	2nd Count Transfer of **Smith** Surplus	3rd Count Transfer of **Cullen, Fay** Votes	4th Count Transfer of **Connolly, Martin** Votes
CONLAN, Margaret (FF)	9,303	*(+1,759)* 11,062	*(+83)* 11,145	*(+2,058)* 13,203
CONNOLLY, Paudge* (Ind)	3,955	*(+79)* 4,034	*(+123)* 4,157	
CRAWFORD, Seymour* (FG)	10,978	*(+79)* 11,057	*(+142)* 11,199	*(+2,559)* 13,758
CULLEN, Des (Lab)	796	*(+53)* 849		
FAY, T.J. (Ind)	113	*(+12)* 125		
MARTIN, Vincent P. (GP)	2,382	*(+63)* 2,445	*(+242)* 2,687	
Ó CAOLÁIN, Caoimhghín* (SF)	13,162			
O'REILLY, Joe (FG)	9,550	*(+345)* 9,895	*(+319)* 10,214	*(+1,024)* 11,238
SMITH, Brendan* (FF)	15,548			
NON-TRANSFERABLE			65	1,203

The Taoiseach Bertie Ahern declines to answer questions and leaves the stage after the announcement of the Fianna Fáil manifesto in Dublin on 29 April 2007.

Clare

Elected

Party Share of Vote

1st Preferences	Number	%	Gain/Loss
Fianna Fáil	24,824	44.03	-1.36%
Fine Gael	19,854	35.21	9.75%
Labour	892	1.58	-1.87%
Prog Democrats	810	1.44	1.44%
Green Party	2,858	5.07	-0.76%
Sinn Féin	1,929	3.42	3.42%
Others	5,218	9.25	-10.62%

Statistics

Electorate	79,555	
Total Poll	56,770	71.36
Spoiled	385	0.68
Total Valid Poll	56,385	70.88
Seats	4	
Quota	11,278	
Candidates	12	

	Quotas	Seats
FF	2.20	2
FG	1.76	2
FG gain from Ind		

Timmy Dooley (FF)

Home Address
8 The Old Forge, Tulla, Co Clare
Constituency Office
8 Mill Road, Ennis, Co Clare
Telephone
Home (065) 683 1732; *Office* (065) 689 1115; *Fax* (065) 689 1116
Birth Place/Date
Limerick. 13 February 1969
Married
Emer McMahon. 1 daughter
Education
Mountshannon National School; Scariff Community College, Co Clare; University College, Dublin
Occupation
Full-time public representative. Formerly businessman

Timmy Dooley is a new deputy.

He was elected to the Administrative panel of the Seanad in 2002; party spokesman in the Seanad on Transport. Member, Joint Oireachtas Committee on Transport in 29th Dáil.

Chairman of the Kevin Barry Cumann of Fianna Fáil in UCD 1989. Founder member of the National Youth Committee 1990–93. Member, Fianna Fáil National Executive. Member of the National Forum on Europe.

Tony Killeen (FF)

Home Address
Kilnaboy, Corofin, Co Clare
Constituency Office
Upper Market Street, Ennis, Co Clare
Telephone
Office (065) 684 1500; *Fax* (065) 684 1514; *Mobile* 087 252 5304
Birth Place/Date
Clare. 9 June 1952
Married
Lily O'Keeffe. 5 sons
Education
St Flannan's College, Ennis; Mary Immaculate College of Education, Limerick
Occupation
Full-time public representative. Formerly national school teacher

Tony Killeen was appointed Minister of State at the Department of Environment, Heritage and Local Government and the Department of Communications, Energy and Natural Resources, with special responsibility for Environment and Energy, on 20 June 2007.

He was first elected to the Dáil in 1992. Minister of State at the Department of Enterprise, Trade and Employment 2004–2007. Chairman, Joint Oireachtas Committee on Education and Science 2002–2004. Member, Dáil Committee on Procedure and Privileges in 29th Dáil. Former Chairman, Committee on Members' Interests. Member, British–Irish Inter-Parliamentary Body.

Member, Clare County Council 1985–97 (Vice-Chairman, 1987–89, and Chairman, 1989–91). Member, County Clare Vocational Education Committee 1979–94 (Chairman, 1991–94).

Former National Chairman of Fianna Fáil Councillors' Association.

Pat Breen (FG)

Home Address
Lisduff, Ballynacally, Co Clare
Constituency Office
Parkview House, Lower Market Street
Car Park, Ennis, Co Clare
Telephone
Home (065) 683 8229; *Office* (065) 686 8466;
Fax (065) 686 8486
Birth Place/Date
Ennis. 21 March 1957
Married
Anne McInerney. 2 sons
Education
Lisheen National School; St Flannan's College,
Ennis; Limerick Technical College
Occupation
Public representative. Farmer. Former
architectural technician

Pat Breen was first elected in 2002. Vice-
Chairman of the Joint Committee on
Enterprise and Small Business 2002–04.

Deputy Fine Gael spokesperson on
Enterprise, Trade and Employment, with
special responsibility for EU Internal Market
Development and Small and Medium
Enterprises. Previously deputy spokesperson
for Transport and Infrastructure.

Member, Clare County Council 1999–2003.

Joe Carey (FG)

Home Address
3 Thomond Villas, Clarecastle, Co Clare
Constituency Office
12 Park Row, Francis Street, Ennis, Co Clare
Telephone
Home (065) 682 9191; *Office* (065) 689 1199
Birth Place/Date
Clarecastle. 24 June 1975
Marital Status
Single
Education
Clarecastle National School, Ennis;
St Flannan's College, Ennis; Galway IT
(1992–93); Athlone IT (1993–97)
Occupation
Full-time public representative

Joe Carey is a new TD.

Member, Clare County Council 1997–2007.
Treasurer, Ennis General Hospital
development committee.

He is a son of Donal Carey, Fine Gael TD for
Clare 1982–2002, Senator 1981–82 and
Minister of State at the Department of the
Taoiseach, the Department of Arts Culture
and the Gaeltacht 1995–97.

Clare

Seats 4 Quota 11,278	1st Count	2nd Count Transfer of **Collins, Fitzgerald** Votes	3rd Count Transfer of **Prior** Votes	4th Count Transfer of **Meaney** Votes
BREEN, James* (Ind)	5,218	*(+122)* 5,340	*(+349)* 5,689	*(+792)* 6,481
BREEN, Pat* (FG)	7,036	*(+168)* 7,204	*(+104)* 7,308	*(+387)* 7,695
CAREY, Joe (FG)	5,818	*(+190)* 6,008	*(+108)* 6,116	*(+548)* 6,664
COLLINS, Murt (PD)	810			
DALY, Brendan (FF)	5,712	*(+158)* 5,870	*(+123)* 5,993	*(+96)* 6,089
DOOLEY, Timmy (FF)	10,791	*(+222)* 11,013	*(+260)* 11,273	*(+361)* 11,634
FITZGERALD, Pascal (Lab)	892			
KILLEEN, Tony* (FF)	8,321	*(+142)* 8,463	*(+197)* 8,660	*(+316)* 8,976
MEANEY, Brian (GP)	2,858	*(+305)* 3,163	*(+442)* 3,605	
MULCAHY, Tony (FG)	3,408	*(+85)* 3,493	*(+118)* 3,611	*(+222)* 3,833
PRIOR, Anna (SF)	1,929	*(+83)* 2,012		
TAYLOR-QUINN, Madeleine (FG)	3,592	*(+127)* 3,719	*(+168)* 3,887	*(+532)* 4,419
NON-TRANSFERABLE		100	143	351

5th Count	6th Count	7th Count	8th Count	9th Count
Transfer of **Mulcahy** Votes	Transfer of **Taylor-Quinn** Votes	Transfer of **Daly** Votes	Transfer of **Killeen** Surplus	Transfer of **Breen, P** Surplus
(+395) 6,876	*(+575)* 7,451	*(+752)* 8,203	*(+1,131)* 9,334	*(+192)* 9,526
(+877) 8,572	*(+1,786)* 10,358	*(+754)* 11,112	*(+555)* 11,667	
(+883) 7,547	*(+1,543)* 9,090	*(+327)* 9,417	*(+384)* 9,801	*(+181)* 9,982
(+189) 6,278	*(+529)* 6,807			
(+408) 9,384	*(+312)* 9,696	*(+4,387)* 14,083		
(+751) 5,170				
330	425	587	735	16

Cork East

Elected

Michael Ahern (FF)*	3rd Count
Ned O'Keeffe (FF)*	4th Count
David Stanton (FG)*	6th Count
Seán Sherlock (Lab)	6th Count

Party Share of Vote

1st Preferences	Number	%	Gain/Loss
Fianna Fáil	20,431	37.97	-3.34%
Fine Gael	16,602	30.85	1.76%
Labour	11,249	20.91	-0.07%
Green Party	1,572	2.92	0.44%
Sinn Féin	3,672	6.82	1.09%
Others	282	0.52	0.12%

Statistics

Electorate	84,354	
Total Poll	54,285	64.35
Spoiled	477	0.88
Total Valid Poll	53,808	63.79
Seats	4	
Quota	10,762	
Candidates	10	

	Quotas	Seats
FF	1.90	2
FG	1.54	1
Lab	1.05	1
No change		

Michael Ahern (FF)

Home Address
Libermann, Barryscourt, Carrigtwohill, Co Cork
Business Address
Department of Enterprise, Trade and Employment, Kildare Street, Dublin 2
Telephone
Home (021) 488 3592; *Fax* (021) 488 3436; *Office* (01) 631 2241; *Fax* (01)631 2808
Birth Place/Date
Dungourney, Co Cork. 20 January 1949
Married
Margaret Monahan. 3 daughters
Education
Rockwell College, Cashel, Co Tipperary; University College, Dublin (BA); Kimmage Manor, Dublin
Occupation
Minister of State. Registered auditor and accountant

Michael Ahern was appointed Minister of State at the Department of Enterprise, Trade and Employment and Education and Science, with special responsibility for Innovation Policy, on 20 June 2007.

First elected to the Dáil in February 1982, he was Minister of State at the Department of Enterprise, Trade and Employment, with special responsibility for Trade and Commerce, 2002–07. Minister of State at the Department of Industry and Commerce, with special responsibility for Science and Technology, 1992–93. Chairperson of the Oireachtas Joint Committee on Finance and the Public Service and of the Committee on Consolidation of Bills 1997–2002. Party deputy spokesperson on Transport 1984–87. Spokesperson on the Office of Public Works and Taxation Policy 1995–97.

Member, Carrigtwohill Community Council; Dungourney Hurling Club; Midleton Gaelic Football Club; Midleton Rugby Club; Muintir na Tíre.

Michael Ahern is a son of the late Liam Ahern, Senator 1957–73 and Dáil deputy for Cork North-East 1973–74.

His granduncle, John Dineen, was Farmers' Party Dáil deputy 1922–27.

Ned O'Keeffe (FF)

Home Address
Ballylough, Mitchelstown, Co Cork
Telephone
Home (022) 25285; *Fax* (022) 25495
Birth Place/Date
Ballylough, Mitchelstown, 1 August 1942
Married
Ann Buckley. 3 sons, 2 daughters
Education
Darra College, Clonakilty, Co Cork; University College, Cork (Diploma in Social and Rural Science)
Occupation
Formerly company director, farmer

Ned O'Keeffe was first elected to the Dáil in November 1982. Minister of State at the Department of Agriculture and Food, with special responsibility for Food, 1997–2001 (resigned following an inquiry into his declaration of personal interests). Senator, Taoiseach's nominee, May–November 1982. Party spokesman on Industry 1982–87. Deputy spokesperson on Enterprise and Employment, with responsibility for Commerce, Science and Technology and Small Businesses, 1994–97.

Member, Cork County Council 1985–97. Chairman, Northern Committee 1985–86; member, Library Committee.

He has served as member, Regional Council and Council of Dairygold Co-operative Society.

Director, Mitchelstown Co-operative Society 1974–82; director, Agricultural Credit Corporation 1980–82; member, Irish Co-operative Organisation Society (ICOS) 1978–81.

Member, Macra na Feirme 1958–71; Irish Farmers' Association 1969–82; Chairman, Cork County Executive 1979–82. Member, Gaelic Athletic Association.

David Stanton (FG)

Home Address
Coppingerstown, Midleton, Co Cork
Constituency Office
29 St Mary's Road, Midleton, Co Cork
Telephone
Constituency office (021) 463 2867;
Fax (021) 462 1133;
Website www.stanton.ie
Birth Place/Date
Cork. 15 February 1957
Married
Mary Lehane. 4 sons
Education
St Colman's Vocational School, Midleton;
Sharman Crawford Technical Institute, Cork;
University College, Cork (BA, MEd, Diploma in
Career Guidance, Diploma in Educational
Administration)
Occupation
Full-time public representative. Former
teacher, career guidance counsellor

David Stanton was elected to the Dáil in 1997
at his first attempt.

Fine Gael front bench spokesperson on Social
and Family Affairs 2004–07 and deputy
spokesperson on Education and Science
2002–04. Front bench spokesperson on
Labour Affairs, Consumer Rights and Trade
1997–2002.

Served as a commissioned officer in An Fórsa
Cosanta Áitiúil. Director and former public
relations officer of Midleton and District Day
Care Centre Ltd, and member of the
Chambers of Commerce at Cobh, Youghal
and Midleton.

Seán Sherlock (Lab)

Home Address
20 Blackwater Drive, Mallow, Co Cork
Telephone
Home (022) 21053; *Mobile* 087 740 2057;
Email seansherlockmcc@gmail.com
Birth Place/Date
Cork. 6 December 1972
Marital Status
Single
Education
Patrician Academy, Mallow; College of
Commerce, Cork; University College, Galway
(BA Economics and Politics)
Occupation
Public representative

Seán Sherlock is a new member of the Dáil.
He was appointed party spokesperson on
Agriculture and Food in September 2007.

He was co-opted to Cork County Council and
Mallow Town Council in 2003 and elected to
both in 2004. Mayor of Mallow, 2004. Former
assistant to Labour Party president and MEP
Proinsias de Rossa.

Member, Blackwater Kayaking Club, Mallow
Rugby Club, and Mountaineering Club of
Ireland.

Seán Sherlock is a son of the late Joe
Sherlock, Sinn Féin, the Workers' Party TD
for Cork East 1981–82, Workers' Party TD
1987–92, Labour Party TD 2002–07, and
member of the Labour Panel of the Seanad
1993–97.

Cork East

	1st Count	2nd Count Transfer of Carr, Cronin, Iremonger Votes	3rd Count Transfer of McLellan Votes	4th Count Transfer of Ahern Surplus	5th Count Transfer of Mulvihill Votes	6th Count Transfer of O'Keeffe Surplus
Seats 4 Quota 10,762						
AHERN, Michael* (FF)	10,350	(+186) 10,536	(+685) 11,221			
BRADFORD, Paul (FG)	8,916	(+194) 9,110	(+265) 9,375	(+23) 9,398	(+439) 9,837	(+26) 9,863
CARR, Christy (Ind)	166					
CRONIN, John (Ind)	116					
IREMONGER, Sarah (GP)	1,572					
McLELLAN, Sandra (SF)	3,672	(+271) 3,943				
MULVIHILL John Snr (Lab)	3,954	(+278) 4,232	(+541) 4,773	(+47) 4,820		
O'KEEFFE, Ned* (FF)	10,081	(+108) 10,189	(+552) 10,741	(+292) 11,033		
SHERLOCK, Seán (Lab)	7,295	(+355) 7,650	(+637) 8,287	(+37) 8,324	(+1,776) 10,100	(+62) 10,162
STANTON, David* (FG)	7,686	(+352) 8,038	(+679) 8,717	(+60) 8,777	(+1,572) 10,349	(+37) 10,386
NON-TRANSFERABLE		110	584		1,033	146

JNP | ARCHITECTS

Design Excellence

DUBLIN OFFICE

30 Northwood Court, Dublin 9

t: **+353 (0) 1 894 0100**

e: **s.finnegan@jnp-architects.net**

BELFAST OFFICE

20 Wildflower Way,

Belfast, BT12 6TA

t: **+44 (0) 28 9033 0111**

e: **g.scott@jnp-architects.com**

Cork North-Central

Elected

Billy Kelleher (FF)*	1st Count
Bernard Allen (FG)*	7th Count
Kathleen Lynch (Lab)*	7th Count
Noel O'Flynn *(FF)	7th Count

Party Share of Vote

1st Preferences	Number	%	Gain/Loss
Fianna Fáil	15,136	35.74	-5.74%
Fine Gael	11,674	27.57	7.18%
Labour	5,221	12.33	0.56%
Prog Democrats	0	0.00	-6.92%
Green Party	1,503	3.55	0.99%
Sinn Féin	3,456	8.16	1.83%
Others	5,357	12.65	2.10%

Statistics

Electorate	67,777	
Total Poll	42,818	63.17
Spoiled	471	1.10
Total Valid Poll	42,347	62.48
Seats	4	
Quota	8,470	
Candidates	13	

	Quotas	Seats
FF	1.79	2
FG	1.38	1
Lab	0.62	1

Previously 5-seat constituency returning 3 FF, 1 FG and 1 Lab

Billy Kelleher (FF)

Home Address
Ballyphilip, White's Cross, Glanmire, Co Cork
Constituency Office
28A Ballyhooley Road, Dillon's Cross, Cork
Telephone
Home (021) 482 1045; *Constituency office* (021) 450 2289; *Mobile* 087 258 0521; *Fax* (021) 502356
Birth Place/Date
Cork. 20 January 1968
Married
Liza Davis. 2 daughters
Education
Sacred Heart College, Carrignavar, Co Cork; Agricultural College, Limerick
Occupation
Minister of State. Farmer

Billy Kelleher was appointed Minister of State at the Department of Enterprise, Trade and Employment, with special responsibility for Labour Affairs, on 20 June 2007.

He was first elected to the Dáil in 1997. Former member of Joint Committees on Agriculture, Food and the Marine: Environment and Local Government: Tourism, Sport and Recreation. He was a Senator, Taoiseach's nominee, 1992–97. He was a candidate in the 1992 general election in Cork North Central, losing out on the last seat by 25 votes. He was also a candidate in the by-election in the same constituency in 1994, caused by the death of Gerry O'Sullivan (Lab).

Bernard Allen (FG)

Home Address
7 Mount Prospect, Shanakiel, Cork
Constituency Office
90 Shandon Street, Cork
Telephone
Home (021) 430 3068; *Fax* (021) 430 4200; *Office* (021) 439 7972; *Fax* (021) 430 4188
Birth Place/Date
Cork. 9 September 1944
Married
Marie Dorney. 3 daughters
Education
North Monastery CBS, Cork; Regional Technical College; University College, Cork (Diploma in Chemical Technology)
Occupation
Full-time public representative. Formerly laboratory technologist

Bernard Allen was Fine Gael spokesperson on Foreign Affairs in the 29th Dáil from 2004 to 2007, and on the Environment and Local Government from 2002 to 2004.

First elected to the Dáil in 1981, he was Chairman of the Dáil's Sub-Committee on European Affairs, 2004–07.

He was Minister of State at the Department of Education, with special responsibility for Youth and Sport, 1994–97; Minister of State at the Department of the Environment, with special responsibility for Local Government Reform and Urban Traffic Management, 1994–97. Front bench spokesperson on Tourism, Sport and Recreation 1997–2002; on Social Welfare 1993–94; on Health 1987–88; on Environmental Protection 1982. Former member of Oireachtas Committee on Health and Children.

Alderman, Cork City Council 1979–95 (Lord Mayor, 1988–89).

Member, Pitch and Putt Union of Ireland; Bol-Chumann na hÉireann; Golfing Union of Ireland.

Kathleen Lynch (Lab)

Home Address
5 Assumption Road, Blackpool, Cork
Telephone
Home/Office (021) 439 9930;
Fax (021) 430 4293
Birth Place/Date
Cork. 7 June 1953
Married
Bernard Lynch. 3 daughters, 1 son
Education
Blackpool School, Cork
Occupation
Full-time public representative

Kathleen Lynch was appointed Labour Party spokesperson on Disability Issues and Equality in September 2007.

She was first elected to the Dáil in 1994 as a Democratic Left candidate in the Cork North-Central by-election caused by the death of the Labour TD, Gerry O'Sullivan. She lost her seat in the 1997 general election and was re-elected in 2002.

Member of Cork City Council 1985–2003.

She is sister-in-law of Ciarán Lynch, new TD for Cork South-Central.

Noel O'Flynn (FF)

Home Address
Melvindale House, Coolowen, Blarney,
Co Cork
Constituency Office
Unit 3A, N.O.F. Commercial Centre, Kilnap,
Mallow Road, Cork
Telephone
Home (021) 438 2500; *Constituency office*
(021) 421 1200; *Fax* (021) 421 1110;
Website www.noeloflynn.ie
Birth Place/Date
Cork. December 1951
Married
Frances O'Keeffe. 3 sons
Education
Regional Technical College, Cork
Occupation
Full-time public representative. Company
director

Noel O'Flynn was first elected a Dáil deputy in 1997. Chairperson of the Joint Committee on Communications, Marine and Natural Resources 2002–07 and ICT sub-committee 2002–07. Member of Oireachtas Committees on Justice, Equality and Women's Rights; Public Enterprise, Enterprise and Small Business; and was Government Whip on Finance and Public Services Committee in 28th Dáil. Was member of Mini CTC Sub-Committee which inquired into CIÉ/Iarnród Éireann.

Member, Cork City Council 1991–2003. Alderman, 1999–2003. Member, Southern Health Board; Institute of Motor Industry; Society of Operations Engineers; Society of Irish Motor Industry.

Cork North-Central

	1st Count	2nd Count Transfer of **Kelleher** Surplus	3rd Count Transfer of **Brennan, McCarthy,** **Saleh, Tynan** Votes
Seats 4 **Quota 8,470**			
ALLEN, Bernard* (FG)	6,866	6,935	7,066
BARRY, Mick (Soc)	1,700	*(+7)* 1,707	*(+134)* 1,841
BRENNAN, Niall (Ind)	84	*(+1)* 85	
KELLEHER, Billy* (FF)	9,456		
KELLY, Gerry (FG)	4,808	*(+82)* 4,890	*(+135)* 5,025
LYNCH, Kathleen* (Lab)	5,221	*(+94)* 5,315	*(+198)* 5,513
McCARTHY, Dave (Ind)	2,492	(+41) 2,533	(+129) 2,662
McCARTHY, John (Ind)	702	(+11) 713	
O'BRIEN, Jonathan (SF)	3,456	(+31) 3,487	(+134) 3,621
O'FLYNN, Noel* (FF)	5,680	*(+618)* 6,298	*(+112)* 6,410
O'LEARY, Chris (GP)	1,503	(+25) 1,528	(+162) 1,690
SALEH, Stephen (Ind)	116	(+3) 119	
TYNAN, Ted (WP)	263	(+4) 267	
NON-TRANSFERABLE			49

4th Count	5th Count	6th Count	7th Count
Transfer of **O'Leary** Votes	Transfer of **Barry** Votes	Transfer of **McCarthy** Votes	Transfer of **O'Brien** Votes
7,267	7,515	8,193	9,258
(+154) 1,995			
(+226) 5,251	(+101) 5,352	(+181) 5,533	(+360) 5,893
(+591) 6,104	(+569) 6,673	(+693) 7,366	(+1,695) 9,061
(+114) 2,776	(+288) 3,064		
(+155) 3,776	(+557) 4,333	(+741) 5,074	
(+121) 6,531	(+81) 6,612	(+431) 7,043	(+603) 7,646
128	151	340	1,351

Cork North-West

Elected

Michael Creed (FG)	3rd Count
Michael Moynihan (FF)*	4th Count
Batt O'Keeffe (FF)*	5th Count

Party Share of Vote

1st Preferences	Number	%	Gain/Loss
Fianna Fáil	24,732	53.05	2.99%
Fine Gael	17,913	38.42	-3.66%
Labour	2,288	4.91	-1.97%
Green Party	1,687	3.62	3.62%
Others	0	0.00	-0.99%

Statistics

Electorate	64,085	
Total Poll	47,021	73.37
Spoiled	401	0.85
Total Valid Poll	46,620	72.75
Seats	3	
Quota	11,656	
Candidates	7	

	Quotas	Seats
FF	2.12	2
FG	1.54	1
No change		

Michael Creed (FG)

Home Address
1 Sullane Weirs, Macroom, Co Cork
Constituency Office
Main Street, Macroom, Co Cork
Telephone
Home (026) 42944; *Office* (026) 41835, *Fax* (026) 41895; *Mobile* (087) 242 4631
Birth Place/Date
Cork. 29 June 1963
Married
Sinéad. 1 daughter, 1 son
Education
St Colman's College, Fermoy, Co Cork; De La Salle College, Macroom; University College, Cork (BA, HDipEd); DIT Rathmines, Dublin (Diploma in Legal Studies)
Occupation
Public representative. Businessman

Michael Creed was re-elected in 2007, having lost his seat in 2002. He had previously sat in the Dáil since 1989. He was appointed party spokesperson on Agriculture, Fisheries and Food in September 2007.

Chairman of the Dáil's Small Business and Services Committee 1995–97. Chairman, Fine Gael Parliamentary Party Committee on Enterprise and Economic Strategy 1993–94; Committee on Health 1989–93. Front bench spokesperson on Education; Arts, Culture and the Gaeltacht 1994, Health 1989–93; Youth and Sport 1993–94.

Co-opted to Cork County Council 1987 and member since then until re-election to Dáil. Chairperson, Cork County Council 2005–06.

Member, Macroom Macra na Feirme, Macroom GAA Club. Won County and Munster National Debating titles in 1987.

Son of Donal Creed, TD for Mid-Cork 1965–81 and Cork North-West 1981–89. Minister of State 1981–86.

Michael Moynihan (FF)

Home Address
Meens, Kiskeam, Mallow, Co Cork
Constituency Office
Percival Street, Kanturk, Co Cork
Telephone
Home (029) 76200; *Constituency office* (029) 51299 and (063) 21088; *Fax* (029) 51300; *Mobile* 087 274 5810
Birth Place/Date
Cork. 12 January 1968
Married
Bríd O'Sullivan
Education
Boherbue Comprehensive School, Mallow
Occupation
Full-time public representative. Farmer

Michael Moynihan was elected to the Dáil in 1997 in his first general election. He was Chairman of the Joint Committee on Education and Science 2004–07. Member of the Committees on Heritage and the Irish Language and Agriculture, Food and the Marine during the 28th Dáil.

Life member, Kiskeam GAA Club. Vice-Chairman, Kiskeam Seán Moylan Commemoration Committee.

Batt O'Keeffe (FF)

Home Address
8 Westcliffe, Ballincollig, Co Cork
Constituency Office
Commercial Park, Ballincollig, Co Cork
Telephone
Home/Office (021) 487 1393;
Fax (021) 487 1393
Birth Place/Date
Cullen, Mallow, Co Cork. 2 April 1945
Married
Mary Murphy. 1 son, 3 daughters
Education
St Brendan's College, Killarney, Co Kerry;
University College, Cork (BA, HDipEd)
Occupation
Minister of State. Formerly lecturer in Cork
Institute of Technology

Batt O'Keeffe was appointed Minister of State
at the Department of the Environment,
Heritage and Local Government, with special
responsibility for Housing, Urban Renewal and
Developing Areas, on 20 June 2007.

He was Minister of State at the Department of
the Environment, Heritage and Local
Government 2004–07; Chairman of the Health
and Children Committee 1997–2002 in the 28th
Dáil; Chairman of the Sustaining Development
Committee 1995–97 in the 27th Dáil.

He was first elected in 1989 but lost his seat
in 1989 and was re-elected 1992. Senator,
Labour panel, 1989–92. Moved from Cork
South-Central constituency to Cork North-
West in the 2007 election because of a
constituency revision.

Member, Cork County Council 1985–2003;
Former Chairman, Southern Health Board.

Cork footballer and holder of Munster medals
at under-21, junior and senior levels. Cork
Intermediate Handball Champion 1980.

Cork North-West

Seats 3 Quota 11,656	1st Count	2nd Count Transfer of **Robinson** Votes	3rd Count Transfer of **Coughlan** Votes	4th Count Transfer of **Moynihan, D** Votes	5th Count Transfer of **Moynihan, M** Votes
COUGHLAN, Martin (Lab)	2,288	(+692) 2,980			
CREED, Michael (FG)	10,516	(+362) 10,878	(+1,542) 12,420		
MOYNIHAN, Donal* (FF)	6,546	(+92) 6,638	(+281) 6,919		
MOYNIHAN, Michael* (FF)	10,146	(+97) 10,243	(+141) 10,384	(+3,617) 14,001	
MURPHY, Gerard* (FG)	7,397	(+148) 7,545	(+425) 7,970	(+339) 8,309	(+348) 8,657
O'KEEFFE, Batt* (FF)	8,040	(+173) 8,213	(+285) 8,498	(+2,170) 10,668	(+1,997) 12,665
ROBINSON, Caroline (GP)	1,687				
NON-TRANSFERABLE		123	306	793	

Fine Gael leader Enda Kenny and Labour leader Pat Rabbitte at a joint press conference in Dublin, 4 May 2007, at the first news conference of the Alliance for Change coalition led by Fine Gael and Labour.

Cork South-Central

Elected

Micheál Martin (FF)*	1st Count
Michael McGrath (FF)	1st Count
Deirdre Clune (FG)	6th Count
Ciarán Lynch (Lab)	6th Count
Simon Coveney (FG)*	6th Count

Party Share of Vote

1st Preferences	Number	%	Gain/Loss
Fianna Fáil	26,154	44.28	-4.29%
Fine Gael	16,782	28.41	9.01%
Labour	5,466	9.25	3.31%
Prog Democrats	1,596	2.70	2.70%
Green Party	4,945	8.37	-0.59%
Sinn Féin	3,020	5.11	1.38%
Others	1,105	1.87	-11.51%

Statistics

Electorate	91,090	
Total Poll	59,660	65.50
Spoiled	592	0.99
Total Valid Poll	59,068	64.85
Seats	5	
Quota	9,845	
Candidates	14	

	Quotas	Seats
FF	2.66	2
FG	1.70	2
Lab	0.56	1

FG and Lab gains from FF and GP

Micheál Martin (FF)

Home Address
16 Silver Manor, Ballincollig, Cork
Business Address
Department of Enterprise, Trade and Employment, Kildare Street, Dublin 2, Ireland
Telephone
Home (021) 432 0088; *Office* (01) 631 2121; *LoCall* 1890 220 222; *Fax*: (01) 631 2827; *Email* info@entemp.ie
Website www.entemp.ie
Birth Place/Date
Cork. 1 August 1960
Married
Mary O'Shea. 4 children
Education
Coláiste Chríosti Rí, Cork; University College, Cork (MA in Political History)
Occupation
Government Minister. Formerly secondary school teacher

Micheál Martin was re-appointed Minister for Enterprise, Trade and Employment on 14 June 2007, a position he also held in the 29th Dáil following a Cabinet re-shuffle in September 2004. He was Minister for Health from January 2000 to September 2004 and Minister for Education and Science from June 1997 to January 2000. First elected to the Dáil in 1989.

Former Chairman of the Oireachtas All-Party Committee on the Irish Language (and a fluent speaker of the language); a former member of the Dáil Committee on Crime and a former member of the Dáil Committee on Finance and General Affairs. He was Opposition spokesperson for Education and the Gaeltacht from 1995 to 1997.

Member, Cork City Council 1985–97 (Lord Mayor, 1992–93, Alderman from 1991). Chairman of Arts Committee 1987–88. Former Chairman, City of Cork Vocational Education Committee. He has served on the Governing Body of University College, Cork, and of Cork Regional Technical College.

Michael McGrath (FF)

Home Address
162 Dun Eoin, Carrigaline, Co Cork
Telephone
Home (021) 491 9689; *Mobile* 086 839 3304
Birth Place/Date
Cork. 23 August 1976
Married
Sarah O'Brien. 2 children
Education
St Peter's Community College, Passage West, Co Cork; University College, Cork (BComm)
Occupation
Chartered accountant

Michael McGrath is a new deputy.

His first election was to Passage West Town Council in 1999 and he was re-elected in 2004; Chairperson of the council 2000–01. Elected to Cork County Council in the local elections in 2004, topping the poll in his electoral area at the first attempt.

Unsuccessful candidate for the Industrial and Commercial panel in the Seanad election 2002. Resigned as Head of Management Information and Systems in UCC in 2005 to concentrate on constituency work.

Deirdre Clune (FG)

Home Address
144 Blackrock Road, Cork
Constituency Office
Douglas Village, East Douglas, Cork
Telephone
Home (021) 436 4934; *Office* (021) 489 0000;
Mobile 087 244 7027;
Website www.deirdreclune.com
Birth Place/Date
Cork. June 1959
Married
Conor Clune. 4 sons
Education
Ursuline Convent, Blackrock, Cork; University
College Cork (BE, Diploma in Management for
Engineers, Higher Diploma in Environmental
Engineering)
Occupation
Public representative. Civil engineer

Deirdre Clune was first elected in 1997 but
lost her seat in 2002.

Former Fine Gael spokesperson on the
Environment and on Arts and Heritage.
Member of the Oireachtas Committee for
Health and Children in 28th Dáil.

Member, Cork City Council 1999–2007. Lord
Mayor, 2005–06.

She is a daughter of Peter Barry, Dáil deputy
for Cork constituencies 1969–97, Tánaiste
1987, Minister for Foreign Affairs 1982–87,
Minister for Environment 1981–82, Minister
for Transport and Power 1973–76, Minister for
Education 1976–77, Deputy Leader of Fine
Gael 1979–87 and 1989–93.

She is granddaughter of Anthony Barry, TD for
Cork Borough 1954–57 and 1961–65, Senator
(Cultural and Educational panel) 1957–61.

Ciarán Lynch (Lab)

Home Address
31 Yewlands, Maryborough Woods, Douglas,
Co Cork
Constituency Office
Labour Party Offices, Bandon Road, Cork
Telephone
Office (021) 431 2705; *Mobile* 086 856 2600;
Email ciaranmail@eircom.net
Website www.ciaranlynch.ie
Birth Place/Date
Cork. 13 June 1964
Married
Bernadette. 2 children
Education
University College, Cork (Social Studies),
Waterford IT (Humanities)
Occupation
Public representative. Adult literacy organiser

Ciarán Lynch is a new deputy. He was
appointed party spokesperson on Housing
and Local Government in September 2007.

He contested the local elections in 1997.
Chairman of Labour Party, Cork South-Central
Constituency.

Member, Teachers' Union of Ireland, Adult
Literacy Organisers' Association National
Executive, National Adult Literacy Agency,
City of Cork VEC Adult Education Board, Cork
City Library Committee, Kinsale Road Dump
Action Group, Carr's Hill Famine Cemetery
Commemorative Committee.

Chairperson, Cork City Community Education
Network.

He is a brother-in-law of Kathleen Lynch, TD
for Cork North-Central.

Simon Coveney (FG)

Home Address
1 Abbotswood, Monastery Road, Cork
Constituency Office
6a Anglesea Street, Cork
Telephone
Constituency office (021) 431 3100;
Fax (021) 431 6696; *Mobile* 087 832 1755;
Website www.simoncoveney.ie
Birth Place/Date
Cork. 16 June 1972
Marital Status
Single
Education
Clongowes Wood College, Co Kildare;
University College, Cork; Gurteen Agricultural
College; Royal Agricultural College,
Gloucestershire, England (BSc Agriculture and
Land Management)
Occupation
Full-time public representative. Formerly
farmer and sailing instructor

Simon Coveney was appointed party
spokesperson on Communications, Energy and
Natural Resources in September 2007. He was
elected to the European Parliament in 2004 but
chose to contest the general election, and gave
up his European seat on election. He was first
elected to the Dáil in a by-election for Cork
South-Central in October 1998 following the
death of his father.

In the European Parliament, he was a
member of the committees on Foreign
Affairs, the Internal Market and Consumer
Protection, and Fisheries. Member,
delegations for relations with the United
States and Iran.

Member, Cork County Council 1999 to 2003.

He is son of Hugh Coveney, TD for Cork
South-Central 1981–87 and 1994–98, Minister
for Defence and Minister for the Marine
1994–95, and Minister of State at the
Department of Finance 1995–97.

Cork South-Central

Seats 5 Quota 9,845	1st Count	2nd Count Transfer of **Martin** Surplus	3rd Count Transfer of **Fitzgerald, Linehan, Neville Stack** Votes	4th Count Transfer of **Cremin, Minihan** Votes	5th Count Transfer of **Buttimer** Votes	6th Count Transfer of **Boyle** Votes
BOYLE, Dan* (GP)	4,945	(+112) 5,057	(+206) 5,263	(+1,055) 6,318	(+676) 6,994	
BUTTIMER, Jerry (FG)	5,180	(+62) 5,242	(+95) 5,337	(+423) 5,760		
CLUNE, Deirdre (FG)	5,739	(+104) 5,843	(+98) 5,941	(+506) 6,447	(+2,118) 8,565	(+1,310) 9,875
COVENEY, Simon* (FG)	5,863	(+97) 5,960	(+98) 6,058	(+393) 6,451	(+1,591) 8,042	(+1,321) 9,363
CREMIN, Henry (SF)	3,020	(+34) 3,054	(+144) 3,198			
DENNEHY, John* (FF)	5,062	(+748) 5,810	(+111) 5,921	(+1,166) 7,087	(+361) 7,448	(+619) 8,067
FITZGERALD, Maurice (Ind)	30	(+1) 31				
LINEHAN, Gerard (Ind)	155	(+1) 156				
LYNCH, Ciarán (Lab)	5,466	(+100) 5,566	(+164) 5,730	(+798) 6,528	(+757) 7,285	(+2,566) 9,851
MARTIN, Micheál* (FF)	11,226					
McGRATH, Michael (FF)	9,866					
MINIHAN, John (PD)	1,596	(+110) 1,706	(+101) 1,807			
NEVILLE, Ted (Ind)	804	(+10) 814				
STACK, Morgan (Ind)	116	(+2) 118				
NON-TRANSFERABLE			102	664	257	1,178

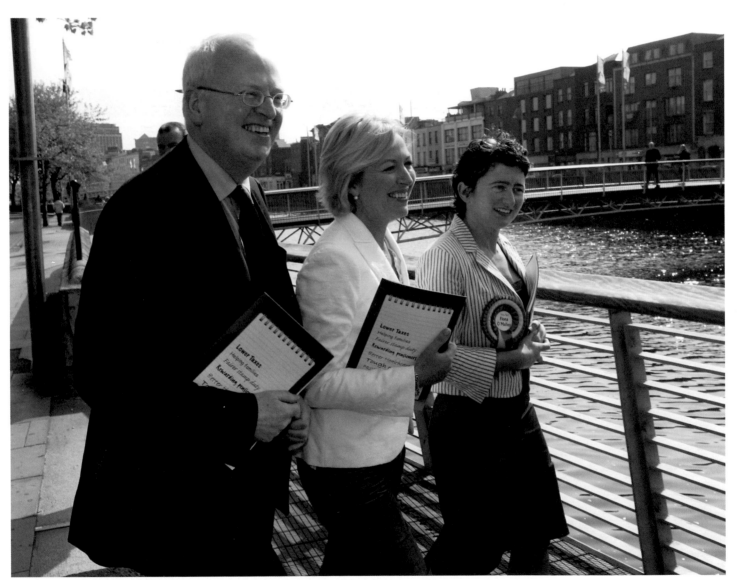

Michael McDowell with Liz O'Donnell and Fiona O'Malley before the launch of the Progressive Democrats manifesto in Dublin, 30 April 2007. All three would lose their seats in the election.

Cork South-West

Elected

Party Share of Vote

1st Preferences	Number	%	Gain/Loss
Fianna Fáil	18,093	42.57	3.10%
Fine Gael	15,299	36.00	3.67%
Labour	4,095	9.64	0.51%
Green Party	2,860	6.73	6.73%
Sinn Féin	2,150	5.06	-0.80%
Others	0	0.00	-13.20%

Statistics

Electorate	61,577	
Total Poll	42,907	69.68
Spoiled	410	0.96
Total Valid Poll	42,497	69.01
Seats	3	
Quota	10,625	
Candidates	7	

	Quotas	Seats
FF	1.70	1
FG	1.44	2
FG gain from FF		

Christy O'Sullivan (FF)

Home Address
Hillside, Tawnies, Clonakilty, Co Cork
Constituency Office
McCurtain Hill, Clonakilty
Telephone
Office (023) 33465; *Mobile* 086 856 5582
Birth Place/Date
Cork. 27 November 1948
Married
Paddi O'Connell. 7 children
Education
De La Salle College, Skibbereen, Co Cork
Occupation
Full-time public representative

Christy O'Sullivan is a new TD. He contested the 2002 election as an Independent and took the seat in 2007 at the expense of the sitting Fianna Fáil deputy, Denis O'Donovan.

He was elected to Cork County Council as an Independent in 1999 and 2004, topping the poll for the Skibbereen electoral area on both occasions. Interests include horses, trotting, sulky racing, road bowling and restoring old cottages.

Jim O'Keeffe (FG)

Home Address
Oldchapel, Bandon, Co Cork
Telephone
Home (023) 41399; *Fax* (023) 41421;
Mobile 087 259 1694
Birth Place/Date
Skibbereen, Co Cork. 31 March 1941
Married
Maeve O'Sullivan. 1 son, 7 daughters
Education
St Fachtna's High School, Skibbereen; University College, Cork; University College, Dublin; Law School of the Incorporated Law Society of Ireland, Dublin
Occupation
Public representative. Solicitor and Notary Public

Jim O'Keeffe was first elected to the Dáil for Cork South-West in 1977.

Minister of State at the Departments of Finance and the Public Service, February 1986–March 1987; Minister of State at the Department of Foreign Affairs, with special responsibility for Development Cooperation, 1982–86 and June 1981–March 1982.

He was chairman of the All-Party Committee on the Constitution in 1993. Fine Gael front bench spokesperson on Justice, Equality and Law Reform in the last Dáil and previously on a large number of portfolios including Social, Community and Family Affairs; Foreign Affairs; Justice; Social Welfare; Agriculture; Health; Security; and Law Reform.

Leader of Fine Gael delegation on the British–Irish Inter-Parliamentary Body, and the Parliamentary Assembly of the Council of Europe. Member of the Oireachtas European Affairs Committee.

Cork South-West

P.J. Sheehan (FG)

Home Address
Main Street, Goleen, Co Cork
Constituency Office
The Quay, Bantry, Co Cork
Telephone
Home (028) 35236; *Office* (027) 52011;
Fax (027) 52013
Birth Place/Date
Kilbrown, Goleen. March 1933
Married
Elizabeth Frances Collins. 1 son, 3 daughters
Education
Kilroy's College, Dublin
Occupation
Full-time public representative. Former
auctioneer, merchant and farmer

P.J. Sheehan was returned to the 30th Dáil
having lost the seat he first won in 1981, in
the 2002 general election.

He was Fine Gael's junior spokesperson on
Agriculture — Livestock Breeding and
Horticulture, 2000 to 2001; party
spokesperson on Agriculture and Forestry, and
Assistant Whip 1997–2000. Former member
of the Dáil Committees on Enterprise and
Economic Strategy; Sustainable Development;
and of the Joint Committee on Small
Businesses.

Member, Cork Council Council 1967–2007.
Member, Muintir na Tíre; Irish Farmers'
Association; Irish Creamery Milk Suppliers'
Association; Carberry Agricultural Society
Show Committee; Schull Agricultural Society
Show Committee; Kealkil Show Society; and
the Munster Agricultural Show Committee.

Seats 3 Quota 10,625	1st Count	2nd Count Transfer of **Ó Súilleabháin** Votes	3rd Count Transfer of **Gargan** Votes	4th Count Transfer of **McCarthy** Votes
GARGAN, Quentin (GP)	2,860	(+433) 3,293		
McCARTHY, Michael (Lab)	4,095	(+376) 4,471	(+1,441) 5,912	
Ó SÚILLEABHÁIN, Cionnaith (SF)	2,150			
O'DONOVAN, Denis* (FF)	7,760	(+248) 8,008	(+409) 8,417	(+1,003) 9,420
O'KEEFFE, Jim* (FG)	7,560	*(+253)* 7,813	*(+658)* 8,471	*(+2,196)* 10,667
O'SULLIVAN, Christy (FF)	10,333	*(+481)* 10,814		
SHEEHAN, P.J. (FG)	7,739)	*(+237* 7,976	*(+411)* 8,387	*(+1,739)* 10,126
NON-TRANSFERABLE		122	374	974

Donegal North-East

Elected

Party Share of Vote

1st Preferences	Number	%	Gain/Loss
Fianna Fáil	19,374	50.26	0.87%
Fine Gael	8,711	22.60	1.59%
Labour	703	1.82	-0.99%
Green Party	520	1.35	1.35%
Sinn Féin	6,733	17.47	7.53%
Others	2,504	6.50	-10.35%

Statistics

Electorate	57,244	
Total Poll	38,931	68.01
Spoiled	386	0.99
Total Valid Poll	38,545	67.33
Seats	3	
Quota	9,637	
Candidates	11	

	Quotas	Seats
FF	2.01	2
FG	0.90	1
FG gain from Ind		

Joe McHugh (FG)

Home Address
Claggan, Carrigart, Letterkenny, Co Donegal
Constituency Office
Grier House, Lower Main Street, Letterkenny
Telephone
Constituency office (074) 916 4787;
Mobile 087 624 1525;
Website www.donegalmatters.com
Birth Place/Date
Carrigart, Co Donegal. 16 July 1971
Married
Olwyn Enright
Education
Umlagh NS; Loreto Convent, Milford; NUI Maynooth (BA Hons Economics and Sociology, HDipEd)
Occupation
Public representative. Formerly teacher

Joe McHugh is a new deputy.

He was a Senator on the Administrative panel from 2002 to 2007. Member of Donegal County Council, 1999–2003.

A geography and maths teacher in Loreto College, Letterkenny, from 1993 to 1995, he also taught in Dubai from 1995 to 1996, where he set up the first GAA club in the area. Former member of Carrigart Boxing Club, Donegal league soccer player, and Gaelic footballer.

He is married to Olwyn Enright, TD for Laois–Offaly since 2002. They are the first married couple to sit in the Dáil at the same time since Fine Gael TDs Alexis Fitzgerald (1982) and Mary Flaherty (1981–97).

James McDaid (FF)

Home Address
The Forest, Thorn Road, Letterkenny, Co Donegal
Constituency Office
Pearse Road, Letterkenny, Co Donegal
Telephone
Office (074) 912 5132; *Fax* (074) 912 6637
Birth Place/Date
Donegal. 3 October 1949
Marital Status
Separated. 3 sons, 1 daughter. Current partner Siobhán O'Donnell, 1 son
Education
Currin National School, Termon; St Eunan's College, Letterkenny; University College, Galway (MB, BCh, BAO) MRCGP
Occupation
Public representative. Formerly medical doctor (GP)

James McDaid was appointed Minister of State at the Department of Transport, with responsibility for Road Traffic, including Road Haulage, 2002–04. Minister for Tourism, Sport and Recreation 1997–2002. Party front bench spokesperson on Equality and Law Reform 1997. Spokesperson on North–South Development 1995–97.

He was elected to the Dáil in 1989 on his first attempt.

He has served as a member of the All-Party Committees on Women's Rights and Public Accounts and the Committee on the Foreign Adoption Bill.

At university he was captain of the UCG soccer team. He was medical officer to Donegal senior Gaelic Athletic Association team 1983–87.

Co-founder of Donegal Hospice (with Dr Tom McGinley, Foyle Hospice, Derry). President of the Donegal Hospice Movement, having served as Chairperson 1988–98.

Niall Blaney (FF)

Home Address
Ballina, Rossnakill, Letterkenny, Co Donegal
Constituency Office
Plunkett O'Boyle Terrace, Letterkenny,
Co Donegal
Telephone
Home (074) 912 7754; *Fax* (074) 912 7783
Birth Place/Date
Letterkenny, 29 January 1974
Married
Rosaleen Shovlin
Education
Mulroy College, Milford, Letterkenny,
Co Donegal; Letterkenny Institute of
Technology (Diploma in Civil Engineering)
Occupation
Public representative. Formerly civil
engineering technician

Niall Blaney was first elected to Dáil Éireann
in 2002. He took over the Independent Fianna
Fáil seat held by his father, Harry, and before
that by his uncle, Neil T. Blaney. Independent
Fianna Fáil and Fianna Fáil amalgamated in
July 2006, bringing an end to a 35-year rift,
and resulting in Niall becoming a Fianna Fáil
TD.

Former member of Donegal County Council,
North Western Health Board and Donegal
VEC.

Niall Blaney is a son of Harry Blaney, who was
a Dáil deputy for Donegal North-East
1997–2002. He is a nephew of Neil T. Blaney,
Dáil deputy 1948–95, as a Fianna Fáil
representative up to 1971 and after that as an
Independent. He held several ministerial posts
during his long career and was also a member
of the European Parliament. Niall Blaney's
grandfather, Neal Blaney, was a Dáil deputy
1927–38 and 1943–48.

Donegal North-East

Seats 3 Quota 9,637	1st Count	2nd Count Transfer of **Doherty, McGuinness** Votes	3rd Count Transfer of **Gallagher** Votes
BLANEY, Niall* (FF)	6,288	*(+44)* 6,332	*(+28)* 6,360
DOHERTY, Mary (CSP)	339		
GALLAGHER, Frank (GP)	520	*(+26)* 546	
HARTE, Jimmy (Ind)	1,313	*(+40)* 1,353	*(+62)* 1,415
KEAVENEY, Cecilia* (FF)	6,362	*(+79)* 6,441	*(+30)* 6,471
MAC LOCHLAINN, Pádraig (SF)	6,733)	*(+56)* 6,789	*(+107)* 6,896
McDAID, Dr James* (FF)	6,724	*(+22)* 6,746	*(+40)* 6,786
McGARVEY, Ian (Ind)	766	*(+29)* 795	*(+28)* 823
McGUINNESS, Arthur (Ind)	86		
McHUGH, Joe (FG)	8,711	*(+89)* 8,800	*(+100)* 8,900
McLAUGHLIN, Siobhán (Lab)	703	*(+20)* 723	*(+121)* 844
NON-TRANSFERABLE		20	30

4th Count	5th Count	6th Count	7th Count	8th Count
Transfer of **McGarvey** Votes	Transfer of **Harte, McLaughlin** Votes	Transfer of **McHugh** Surplus	Transfer of **Keaveney** Votes	Transfer of **McDaid** Surplus
(+178) 6,538	(+264) 6,802	(+86) 6,888	(+2,235) 9,123	(+316) 9,439
(+54) 1,469				
(+10) 6,481	(+193) 6,674	(+70) 6,744		
(+101) 6,997	(+318) 7,315	(+95) 7,410	(+1,411) 8,821	(+55) 8,876
(+146) 6,932	(+411) 7,343	(+146) 7,489	(+2,519) 10,008	
(+234) 9,134	(+900) 10,034			
(+40) 884				
60	267		579	

Donegal South-West

Elected

Mary Coughlan (FF)*	1st Count
Pat Gallagher (FF)*	2nd Count
Dinny McGinley (FG)*	3rd Count

Party Share of Vote

1st Preferences	Number	%	Gain/Loss
Fianna Fáil	20,136	50.53	8.44%
Fine Gael	9,167	23.00	-2.42%
Labour	1,111	2.79	-0.24%
Green Party	589	1.48	1.48%
Sinn Féin	8,462	21.23	10.49%
Others	388	0.97	-17.75%

Statistics

Electorate	60,829	
Total Poll	40,274	66.21
Spoiled	421	1.05
Total Valid Poll	39,853	65.52
Seats	3	
Quota	9,964	
Candidates	7	

	Quotas	Seats
FF	2.02	2
FG	0.92	1
No change		

Mary Coughlan (FF)

Home Address
Ballybrillighan, Mount Charles PO, Co Donegal
Business Address
Department of Agriculture, Fisheries and Food, Kildare Street, Dublin 2
Constituency Office
Cranny, Inver, Co Donegal
Telephone
Office (01) 607 2000; *Constituency office* (073) 36002/36535
Birth Place/Date
Donegal. May 1965
Married
David Charlton. 1 son, 1 daughter
Education
Ursuline Convent, Sligo; University College, Dublin (BSocSc)
Occupation
Government minister. Formerly social worker

Mary Coughlan was re-appointed Minister for Agriculture, Fisheries and Food on 14 June 2007, having been Minister for Agriculture and Food from September 2004 to June 2007 and Minister for Social and Family Affairs from June 2002.

She was first elected to the Dáil in 1987. Minister of State at the Department of Arts, Heritage, Gaeltacht and the Islands 2001–02. Vice-Chairperson of Oireachtas Committee on Tourism, Sport and Recreation and member of Committee on Justice, Equality and Law Reform. Member of British–Irish Inter-Parliamentary Body.

President of Killybegs Coast and Cliff Rescue Service.

She is daughter of the late Cathal Coughlan, Dáil deputy for Donegal South-West 1983–86, and niece of the late Clement Coughlan, Dáil deputy for the same constituency 1980–83.

Pat 'the Cope' Gallagher (FF)

Home Address
Dungloe, Co Donegal
Constituency Office
Dungloe
Telephone
Home (075) 21364; *Constituency office* (075) 21176; *Fax* (075) 21133;
Website www.patthecope.com
Birth Place/Date
Burtonport, Co Donegal. 10 March 1948
Married
Ann Gillespie
Education
Roshine National School, Dungloe; Luinneach National School, Gweedore; High School, Dungloe; St Enda's College, Galway; University College, Galway (BComm)
Occupation
Minister of State. Formerly fish exporter.

Pat the Cope Gallagher was appointed Minister of State at the Department of Health and Children, with special responsibility for Health Promotion and Food Safety, on 20 June 2007.

Previously Minister of State at the Department of Transport, February 2006–07; at the Department of Communications, Marine and Natural Resources, with responsibility for the Marine, 2004–06; at the Department of the Environment and Local Government 2002–04; at the Department of the Marine 1987–89; for Arts, Culture and the Gaeltacht 1989–94.

First elected to the Dáil in 1981 and at all subsequent elections until 1997 when he gave up his seat to remain as a member of the European Parliament. He was re-elected to the Dáil in 2002 and stepped down as MEP for Connacht–Ulster. Member of the European Parliament 1994–2002.

Elected to Donegal County Council 1979 (Chairman, 1985–86).

His grandfather, Paddy the Cope, was a leading figure in the co-operative movement early in the last century.

Dinny McGinley (FG)

Home Address
Bunbeg, Co Donegal
Telephone
Home (075) 31719; *Constituency office*
(074) 953 1025/1719; *Fax* (074) 953 1025;
Mobile 087 241 4809
Birth Place/Date
Gweedore, Co Donegal. 27 April 1945
Marital Status
Single
Education
Coláiste Íosagáin, Ballyvourney, Co Cork;
St Patrick's Teachers' Training College,
Drumcondra, Dublin; University College,
Dublin (BA, HDipEd)
Occupation
Full-time public representative. Formerly
principal national school teacher

Dinny McGinley has been re-elected at every
election since 1982. He was Fine Gael front
bench spokesperson on Community, Rural
and Gaeltacht Affairs from 2004 to 2007, and
previously spokesperson on Defence from
2002. He was spokesperson for Arts,
Heritage and the Islands, February 2001–02.

Chairperson, Joint Oireachtas Committee on
the Irish Language 1995–97. Member,
British–Irish Parliamentary Body 1993–97.
Former member of the Joint Oireachtas
Committees on Social Affairs and on Small
Business.

Member, Donegal Vocational Education
Committee 1991–99. Member of the Irish
National Teachers' Organisation since 1965.
Member of Comhairle Raidio na Gaeltachta
1977–80.

Seats 3 Quota 9,964	1st Count	2nd Count Transfer of **Coughlan** Surplus	3rd Count Transfer of **Doherty, Ó Maolchallann, Rodgers** Votes
COUGHLAN, Mary* (FF)	10,530		
DOHERTY, John (Ind)	388	(+9) 397	
DOHERTY, Pearse (SF)	8,462	(+89) 8,551	(+712) 9,263
GALLAGHER, Pat* (FF)	9,606	(+370) 9,976	
McGINLEY, Dinny* (FG)	9,167	(+82) 9,249	(+1,032) 10,281
Ó MAOLCHALLANN, Seán (GP)	589	(+7) 596	
RODGERS, Seamus (Lab)	1,111	(+9) 1,120	
NON-TRANSFERABLE			369

Dublin Central

Elected

Party Share of Vote

1st Preferences	Number	%	Gain/Loss
Fianna Fáil	15,398	44.45	4.88%
Fine Gael	3,302	9.53	-1.52%
Labour	4,353	12.57	0.39%
Prog Democrats	193	0.56	0.56%
Green Party	1,995	5.76	1.45%
Sinn Féin	3,182	9.19	-5.42%
Others	6,216	17.95	-0.33%

Statistics

Electorate	63,423	
Total Poll	35,149	55.42
Spoiled	510	1.45
Total Valid Poll	34,639	54.62
Seats	4	
Quota	6,928	
Candidates	13	

	Quotas	Seats
FF	2.22	2
Lab	0.63	1
Ind	0.67	1
No change		

Bertie Ahern (FF)

Home Address
44 Beresford Avenue, Dublin 9
Business Address
Department of the Taoiseach, Government Buildings, Merrion Street, Dublin 2
Constituency Office
St Luke's, 161 Drumcondra Road, Dublin 9
Telephone
Constituency office (01) 837 4129;
Office (01) 662 4888
Birth Place/Date
Dublin. 12 September 1951
Marital Status
Separated. 2 daughters
Education
St Aidan's CBS, Whitehall, Dublin; Rathmines College of Commerce, Dublin; University College, Dublin
Occupation
Full-time public representative.

Bertie Ahern was re-elected Taoiseach on 14 June 2007, the first person to be re-elected Taoiseach for a third consecutive term since Eamon de Valera in the 1930s and 1940s. He was elected at the head of a three-party government of Fianna Fáil, the Green Party and the Progressive Democrats, the first three-party coalition involving Fianna Fáil.

Leader of Fianna Fáil from 1994, Taoiseach from June 1997. He was Tánaiste November–December 1994; Minister for Finance November 1991–94; Minister for Industry and Commerce, January 1993; Minister for Arts, Culture and the Gaeltacht, November–December 1994; Minister for Labour 1987– 91; Minister of State at the Department of the Taoiseach and at the Department of Defence, and Government Chief Whip, March–December 1982; Assistant Government Whip 1980–81; Opposition Chief Whip, December 1982–84. Fianna Fáil front bench Spokesman on Labour 1984–87; on Youth 1981–82.

He was first elected to the Dáil in 1977 for the constituency of Dublin-Finglas and has represented Dublin Central since 1981.

Tony Gregory (Ind)

Home Address
5 Sackville Gardens, Ballybough, Dublin 3
Telephone
Dáil office (01) 618 3488
Birth Place/Date
Dublin. 5 December 1947
Marital Status
Single
Education
St Canice's National School; Christian Brothers' O'Connell School, Dublin; University College, Dublin (BA, HDipEd)
Occupation
Full-time public representative. Formerly secondary school teacher

Tony Gregory has been a Dáil deputy since February 1982 and is the longest-sitting Independent in the house. He was the initiator and Chief Whip of the Technical Group, incorporating the Green Party, Sinn Féin, the Socialist Party and 10 Independents in the 29th Dáil.

Member of Dáil Committee on Procedures and Privileges and Oireachtas Committee on Foreign Affairs 2002–07. Served on Oireachtas Committee on European Affairs 1997–2002, Dáil Security Committee 1992–97.

Member, Dublin City Council 1979–2004. Chairman, North Centre City Community Policing Forum. Former member, Official Sinn Féin and the Irish Republican Socialist Party. Member, Association of Secondary Teachers of Ireland.

In both March 1982 and March 1987, Tony Gregory's vote was a key factor in the election of Taoiseach. In 1982, he voted for Charles Haughey and in 1987 his abstention in the vote was crucial to the success of Mr Haughey.

Joe Costello (Lab)

Home Address
66 Aughrim Street, Dublin 7
Constituency Office
334 North Circular Road, Dublin 7
Telephone
Home (01) 838 5355;
Constituency office (01) 830 8182;
Website joecostellotd.blogspot.com
Birth Place/Date
Sligo. 13 July 1945
Married
Emer Malone
Education
Summerhill College, Sligo; St Patrick's
College, Maynooth; University College, Dublin
Occupation
Public representative. Formerly secondary
school teacher

Joe Costello was first elected to the Dáil in
1992, lost his seat in 1997 and regained it in
2002. He was appointed party spokesperson
on Europe and Human Rights in September
2007.

Member, Dáil Sub-Committee on the Barron
Report on the Dublin and Monaghan
Bombings of 1974; Dáil Select Committee on
European Affairs 2006–07. Senator,
Administrative panel, 1989–92. Party Leader
in Seanad 1997–2002. Spokesperson on
Education, Science, Trade and Employment,
Sport and Finance. Member, Joint Committee
on Family, Community and Social Affairs.

Former Vice-Chairman, Parliamentary Labour
Party. Member, British–Irish Inter-
Parliamentary Body.

Member, Dublin City Council 1991–2003.
Deputy Lord Mayor, 1991–92. Former
President of Association of Secondary
Teachers of Ireland. Prisoners' Rights
Organisation 1973–87 (Chairman, 1975–85).
Member, Seán McDermott Street Community
Association; Save Temple Street Children's
Hospital Campaign; Amnesty International;
Irish Council for Civil Liberties.

Cyprian Brady (FF)

Home Address
Donaghmede, Dublin 13
Constituency Office
St Luke's, 161 Lower Drumcondra Road,
Dublin 9
Telephone
Office (01) 837 4129
Birth Place/Date
Dublin. 26 June 1962
Married
Valerie Rooney. 1 daughter, 1 son
Education
St Mary's NS, Fairview; St Joseph's CBS,
Fairview, Dublin
Occupation
Public representative. Formerly civil servant

Cyprian Brady is a new deputy, elected by
Bertie Ahern's surplus, having received fewer
than a thousand first preference votes.

He was a Taoiseach's nominee to the Seanad
2002–07 where he was party spokesperson
on the Environment and Local Government,
with responsibility for Drugs Strategy and
Community Affairs.

Dublin Central

Seats 4 Quota 6,928	1st Count	2nd Count Transfer of **Ahern** Surplus	3rd Count Transfer of **Beirne, Hannon, O'Loughlin, Talbot** Votes
AHERN, Bertie* (FF)	12,734		
BEIRNE, Alan (Ind)	116	*(+86)* 202	
BRADY, Cyprian (FF)	939	*(+2,403)* 3,342	*(+168)* 3,510
COSTELLO, Joe* (Lab)	4,353	*(+440)* 4,793	*(+77)* 4,870
DONOHOE, Paschal (FG)	3,302	*(+139)* 3,441	*(+107)* 3,548
FITZPATRICK, Mary (FF)	1,725	*(+1,362)* 3,087	*(+149)* 3,236
GREGORY, Tony* (Ind)	4,649	*(+804)* 5,453	*(+169)* 5,622
HANNON, Jerry (PD)	193	*(+33)* 226	
McDONALD, Mary Lou (SF)	3,182	*(+289)* 3,471	*(+48)* 3,519
McKENNA, Patricia (GP)	1,995	*(+121)* 2,116	*(+105)* 2,221
O'LOUGHLIN, Paul (CSP)	260	*(+9)* 269	
PERRY, Cieran (Ind)	952	*(+106)* 1,058	*(+75)* 1,133
TALBOT, Patrick (Ind)	239	*(+14)* 253	
NON-TRANSFERABLE			52

4th Count	5th Count	6th Count	7th Count	8th Count
Transfer of **Perry** Votes	Transfer of **McKenna** Votes	Transfer of **Fitzpatrick** Votes	Transfer of **Gregory** Surplus	Transfer of **McDonald** Votes
(+44) 3,554	*(+62)* 3,616	*(+1,992)* 5,608	*(+156)* 5,764	*(+584)* 6,348
(+158) 5,028	*(+781)* 5,809	*(+264)* 6,073	*(+132)* 6,205	*(+1,813)* 8,018
(+52) 3,600	*(+296)* 3,896	*(+251)* 4,147	*(+69)* 4,216	*(+340)* 4,556
(+94) 3,330	*(+117)* 3,447			
(+440) 6,062	*(+737)* 6,799	*(+586)* 7,385		
(+225) 3,744	*(+204)* 3,948	*(+172)* 4,120	*(+58)* 4,178	
(+73) 2,294				
47	97	182	42	1,441

Dublin Mid-West

Elected

John Curran (FF)*	1st Count
Paul Gogarty (GP)*	6th Count
Mary Harney (PD)*	6th Count
Joanna Tuffy (Lab)	6th Count

Party Share of Vote

1st Preferences	Number	%	Gain/Loss
Fianna Fáil	12,321	33.00	0.94%
Fine Gael	4,480	12.00	0.49%
Labour	4,075	10.91	1.91%
Prog Democrats	4,663	12.49	-7.56%
Green Party	4,043	10.83	-1.50%
Sinn Féin	3,462	9.27	2.75%
Others	4,295	11.50	2.98%

Statistics

Electorate	61,347	
Total Poll	37,659	61.39
Spoiled	320	0.85
Total Valid Poll	37,339	60.87
Seats	4	
Quota	7,468	
Candidates	11	

	Quotas	Seats
FF	1.65	1
Lab	0.55	1
PD	0.62	1
GP	0.54	1

Lab gain; previously a 3-seat constituency with 1 FF, 1 PD, 1 GP

John Curran (FF)

Home Address
15 Knockmeenagh Road, Clondalkin, Dublin 22
Constituency Office
2A Main Street, Clondalkin; 1 Church View, Lower Main Street, Lucan
Telephone
Home (01) 459 2803; *Office* (01) 457 9913
Birth Place/Date
Dublin. 17 June 1960
Married
Shauna O'Higgins. 2 sons, 1 daughter
Education
Moyle Park College, Clondalkin; University College, Dublin (BComm)
Occupation
Public representative. Formerly company director

John Curran was first elected to the Dáil in 2002. Member of the Public Accounts Committee, the Education and Science Committee, and the Committee on Child Protection in the last Dáil.

Member of South Dublin County Council 1999–2003.

Member, Board of Management of Scoil Mhuire; Gaelic Athletic Association.

Paul Gogarty (GP)

Home Address
34 Cherbury Park Road, Lucan, Co Dublin
Constituency Office
Room 4, Muintir na Tíre Hall, Lower Main Street, Lucan
Telephone
Constituency office (01) 621 9966;
Mobile 087 275 2489;
Email office@paulgogarty.com
Website www.paulgogarty.com
Birth Place/Date
Castlepollard, Co Westmeath. 20 December 1968
Married
Heidi Mahon. 2 children
Education
St Mary's Boys' National School, Lucan; Coláiste Phádraig, Lucan; College of Commerce, Rathmines (Diploma in Journalism)
Occupation
Full-time public representative. Formerly editor/journalist

Paul Gogarty was first elected to the Dáil in 2002.

He was Green Party spokesperson for Education and Science, Arts, Sports and Tourism, and Youth Affairs, in the 29th Dáil. Member of the Education and Science Committee in the last Dáil. Former member of the National Forum of Europe.

Only Green Party member of South Dublin County Council 1999–2003.

Member, Lucan Sarsfields GAA club.

Mary Harney (PD)

Home Address
Clonskeagh, Dublin 6
Business Address
Department of Health and Children, Hawkins
House, Dublin 2
Telephone
Business (01) 635 4148 / 671 1026;
Website www.maryharney.ie
Birth Place/Date
Ballinasloe, Co Galway. 11 March 1953
Married
Brian Geoghegan
Education
Convent of Mercy, Goldenbridge, Inchicore,
Dublin; Coláiste Bhríde, Clondalkin, Co Dublin;
Trinity College, Dublin (BA [Mod])
Occupation
Government Minister. Formerly research
worker

Mary Harney was re-appointed Minister for
Health and Children on 14 June 2007, a
portfolio she had held since September 2004.

As Leader of the Progressive Democrats, she
was Tánaiste from June 1997 to September
2006 when she stepped down as party
Leader and was replaced by Michael
McDowell. Following his defeat in the 2007
election, she became acting party Leader
pending the appointment of a new leader. She
was the first woman to become Tánaiste.

She was Minister for Enterprise, Employment
and Trade from 1997 to 2004, and Minister of
State at the Department of the Environment,
with responsibility for Environmental
Protection, 1989–92.

A founder member of the Progressive
Democrats with Desmond O'Malley in 1985,
she became Leader of the party in 1993. She
was first elected to the Dáil in 1981 as a
Fianna Fáil candidate and, from 1987, as a PD
candidate. She is one of only two PD
members of the 30th Dáil.

She was the youngest ever member of the
Seanad when nominated by the Taoiseach,
Jack Lynch, as a Senator, in 1977–81. She had
been a candidate in the 1977 general election
in Dublin South-East.

Joanna Tuffy (Lab)

Home Address
111 Esker Lawns, Lucan, Co Dublin
Telephone
Home (01) 628 0765;
Website www.joannatuffy.ie
Birth Place/Date
England. 9 March 1965
Marital Status
Partner, Philip Long. 1 daughter
Education
St Joseph's College, Lucan; Trinity College,
Dublin (BA [Mod] Hons); Diploma Legal
Studies, DIT Rathmines.
Occupation
Public representative.

Joanna Tuffy is a new deputy. She was
appointed party spokesperson on
Environment and Heritage in September
2007.

She contested the 2002 election in Dublin
Mid-West and was subsequently elected to
the Seanad on the Administrative panel
2002–07. Member, Joint Oireachtas
Committee on Justice, Equality, Defence and
Women's Rights, and Joint Committee on
Education and Science 2002–07. Labour Party
spokesperson in the Seanad on Education and
Science, Justice, Equality and Law Reform,
and Defence.

Member, South Dublin County Council
1999–2003.

Dublin Mid-West

Seats 4 Quota 7,468	1st Count	2nd Count Transfer of **Curran** Surplus	3rd Count Transfer of **Finnegan, Kenny, McHale** Votes	4th Count Transfer of **Keating** Votes	5th Count Transfer of **Spain** Votes	6th Count Transfer of **Moriarty** Votes
CURRAN, John* (FF)	8,650					
FINNEGAN, Mick (WP)	366	*(+12)* 378				
FITZGERALD, Frances (FG)	4,480	*(+52)* 4,532	*(+148)* 4,680	*(+295)* 4,975	*(+369)* 5,344	*(+320)* 5,664
GOGARTY, Paul* (GP)	4,043	*(+80)* 4,123	*(+270)* 4,393	*(+1,164)* 5,557	*(+1,143)* 6,700	*(+1,220)* 7,920
HARNEY, Mary* (PD)	4,663	*(+293)* 4,956	*(+110)* 5,066	*(+388)* 5,454	*(+214)* 5,668	*(+2,118)* 7,786
KEATING, Derek (Ind)	2,701	*(+28)* 2,729	*(+178)* 2,907			
KENNY, Gino (Ind)	1,058	*(+41)* 1,099				
McHALE, Jim (Ind)	170	*(+10)* 180				
MORIARTY, Luke (FF)	3,671	*(+529)* 4,200	*(+133)* 4,333	*(+333)* 4,666	*(+519)* 5,185	
SPAIN, Joanne (SF)	3,462	*(+67)* 3,529	*(+441)* 3,970	*(+168)* 4,138		
TUFFY, Joanna (Lab)	4,075	*(+70)* 4,145	*(+295)* 4,440	*(+455)* 4,895	*(+1,109)* 6,004	*(+668)* 6,672
NON-TRANSFERABLE			82	104	784	859

Dublin North

Elected

Party Share of Vote

1st Preferences	Number	%	Gain/Loss
Fianna Fáil	22,998	42.09	3.85%
Fine Gael	7,667	14.03	2.22%
Labour	5,256	9.62	-4.85%
Prog Democrats	1,395	2.55	2.55%
Green Party	9,107	16.67	0.07%
Sinn Féin	1,454	2.66	-0.41%
Others	6,764	12.38	-3.43%

Statistics

Electorate	80,221	
Total Poll	55,052	68.63
Spoiled	411	0.75
Total Valid Poll	54,641	68.11
Seats	4	
Quota	10,929	
Candidates	13	

	Quotas	Seats
FF	2.10	2
FG	0.70	1
GP	0.83	1

FG gain from Lab

Michael Kennedy (FF)

Home Address
84 The Dunes, Portmarnock, Co Dublin
Constituency Office
The Plaza, Swords, Co Dublin
Telephone
Home (01) 846 2403; *Office* (01) 890 2277;
Fax (01) 890 2296; *Mobile* 087 243 2995;
Email mjkennedy@eircom.net
Website www.michaelkennedy.ie
Birth Place/Date
Roundwood, Co Wicklow
Married
Maria Byrne. 1 son, 2 daughters
Education
St Vincent's CBS, Glasnevin, Dublin;
Associate of Insurance Institute of London
(ACII), Chartered Insurance Broker (CIB)
Occupation
Public representative. Insurance broker

Michael Kennedy is a new deputy. He
contested the by-election in 2002, caused by
the resignation of former Minister Ray Burke,
and the 2002 general election.

He was first elected to Dublin County Council
in 1991 representing Malahide/Portmarnock/
Kinsealy ward. Re-elected to Fingal County
Council for the Swords ward in 1999 and
2004. Cathaoirleach, Fingal County Council
2002–03; Leas Cathaoirleach 2001–02.

A former inter-county Dublin hurler and
footballer, he is a member of Na Fianna GAA
Club. He is also a member of Naomh
Mearnog GAA Club and The Island Golf Club,
Donabate.

Trevor Sargent (GP)

Home Address
37 Tara Cove, Balbriggan, Co Dublin
Constituency Office
35 Main Street, Swords, Co Dublin
Telephone
Home/Fax (01) 841 2371; *Office* (01) 890 0360;
Fax (01) 890 0361; *Mobile* 087 254 7836
Birth Place/Date
Dublin. 1 July 1960
Married
Heidi Bedell
Education
The High School, Dublin; Church of Ireland
College, Rathmines, Dublin; Trinity College,
Dublin (BEd)
Occupation
Full-time public representative. Formerly
national school teacher and principal

Trevor Sargent was appointed Minister of
State at the Department of Agriculture, Food
and Fisheries, with special responsibility for
Food and Horticulture, on 20 June 2007.

The first Leader of the Green Party, elected in
October 2001. He resigned the position after
leading his party into coalition government with
Fianna Fáil and the Progressive Democrats.

He was first elected to the Dáil in 1992. He
contested the general election of 1987 as a
Green Alliance candidate in the old 3-seat
constituency of Dublin North, and the 1989
general election as a Green Party candidate in
the same constituency.

Member, Dublin County Council 1991–93.
Cathaoirleach, Fingal Area 1991–92 and of
Coiste Stiúrtha na Gaeilge.

Former chairman, Tara Cove Residents'
Association; Fingal Council Against Blood
Sports. Member, Fingal Committee of An
Taisce; Amnesty International; Irish Wildbird
Conservancy; Greenpeace; Irish Organic
Society; Dublin Food Cooperative; Alternative
Technology Association. Director of Sonairte
(Ecology Centre). Member, Earthwatch.

Cathaoirleach, Craobh Shéamuis Ennis,
Conradh na Gaeilge. Member, Balbriggan
Rugby Club.

Darragh O'Brien (FF)

Home Address
49 Galtrim Grange, Malahide, Co Dublin
Constituency Office
1 Church Road, Malahide, Co Dublin
Telephone
Office (01) 845 0710; *Mobile* 086 251 9893
Birth Place/Date
Malahide, Co Dublin. 8 July 1974
Marital Status
Single
Education
Pope John Paul National School. Malahide
Community School
Occupation
Public representative. Formerly financial
manager with Friends First.

Darragh O'Brien is a new deputy.

He has been active in local politics since
leaving secondary school and was elected to
Fingal County Council in June 2004. Protégé
of retiring Fianna Fáil deputy for Dublin North,
G.V. Wright.

Member of Malahide Cricket Club, St
Sylvester's GAA Club and Malahide United.

James Reilly (FG)

Home Address
Seafoam, South Shore Road, Rush, Co Dublin
Constituency Office
Lusk Towncentre, Market Square, Lusk,
Co Dublin
Telephone
Office/Fax (01) 843 7014
Birth Place/Date
Dublin. 16 August 1955
Married
Dorothy McEvoy. 1 daughter, 4 sons
Education
St Conleth's and CUS Dublin; Ring, Waterford;
Gormanston, Co Meath; Royal College of
Surgeons; Royal College of General
Practitioners; Irish College of General
Practitioners; Master of Medical Science at
University College, Dublin
Occupation
Full-time public representative. General
practitioner

James Reilly is a new deputy. He was
appointed party spokesperson on Health in
September 2007.

He is a former President of the Irish Medical
Organisation, Chairman and President of the
GP Committee of the IMO. Chairman of the
GP Development Team and the IMO
representative at the World Medical
Association.

Former member, Eastern Health Board;
Chairman of its Community Care Committee
and Psychiatric Hospitals and Mental Health
Committee. He subsequently served on the
Eastern Regional Health Authority and on the
Northern Area Health Board. Former member
of the Council of the Society for Autistic
Children

Dublin North

Seats 4
Quota 10,929

	1st Count	2nd Count Transfer of **Donnelly, Loftus** Votes	3rd Count Transfer of **Morrissey** Votes	4th Count Transfer of **Kennedy** Surplus
CORR, Joe (GP)	1,659	*(+22)* 1,681	*(+35)* 1,716	*(+5)* 1,721
DALY, Clare (SP)	4,872	*(+88)* 4,960	*(+61)* 5,021	*(+11)* 5,032
DONNELLY, John (Ind)	286			
KENNEDY, Michael (FF)	10,869	*(+42)* 10,911	*(+355)* 11,266	
LOFTUS, Cathal (CSP)	210			
McCORMACK, Matt (SF)	1,454	*(+39)* 1,493	*(+4)* 1,497	*(+1)* 1,498
MORRISSEY, Tom (PD)	1,395	*(+30)* 1,425		
O'BRIEN, Darragh (FF)	7,055	*(+28)* 7,083	*(+322)* 7,405	*(+148)* 7,553
O'CONNOR, David (Ind)	1,396	*(+57)* 1,453	*(+40)* 1,493	*(+10)* 1,503
O'LEARY, John (FF)	5,074	*(+34)* 5,108	*(+176)* 5,284	*(+100)* 5,384
REILLY, Dr James (FG)	7,667	*(+51)* 7,718	*(+209)* 7,927	*(+24)* 7,951
RYAN, Brendan (Lab)	5,256	*(+38)* 5,294	*(+49)* 5,343	*(+14)* 5,357
SARGENT, Trevor* (GP)	7,448	*(+51)* 7,499	*(+157)* 7,656	*(+24)* 7,680
NON-TRANSFERABLE		16	17	

5th Count	6th Count	7th Count	8th Count	9th Count	10th Count
Transfer of **McCormack** Votes	Transfer of **O'Connor** Votes	Transfer of **Corr** Votes	Transfer of **Daly** Votes	Transfer of **O'Leary** Votes	Transfer of **O'Brien** Surplus
(+97) 1,818	(+79) 1,897				
(+472) 5,504	(+181) 5,685	(+202) 5,887			
(+147) 7,700	(+153) 7,853	(+72) 7,925)	(+502) 8,427	(+4,143) 12,570	
(+90) 1,593					
(+152) 5,536	(+275) 5,811	(+108) 5,919	(+485) 6,404		
(+85) 8,036	(+245) 8,281	(+173) 8,454	(+693) 9,147	(+559) 9,706	(+633) 10,339
(+157) 5,514	(+244) 5,758	(+131) 5,889	(+1,434) 7,323	(+835) 8,158	(+1,008) 9,166
(+234) 7,914	(+341) 8,255	(+1,159) 9,414	(+2,197) 11,611		
64	75	52	576	867	

Dublin North-Central

Elected

Richard Bruton (FG)*   1st Count
Seán Haughey (FF)*   3rd Count
Finian McGrath (Ind)*   5th Count

Party Share of Vote

1st Preferences	Number	%	Gain/Loss
Fianna Fáil	16,029	44.02	-6.03%
Fine Gael	9,303	25.55	8.54%
Labour	2,649	7.27	-3.22%
Green Party	1,891	5.19	-0.49%
Sinn Féin	1,375	3.78	-1.96%
Others	5,169	14.19	3.16%

Statistics

Electorate	53,443	
Total Poll	36,758	68.78
Spoiled	342	0.93
Total Valid Poll	36,416	68.14
Seats	3	
Quota	9,105	
Candidates	7	

	Quotas	Seats
FF	1.76	1
FG	1.02	1
Ind	0.57	1

Previously a 4-seat constituency with 2 FF, 1 FG, 1 Ind

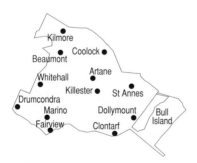

Richard Bruton (FG)

Home Address
210 Griffith Avenue, Drumcondra, Dublin 9
Telephone
Home (01) 836 8185; *Fax* (01) 836 8185;
Website www.richardbruton.com
Birth Place/Date
Dublin. 15 March 1953
Married
Susan Meehan. 2 sons, 2 daughters
Education
Belvedere College, Dublin; Clongowes Wood College, Co Kildare; University College, Dublin; Nuffield College, Oxford (BA, MA, MPhil [Oxon] Economics)
Occupation
Full-time public representative. Formerly economist

Richard Bruton is Deputy Leader of Fine Gael and was reappointed as spokesperson on Finance in September 2007.

He was first elected to the Dáil in February 1982. He was Minister for Enterprise and Employment 1994–97, and Minister of State at the Department of Industry and Commerce 1986–87. Director of Policy 2000–02. Front bench spokesperson on Education and Science 1997–2002; on Enterprise and Employment 1993–94; Director of Policy 1994. Spokesperson on Employment 1992–93; Health 1990–92; Energy and Natural Resources 1989–90; Energy and Communications 1987–89. He was a Senator, Agricultural panel, August 1981–February 1982.

Member, Dublin City Council 1991–94. Re-elected 1999–2003.

Member, Meath County Council 1979–82.

He is a brother of John Bruton, Taoiseach 1994–97; Dáil deputy for Meath 1969–2004; Minister for Finance 1981–82 and 1986–87, Minister for Public Service 1987; Minister for Industry, Trade, Commerce and Tourism 1983–86; Minister for Industry and Energy 1982–83; Leader of Fine Gael 1990–2001, EU Ambassador to the United States since 2004.

Seán Haughey (FF)

Home Address
Chapelfield Lodge, Baskin Lane, Kinsealy, Dublin 17
Constituency Office
5 Mornington Park, Malahide Road, Artane, Dublin 5
Telephone
Home (01) 846 4004; *Fax* (01) 845 1444;
Constituency office (01) 845 0111;
Mobile 087 286 9542;
Website www.seanhaughey.com
Birth Place/Date
Dublin. 8 November 1961
Married
Orla O'Brien. 3 sons, 1 daughter
Education
St Paul's College, Raheny, Dublin; Trinity College, Dublin (BA [Mod])
Occupation
Full-time public representative

Seán Haughey was appointed Minister of State at the Department of Education and Science and Enterprise Trade and Employment, with special responsibility for Lifelong Learning, Youth Work and School Transport, on 20 June 2007. He was first appointed a Minister of State at the Department of Education and Science in December 2006.

He has been a member of the Dáil since 1992. Senator, Administrative panel, 1987–92 and candidate in Dublin North-East in the general elections of 1987 and 1989.

Alderman, Dublin City Council 1985–2003. Lord Mayor, 1989–90. National Chairman, Ógra Fianna Fáil 1995–97.

He is a son of Charles J. Haughey, Taoiseach December 1979–June 1981, March–December 1982, March 1987–June 1989; Acting Taoiseach June–July 1989; Taoiseach July 1989–February 1992. Dáil deputy 1957–92.

He is a grandson of Seán Lemass, Taoiseach 1959–66 and TD for Dublin South 1924–48 and Dublin South-Central 1948–69.

Finian McGrath (Ind)

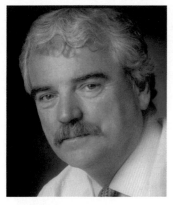

Home Address
342 Charlemont, Griffith Avenue, Dublin 9
Telephone
Home/Office (01) 837 8028;
Mobile 087 673 8041;
Website www.finianmcgrath.ie
Birth Place/Date
Tuam. 9 April 1953
Married
Anne Russell. 2 daughters
Education
Tuam CBS; St Patrick's Training College,
Drumcondra, Dublin
Occupation
Public representative. Formerly school
principal and full-time worker with the Simon
Community

Finian McGrath was first elected in 2002. In
2007, he supported the Fianna Fáil / Green
Party / Progressive Democrats government
after negotiations with Fianna Fáil.

In the 2002 election, he campaigned as a
member of the Independent Health Alliance,
calling for improved health services. He also
contested the 1997 general election.

Member, Dublin City Council 1999–2003.
Board member of Northside Centre for the
Unemployed, Coolock; Board member of the
Orthopaedic Hospital, Clontarf.

Member, Irish National Teachers'
Organisation.

Dublin North-Central

Seats 3 Quota 9,105	1st Count	2nd Count Transfer of **Bruton** Surplus	3rd Count Transfer of **Lawlor** Votes	4th Count Transfer of **Haughey** Surplus	5th Count Transfer of **Maher, McDowell** Votes
BRUTON, Richard* (FG)	9,303				
CALLELY, Ivor* (FF)	7,003	(+16) 7,019	(+148) 7,167	(+85) 7,252	(+700) 7,952
HAUGHEY, Seán* (FF)	9,026	(+20) 9,046	(+234) 9,280		
LAWLOR, Peter (SF)	1,375	(+5) 1,380			
MAHER, Bronwen (GP)	1,891	(+22) 1,913	(+247) 2,160	(+26) 2,186	
McDOWELL, Derek (Lab)	2,649	(+92) 2,741	(+143) 2,884	(+13) 2,897	
McGRATH, Finian* (Ind)	5,169	(+43) 5,212	(+556) 5,768	(+51) 5,819	(+3,578) 9,397
NON-TRANSFERABLE			52		805

Brian Cowen in relaxed mood at an election press conference on 21 May 2007.

Dublin North-East

Elected

Party Share of Vote

1st Preferences	Number	%	Gain/Loss
Fianna Fáil	13,864	39.69	-0.42%
Fine Gael	8,012	22.94	7.58%
Labour	5,294	15.16	-1.07%
Prog Democrats	749	2.14	-2.01%
Green Party	2,349	6.73	1.08%
Sinn Féin	4,661	13.34	3.10%
Others	0	0.00	-8.24%

Statistics

Electorate	53,778	
Total Poll	35,252	65.55
Spoiled	323	0.92
Total Valid Poll	34,929	64.95
Seats	3	
Quota	8,733	
Candidates	8	

	Quotas	Seats
FF	1.59	1
FG	0.92	1
Lab	0.61	1
FG gain from FF		

Tommy Broughan (Lab)

Home Address
18 Thormanby Lawns, Howth, Dublin 13
Telephone
Home (01) 847 7634
Birth Place/Date
Clondalkin, Co Dublin. August 1947
Married
Carmel Healy
Education
Moyle Park College, Clondalkin; University College, Dublin (BA, HDipEd); London University (BSc, MSc [Econ])
Occupation
Full-time public representative. Formerly teacher

Tommy Broughan was appointed Labour Party spokesperson on Transport in September 2007.

He was a member of the Joint Services Committee and the Joint Committee on Enterprise and Small Business in the 29th Dáil. In the previous Dáil, he was Vice-Chairperson of the Oireachtas Committee on Family, Community and Social Affairs and a member of the Committee on Enterprise and Small Business. He was first elected to the Dáil in 1992, having been an unsuccessful candidate in Dublin North-East in the 1989 election.

Member, Dublin City Council 1991–2003.

Founding secretary, Community Enterprise, Donaghmede and Artane. Founding Chairman of Coolock Development Council. Director, Northside Centre for the Unemployed.

Member of several north-side Gaelic football and soccer clubs.

Terence Flanagan (FG)

Home Address
75 Old Malahide Road, Dublin 5
Telephone
Mobile (087) 995 2031
Birth Place/Date
Dublin. January 1975
Marital Status
Single
Education
St David's BNS, Kilmore Road, Dublin 5; Chanel College, Malahide Road, Dublin 5; Dublin Business School, Aungier Street, Dublin 2
Occupation
Public representative. Accountant

Terence Flanagan is a new deputy, elected on his first attempt.

He was co-opted to Dublin City Council in October 2003 to replace Deputy Richard Bruton for whom he was a campaign worker for many years. He was subsequently elected to the Council to represent the Artane Electoral Area in the 2004 local elections.

Michael J. Woods (FF)

Home Address
13 Kilbarrack Grove, Raheny, Dublin 5
Telephone
Home (01) 832 3357; Fax (01) 832 5222
Birth Place/Date
Bray, Co Wicklow. 8 December 1935
Married
Margaret Maher. 3 sons, 2 daughters
Education
Synge Street CBS, Dublin; University College,
Dublin (BAgrSc, MAgrSc, PhD, DSc); Institute
of Public Administration (Diploma in Central
Administration and Fellowship in Public
Administration); Harvard Business School
(Diploma in Marketing)
Occupation
Full-time public representative. Formerly
Principal Officer and Head of Glasshouse
Crops and Mushroom Department, An Foras
Talúntais

Michael Woods was first elected to the Dáil in
1977 and was a Cabinet Minister for 14 years
up to 2002. Chairman, Foreign Affairs
Committee in the last Dáil.

Minister for Education 2000–02. Minister for
the Marine and Natural Resources 1997–2000.
Minister for Social Welfare 1993–December
1994 and Minister for Health,
November–December 1994. He was Minister
for the Marine 1992–93; Minister for Agriculture
and Food 1991–92; Minister for Social Welfare
1987–91. He was Minister for Health and
Minister for Social Welfare March–December
1982 and 1979–81. He was Minister of State at
the Department of the Taoiseach and the
Department of Defence, and Government Chief
Whip in 1979. Party spokesperson on Justice
1982–87, on Equality and Law Reform
1993–94; on Social Welfare 1994.

He is the author of *Research in Ireland, Key to
Economic and Social Development* and
numerous technical and scientific papers.

Seats 3 Quota 8,733	1st Count	2nd Count Transfer of **Healy,** **Redmond** Votes	3rd Count Transfer of **Sweeney** Votes	4th Count Transfer of **O'Toole** Votes
BRADY, Martin* (FF)	6,861	(+391) 7,252	(+143) 7,395	(+700) 8,095
BROUGHAN, Tommy* (Lab)	5,294	(+927) 6,221	(+688) 6,909	(+2,002) 8,911
FLANAGAN, Terence (FG)	4,483	(+517) 5,000	(+2,751) 7,751	(+843) 8,594
HEALY, David (GP)	2,349			
O'TOOLE, Larry (SF)	4,661	(+322) 4,983	(+106) 5,089	
REDMOND, Keith (PD)	749			
SWEENEY, Brody (FG)	3,529	(+417) 3,946		
WOODS, Michael* (FF)	7,003	(+399) 7,402	(+186) 7,588	(+842) 8,430
NON-TRANSFERABLE		125	72	702

Dublin North-West

Elected

Party Share of Vote

1st Preferences	Number	%	Gain/Loss
Fianna Fáil	15,124	48.84	1.31%
Fine Gael	3,083	9.96	2.00%
Labour	6,286	20.30	3.51%
Green Party	853	2.75	0.43%
Sinn Féin	4,873	15.74	-2.54%
Others	745	2.41	-4.71%

Statistics

Electorate	51,951	
Total Poll	31,387	60.42
Spoiled	423	1.35
Total Valid Poll	30,964	59.60
Seats	3	
Quota	7,742	
Candidates	8	

	Quotas	Seats
FF	1.95	2
Lab	0.81	1
No change		

Noel Ahern (FF)

Home Address
25 Church Avenue, Drumcondra, Dublin 9
Telephone
Home (01) 832 5911; *Fax* (01) 832 5911
Birth Place/Date
Dublin. December 1944
Married
Helen Marnane. 2 sons, 1 daughter
Education
Christian Brothers O'Connell School, Dublin; University College, Dublin; College of Commerce, Rathmines, Dublin (DPA, MCIT)
Occupation
Minister of State. Formerly official with CIÉ

Noel Ahern was appointed Minister of State at the Department of Finance, with special responsibility for the Office of Public Works, on 20 June 2007.

He was previously Minister of State at the Department of Environment and Local Government, with responsibility for Housing and Urban Renewal, and at the Department of Community, Rural and Gaeltacht Affairs, with responsibility for Drugs Strategy and Community Affairs, from 2002 to 2007. Chairperson of the Oireachtas Committee on Social Community and Family Affairs 1997–2002. Member of the Cabinet Committee on Social Inclusion.

He was first elected to the Dáil in 1992. Party spokesperson on the Environment, with special responsibility for Housing, 1994–97. Chairperson, Oireachtas Committee on Social, Community and Family Affairs 1997–2002.

Member, Dublin City Council 1985–2002. Former Chairperson of Housing and Traffic Committees and Chairperson of the North-West Area Committee 2001–02.

Former branch officer and member of National Executive of the Transport Salaried Staffs Association.

He is brother of Bertie Ahern, Taoiseach since 1997, Leader of the Fianna Fáil party since 1994, former Minister and Dáil deputy since 1977.

Róisín Shortall (Lab)

Home Address
12 Iveragh Road, Gaeltacht Park, Dublin 9
Telephone
Home (01) 837 0563; *Dáil office* (01) 618 3593; *Fax* (01) 618 4380
Birth Place/Date
Dublin. 25 April 1954
Married
Seamus O'Byrne. 3 daughters
Education
Dominican College, Eccles Street, Dublin; University College, Dublin; St Mary's College of Education, Marino, Dublin (BA, NTDip Teacher of the Deaf)
Occupation
Full-time public representative. Formerly primary school teacher for the deaf at St Joseph's School, Cabra, Dublin

Róisín Shortall has been a Dáil deputy since 1992. Labour Party spokesperson on Social and Family Affairs, spokesperson on Transport in the last Dáil (from 2003) and on Education and Children 1997–2002. Member, Joint Oireachtas Committee on Transport 2003–07.

Member, Dublin City Council 1991–2003; Eastern Health Board 1991–2003 (Chairperson, 1997). Board member, Ballymun Neighbourhood Council; Ballymun Local Drugs Task Force; Finglas Crime Task Force.

Pat Carey (FF)

Home Address
69 Bourne View, Ashbourne, Co Meath
Constituency Office
2 Finglas Town Centre, Dublin 11
Telephone
Home (01) 835 0544; *Fax* (01) 835 0430;
Constituency office (01) 864 4118;
Fax (01) 864 4119; *Mobile* 087 257 4393
Birth Place/Date
Castlemaine, Co Kerry. 9 November 1947
Marital Status
Single
Education
Presentation Brothers College, Milltown, Co
Kerry; St Patrick's Teachers' Training College,
Drumcondra, Dublin; University College,
Dublin; Trinity College, Dublin (BA HDipEd)
Occupation
Full-time public representative. Formerly
primary school teacher, vice-principal

Pat Carey was appointed Minister of State at
the Department of Community, Rural and
Gaeltacht Affairs, with special responsibility
for Drug Strategy and Community Affairs, on
20 June 2007.

He was first elected as a Dáil deputy in 1997.
Co-Chairperson of the British–Irish Inter-
Parliamentary Body and Vice-Chairperson of
the European Movement, Ireland. Member of
the Joint Oireachtas Committee on Foreign
Affairs and sub-committee on Human Rights,
in last Dáil. Member of the Forum on Europe,
the Euro-Mediterranean Parliamentary
Assembly and the National Economic and
Social Forum. Member of the Joint Oireachtas
Committee on European Affairs and the
Oireachtas Committee on the Scrutiny of EU
Legislation, until November 2004. Member,
Oireachtas Committees for Education and
Science; Language and Heritage and European
Affairs (Government convenor) 1997–2002.

Member of Dublin City Council 1985–2001.

Chairman, School Committee of Coláiste Éoin
and Coláiste Íde, Finglas, since 1985; Plunkett
College, Whitehall, 1985–91. Member, Sports
Advisory Council, City of Dublin VEC and City
of Dublin Youth Service Board. Former
Chairman, Catholic Youth Council. Council
member, NCEA 1991–96.

Seats 3 Quota 7,742	1st Count	2nd Count Transfer of **Fitzgerald, Martin, O'Neill** Votes	3rd Count Transfer of **Tormey** Votes
AHERN, Noel* (FF)	7,913		
CAREY, Pat* (FF)	7,211	*(+228)* 7,439	*(+411)* 7,850
ELLIS, Dessie (SF)	4,873	*(+378)* 5,251	*(+406)* 5,657
FITZGERALD, Declan (GP)	853		
MARTIN, Owen (WP)	240		
O'NEILL, John (Ind)	505		
SHORTALL, Róisín* (Lab)	6,286	*(+678)* 6,964	*(+2,291)* 9,255
TORMEY, Dr Bill (FG)	3,083	*(+208)* 3,291	
NON-TRANSFERABLE		106	183

Dublin South

Elected

Party Share of Vote

1st Preferences	Number	%	Gain/Loss
Fianna Fáil	25,298	41.33	4.69%
Fine Gael	16,686	27.26	7.48%
Labour	6,384	10.43	0.94%
Prog Democrats	4,045	6.61	-8.39%
Green Party	6,768	11.06	1.61%
Sinn Féin	1,843	3.01	-0.92%
Others	180	0.29	-5.41%

Statistics

Electorate	89,464	
Total Poll	61,622	68.88
Spoiled	418	0.68
Total Valid Poll	61,204	68.41
Seats	5	
Quota	10,201	
Candidates	13	

	Quotas	Seats
FF	2.48	2
FG	1.64	2
GP	0.66	1
FG gain from PD		

Séamus Brennan (FF)

Home Address
31 Finsbury Park, Churchtown, Dublin 14
Business Address
Department of Arts, Sport and Tourism,
23 Kildare Street, Dublin 2
Constituency Office
9 Braemor Road, Churchtown, Dublin 14
Telephone
Constituency office (01) 295 7171;
Ministerial office (01) 631 3800
Birth Place/Date
Galway. 16 February 1948
Married
Ann O'Shaughnessy. 2 sons, 4 daughters
Education
St Joseph's Secondary School, Galway;
University College, Galway (BA, BComm);
University College, Dublin (MComm)
Occupation
Full-time public representative. Formerly
accountant and management consultant

Séamus Brennan was appointed Minister for
Arts, Sport and Tourism, on 14 June 2007. He
was previously Minister for Social and Family
Affairs 2004–07; Minister for Transport
2002–04; Minister of State for Public
Enterprise 6–18 June 2002.

He was Minister of State at the Department of
the Taoiseach and at the Department of
Defence, and Chief Whip 1997–2002; Minister
of State at the Department of Enterprise and
Employment, with special responsibility for
Commerce and Technology, 1993–94; Minister
for Education 1992–93. Minister for Tourism,
Transport and Communications 1991–92;
Minister for Tourism and Transport 1989–91;
Minister of State at the Department of Industry
and Commerce, with special responsibility for
Trade and Marketing, 1987–89.

Member, Dublin County Council 1985–87.

Tom Kitt (FF)

Home Address
3 Pine Valley, Rathfarnham, Dublin 16
Constituency Office
Pembroke House, 2 Glenville Terrace,
Main Street, Dundrum, Dublin 14
Telephone
Home (01) 493 8200; *Fax* (01) 493 2207;
Constituency office (01) 298 2304;
Email tomkitt@tomkitt.ie
Website www.tomkitt.ie
Birth Place/Date
Galway. 11 July 1952
Married
Jacinta Burke-Walsh. 3 sons, 1 daughter
Education
St Jarlath's College, Tuam, Co Galway;
St Patrick's Teachers' Training College,
Drumcondra, Dublin
Occupation
Minister of State. Formerly national school
teacher

Tom Kitt was appointed Government Chief
Whip and Minister of State at the Department of
Defence, on 14 June 2007.

He was Government Chief Whip and Minister of
State at the Department of the Taoiseach, with
responsibility for eGovernment, 2004–07.
Minister of State at the Department of Foreign
Affairs, with responsibility for Overseas
Development and Human Rights, 2002–04.

He was first elected to the Dáil in 1987. Minister
of State at the Department of Enterprise, Trade
and Employment, 1997–2002; at the
Department of the Taoiseach and the
Department of Foreign Affairs, 1993–94; at the
Department of the Taoiseach, 1992–93.

He is son of Michael F. Kitt, Dáil deputy for
Galway East constituencies 1948–51, 1957–75,
and brother of Michael Kitt, Minister of State.

Olivia Mitchell (FG)

Home Address
18 Ballawley Court, Dundrum, Dublin 16
Telephone
Home (01) 295 3033; *Fax* (01) 295 3033
Birth Place/Date
Birr, Co Offaly. 31 July 1947
Married
James Mitchell. 2 sons, 1 daughter
Education
Dominican Convent, Eccles Street, Dublin;
Trinity College, Dublin (BA, HDipEd)
Occupation
Full-time public representative. Formerly
secondary school teacher

Olivia Mitchell was appointed party
spokesperson on Arts, Sport and Tourism in
September 2007. She was Fine Gael
spokesperson on Health and Children and,
from 2004, spokesperson on Transport in the
29th Dáil.

She was first elected as a Dáil deputy in 1997,
having been a candidate in Dublin South in the
1989 and 1992 general elections. Party
spokesperson on Local Development,
National Drugs Strategy and Dublin Traffic
(1997–February 2001); on Local Government
and Housing (2001–02).

Member of Oireachtas Committees on
Transport (2004–07); Health (2002–04); and of
the Committees on Heritage and the Irish
Language, Environment and Local
Government during the 28th Dáil.

Member, Dublin County Council 1985–93 and
of Dún Laoghaire–Rathdown County Council
1994–2003 (Cathaoirleach, 1995–96).

Former member, Eastern Health Board;
Dublin Regional Authority; Dublin Transport
Office Steering Committee.

She was a member of the Fine Gael
delegation to the Forum for Peace and
Reconciliation. Former member, Co-ordinating
Committee of the European Sustainable Cities
and Towns Campaign.

Eamon Ryan (GP)

Home Address
66 Whitebeam Road, Clonskeagh, Dublin 14
Telephone
Home (01) 269 0473; *Constituency office*
(01) 618 3000; *Mobile* 087 829 4429
Birth Place/Date
Dublin. 28 July 1963
Married
Victoria White. 3 sons, 1 daughter
Education
Holy Cross National School, Dundrum;
Gonzaga College, Ranelagh, Dublin; University
College, Dublin (BComm)
Occupation
Government Minister. Formerly tour operator
and founder of activity holiday company

Eamon Ryan was appointed Minister for
Communications, Energy and Natural
Resources, on 14 June 2007.

He was first elected to the Dáil in 2002. Co-
opted to Dublin City Council to replace Green
Party colleague John Gormley in 1998,
elected 1999–2003.

Green Party spokesperson on Transport,
Enterprise, Trade and Employment, and
Communications, Marine and Natural
Resources in the 29th Dáil. Opposition
convenor on the Joint Oireachtas Committee
for Communications, Marine and Natural
Resources in the last Dáil.

Founding chairman of the Dublin Cycling
Campaign. Member of the Dublin
Transportation Office Advisory Committee.
Editor of Lord Mayor's Commission Report on
Cycling in Dublin, 1996. Special interest in
energy, transport and enterprise issues.

Alan Shatter (FG)

Home Address
57 Delbrook Manor, Ballinteer, Dublin 16
Constituency Office
4 Upper Ely Place, Dublin 2
Telephone
Home (01) 298 3045; *Office* (01) 613 0051;
Email alan@alanshatter.com
Website www.alanshatter.com
Birth Place/Date
Dublin. February 1951
Married
Carol Danker. 1 son, 1 daughter
Education
High School, Dublin; Trinity College, Dublin;
University of Amsterdam; Law School of the
Incorporated Law Society
Occupation
Public representative. Solicitor, author

Alan Shatter was appointed party
spokesperson on Children in September 2007.
He was re-elected in 2007, having lost his
seat in the 2002 general election. He had
previously been returned for Dublin South at
every election since 1981.

He was Fine Gael spokesperson on Law
Reform 1982, 1987–88, on the Environment
1989–91; on Labour 1991; on Justice
1992–93; on Equality and Law Reform
1993–94; on Health and Children 1997–2000;
Justice, Law Reform and Defence 2000–02.

Chairman of the Foreign Affairs Committee
1996–97. Former member of Dáil Committees
on Women's Rights, Marital Breakdown,
Building Land, Childcare, Bankruptcy and
Crime.

Member, Dublin County Council 1979–93,
South Dublin County Council 1994–99.

Director and former chairman of Free Legal
Advice Centres (FLAC). Former Chairman of
CARE (Campaign for Deprived Children).
President, Irish Council Against Blood Sports
1986–93.

Author of two books, *Shatter's Family Law in
the Republic of Ireland* (4th Edition, published
1997) and *Laura* (1990), a novel.

Dublin South

	1st Count	2nd Count Transfer of **Brennan** Surplus	3rd Count Transfer of **Nic Cormaic, Ó Gógáin, Tracey** Votes	4th Count Transfer of **Kitt** Surplus
Seats 5 Quota 10,201				
BRENNAN, Séamus* (FF)	13,373			
CORRIGAN, Maria (FF)	3,438	(+840) 4,278	(+237) 4,515	(+140) 4,655
CULHANE, Aidan (Lab)	2,809	(+58) 2,867	(+185) 3,052	(+17) 3,069
KITT, Tom* (FF)	8,487	(+1,637) 10,124	(+301) 10,425	
MITCHELL, Olivia* (FG)	8,037	(+111) 8,148	(+79) 8,227	(+9) 8,236
NIC CORMAIC, Sorcha (SF)	992	(+29) 1,021		
Ó GÓGÁIN, Liam (Ind)	180	(+5) 185		
O'DONNELL, Liz* (PD)	4,045	(+209) 4,254	(+74) 4,328	(+9) 4,337
O'LEARY, Jim (FG)	2,897	(+31) 2,928	(+63) 2,991	(+6) 2,997
RYAN, Eamon* (GP)	6,768	(+117) 6,885	(+598) 7,483	(+28) 7,511
SHATTER, Alan (FG)	5,752	(+68) 5,820	(+51) 5,871	(+4) 5,875
TRACEY, Shaun (SF)	851	(+13) 864		
WHITE, Alex (Lab)	3,575	(+54) 3,629	(+214) 3,843	(+11) 3,854
NON-TRANSFERABLE		268	44	

5th Count	6th Count	7th Count	8th Count	9th Count
Transfer of **O'Leary** Votes	Transfer of **Culhane** Votes	Transfer of **O'Donnell** Votes	Transfer of **White** Votes	Transfer of **Ryan** Surplus
(+93) 4,748	(+145) 4,893	(+1,923) 6,816	(+501) 7,317	(+339) 7,656
(+186) 3,255				
(+1,308) 9,544	(+447) 9,991	(+855) 10,846		
(+89) 4,426	(+94) 4,520			
(+303) 7,814	(+565) 8,379	(+802) 9,181	(+2,708) 11,889	
(+783) 6,658	(+234) 6,892	(+474) 7,366	(+2,090) 9,456	(+1,349) 10,805
(+191) 4,045	(+1,694) 5,739	(+223) 5,962		
44	76	243	663	

Dublin South-Central

Dublin South-Central

Elected

Seán Ardagh (FF)*	1st Count
Michael Mulcahy (FF)*	3rd Count
Mary Upton (Lab)*	9th Count
Catherine Byrne (FG)	10th Count
Aengus Ó Snodaigh (SF)*	10th Count

Party Share of Vote

1st Preferences	Number	%	Gain/ Loss
Fianna Fáil	15,725	33.08	-1.24%
Fine Gael	6,838	14.39	-2.55%
Labour	10,041	21.13	1.41%
Prog Democrats	912	1.92	-1.21%
Green Party	2,756	5.80	0.58%
Sinn Féin	4,825	10.15	-2.55%
Others	6,434	13.54	5.57%

Statistics

Electorate	86,710	
Total Poll	48,320	55.73
Spoiled	789	1.63
Total Valid Poll	47,531	54.82
Seats	5	
Quota	7,922	
Candidates	16	

	Quotas	Seats
FF	1.98	2
FG	0.86	1
Lab	1.27	1
SF	0.61	1
No change		

Seán Ardagh (FF)

Home Address
168 Walkinstown Road, Dublin 12
Constituency Office
168 Walkinstown Road, Dublin 12
Telephone
Home/Office (01) 456 8736; *Fax* (01) 408 0436
Birth Place/Date
Dublin. 25 November 1947
Married
Marie Bhreathnach. 2 sons, 1 daughter
Education
Marian College, Sandymount, Dublin;
University College, Dublin (BSc); University of Toronto
Occupation
Public representative. Chartered accountant

Seán Ardagh was first elected to the Dáil in 1997. He was a member of the Public Accounts Committee and of the Committee on Procedure and Privileges, and Chairperson, Oireachtas Committee on Justice, Equality, Defence and Women's Rights in the last Dáil and the 28th Dáil. Chairman of the Sub-Committee on the Barron Report in 29th Dáil.

Member, Dublin City Council 1999–2003; Dublin County Council 1985–91; South Dublin County Council 1985–99.

Member, St Jude's GAA Club.

Michael Mulcahy (FF)

Home Address
3 Beechwood Road, Ranelagh, Dublin 6
Constituency Office
102A Cork Street, Dublin 8
Telephone
Home (01) 497 2758; *Office* (01) 454 6223;
Fax (01) 454 6223;
Website www.michaelmulachy.ie
Birth Place/Date
Dublin. 23 June 1960
Married
Veronica Gates
Education
St Conleth's College, Dublin 4; Trinity College, Dublin, 1977–81 (Degree in Mental and Moral Science); Trinity College 1981–83 (Degree in Legal Science); King's Inns, Dublin
Occupation
Public representative. Barrister-at-Law

Michael Mulcahy was first elected to the Dáil in 2002, having contested the Dublin South-Central constituency in the general elections of 1992 and 1997 and by-elections in the constituency in 1994 and 1999. Taoiseach's nominee to Seanad 1994–97, where he was party spokesperson on Justice.

Member of the Joint Oireachtas Committees on Education and Science and European Affairs, in last Dáil. Member of Fianna Fáil National Executive 1990–92.

Member, Dublin City Council 1985–2003 (Lord Mayor of Dublin, 2001–02).

Chairman of Dublin Regional Authority 1999.

Member of the Board, Hugh Lane Municipal Gallery of Modern Art, Dublin, 1985–2002.

Mary Upton (Lab)

Home Address
9 Fortfield Grove, Terenure, Dublin 6W
Telephone
Dáil office (01) 618 3756
Birth Place/Date
Derrylough, Kilrush, Co Clare. 30 May 1946
Marital Status
Single
Education
Coláiste Mhuire, Ennis; University College, Galway (MSc in Microbiology); University College, Dublin (PhD)
Occupation
Public representative. University lecturer

Mary Upton was appointed party spokesperson on Arts, Sport and Tourism in September 2007. In the last Dáil she was spokesperson on Agriculture and Food and a member of the Joint Oireachtas Committee on Agriculture and Food. Previously party spokesperson for Food Safety, Consumer Affairs and Health Promotion.

She was first elected to the Dáil in October 1999 in the by-election caused by the death of her brother, Pat Upton, who was the Labour TD in Dublin South-Central 1992–99.

Member of the Fatima Mansions Regeneration Board and the board of management of St James's Street CBS.

Catherine Byrne (FG)

Home Address
30 Bulfin Road, Inchicore, Dublin 8
Telephone
Home (01) 454 0920; *Mobile* 086 854 3276
Birth Place/Date
Dublin. 26 February 1956
Married
Joseph Byrne. 4 daughters, 1 son
Education
Our Lady of the Wayside National School, Bluebell, Dublin 12; Holy Faith, The Coombe, Dublin 8; Cathal Brugha Catering College, Dublin 1
Occupation
Public representative

Catherine Byrne is a new member of the Dáil.

She was elected to Dublin City Council for the South-West Inner-City Ward on her first attempt in 1999 and topped the poll in the area in the 2004 local elections. Lord Mayor of Dublin 2005–06.

Former Chairperson of St Michael's Community Centre; member of the Board of Management of the Mercy Convent Secondary School, Goldenbridge; Leader of St Michael's Folk/Gospel Group for 15 years. Played ladies' soccer at the highest level and previously managed schoolboy soccer teams in her locality. Completed a two-year Lay Ministry course in All Hallows and also has a City and Guilds Diploma in Catering.

Aengus Ó Snodaigh (SF)

Constituency Office
347 Ballyfermot Road, Dublin 10
Telephone
Constituency office (01) 625 9320;
Fax (01) 620 3931
Birth Place/Date
Dublin. 31 July 1964
Married
Aisling Ó Dálaigh. 2 sons
Education
Scoil Lorcain, Monkstown, Co Dublin; Coláiste Eoin, Booterstown, Co Dublin; University College, Dublin (BA, HDipEd)
Occupation
Full-time public representative. Formerly officer, Bord na Gaeilge

Aengus Ó Snodaigh was first elected in 2002. He was Sinn Féin Whip in the last Dáil and party spokesperson on Justice and Equality, Culture, Gaeilge and Gaeltacht, International Affairs and Defence. He contested the constituency of Dublin South-East in the general election of 1987 and the by-election in Dublin South-Central in 1999.

Member, Sinn Féin Ard-Comhairle since 1999; National Forum on Europe; Sinn Féin delegation in talks with the British Government at Lancaster House in 2000 and Weston Park 2001.

Dublin South-Central

	1st Count	2nd Count	3rd Count	4th Count
Seats 5 Quota 7,922		Transfer of **Ardagh** Surplus	Transfer of **Doyle, Gunning, McGuinness,** Votes	Transfer of **Mulcahy** Surplus
ARDAGH, Seán* (FF)	8,286			
BYRNE, Catherine (FG)	4,713	*(+15)* 4,728	*(+119)* 4,847	*(+43)* 4,890
BYRNE, Eric (Lab)	4,054	*(+17)* 4,071	*(+73)* 4,144	*(+21)* 4,165
COLLINS, Joan (Ind)	2,203	*(+9)* 2,212	*(+65)* 2,277	*(+11)* 2,288
DOYLE, Ben (PD)	438	*(+11)* 449		
GUNNING, Con (Ind)	121	*(+1)* 122		
HEALY, Dr Róisín (Ind)	1,613	*(+6)* 1,619	*(+107)* 1,726	*(+40)* 1,766
MARTIN, Anne Marie (FG)	2,125	*(+6)* 2,131	*(+99)* 2,230	*(+39)* 2,269
McDERMOTT, Tony (GP)	2,756	*(+8)* 2,764	*(+108)* 2,872	*(+32)* 2,904
McGUINNESS, Andrew (WP)	256	*(+1)* 257		
McNAMARA, Frank (PD)	474	*(+6)* 480		
MULCAHY, Michael* (FF)	7,439	*(+248)* 7,687	*(+499)* 8,186	
Ó SNODAIGH, Aengus* (SF)	4,825	*(+13)* 4,838	*(+75)* 4,913	*(+9)* 4,922
REDMOND, Michael (CSP)	155	*(+)* 155		
SMITH, Bríd (Ind)	2,086	*(+4)* 2,090	*(+115)* 2,205	*(+16)* 2,221
UPTON, Mary* (Lab)	5,987	*(+19)* 6,006	*(+127)* 6,133	*(+53)* 6,186
NON-TRANSFERABLE			76	

5th Count	6th Count	7th Count	8th Count	9th Count	10th Count
Transfer of **Healy** Votes	Transfer of **Smith** Votes	Transfer of **Martin** Votes	Transfer of **Collins** Votes	Transfer of **McDermott** Votes	Transfer of **Upton** Surplus
(+178) 5,068	(+163) 5,231	(+1,488) 6,719	(+331) 7,050	(+613) 7,663	(+258) 7,921
(+172) 4,337	(+156) 4,493	(+261) 4,754	(+578) 5,332	(+895) 6,227	(+705) 6,932
(+264) 2,552	(+701) 3,253	(+109) 3,362			
(+172) 2,441	(+117) 2,558				
(+235) 3,139	(+139) 3,278	(+138) 3,416	(+365) 3,781		
(+117) 5,039	(+609) 5,648	(+124) 5,772	(+737) 6,509	(+423) 6,932	(+69) 7,001
(+162) 2,383					
(+346) 6,532	(+286) 6,818	(+318) 7,136	(+623) 7,759	(+1,261) 9,020	
120	212	120	728	589	66

Dublin South-East

Elected

Chris Andrews (FF)	3rd Count
Lucinda Creighton (FG)	5th Count
Ruairí Quinn (Lab)*	5th Count
John Gormley (GP)*	5th Count

Party Share of Vote

1st Preferences	Number	%	Gain/Loss
Fianna Fáil	9,720	28.72	1.69%
Fine Gael	6,311	18.65	2.58%
Labour	5,636	16.65	4.22%
Prog Democrats	4,450	13.15	-5.64%
Green Party	4,685	13.84	-2.39%
Sinn Féin	1,599	4.72	-2.67%
Others	1,441	4.26	2.20%

Statistics

Electorate	63,468	
Total Poll	34,134	53.78
Spoiled	292	0.86
Total Valid Poll	33,842	53.32
Seats	4	
Quota	6,769	
Candidates	13	

	Quotas	Seats
FF	1.44	1
FG	0.93	1
Lab	0.83	1
GP	0.69	1
FG gain from PD		

Chris Andrews (FF)

Home Address
39 Dun Emer Road, Dundrum, Dublin 14
Telephone
Mobile (087) 285 1515
Birth Place/Date
Dublin. 25 May 1964
Married
Tina Brosnan. 2 children
Education
Willow Park, Blackrock; Newpark, Blackrock, Co Dublin
Occupation
Public representative

Chris Andrews is a new TD. He was elected to the seat vacated by Eoin Ryan MEP who did not contest the 2007 election.

He was elected to Dublin City Council for the Pembroke ward on his first attempt in 1997 but narrowly lost his seat in 2004, while maintaining his vote. Co-opted on to the Council in October 2006 to represent Dublin South inner-city ward. Unsuccessful candidate in the 2002 general election.

He is a cousin of Barry Andrews, TD for Dún Laoghaire since 2002, and son of the late Niall Andrews, TD from 1977 to 1987 and MEP from 1984 to 2004. Nephew of David Andrews who was a TD for Dún Laoghaire 1965–2002 and Minister for Foreign Affairs 1992–93 and 1997–2000, Minister for the Marine 1993–94. He is a grandson of Todd Andrews, former chairman of RTÉ and CIÉ and first managing director of Bord na Móna.

Lucinda Creighton (FG)

Home Address
8 Herbert Park Mews, Donnybrook, Dublin 4
Business Address
Law Library, The Four Courts, Dublin 1
Telephone
Home (01) 219 5841; *Mobile* (086) 600 9296
Website www.lucindacreighton.ie
Birth Place/Date
Mayo. 20 January 1980
Marital Status
Single
Education
Convent of Mercy, Claremorris, Co Mayo; Trinity College Dublin (LLB); New York Bar; King's Inns, Dublin (Barrister-at-Law)
Occupation
Barrister. Former public relations officer for Health and Safety Authority and researcher for European Movement.

Lucinda Creighton is a new deputy, taking the seat of the former Progressive Democrats Leader and Minister for Justice, Michael McDowell.

Member of Fine Gael National Executive. Representative of Young Fine Gael and Fine Gael at European level. Vice-Chairperson of Fine Gael taskforce charged with rejuvenating the party in Dublin in 2003.

Elected as the youngest member of Dublin City Council in 2004. Youngest member of the 30th Dáil.

Ruairí Quinn (Lab)

Home Address
23 Strand Road, Sandymount, Dublin 4
Telephone
Office (01) 618 3434; *Fax* (01) 618 4153;
Website www.ruairiquinn.ie
Birth Place/Date
Dublin. 2 April 1946
Married
Liz Allman. 1 son, and 1 son, 1 daughter from
previous marriage
Education
Blackrock College, Dublin; University College,
Dublin (BArch); Athens Centre of Ekistics,
Greece (HCE)
Occupation
Public representative. Architect and town
planner

Ruairí Quinn was appointed party
spokesperson on Education and Science in
September 2007. He was Leader of the
Labour Party 1997–2002 and Deputy Leader
1989–97. He was Minister for Finance
1994–97; Minister for Enterprise and
Employment 1993–94; Minister for Labour,
December 1983–87; Minister for the Public
Service, February 1986–87; Minister of State at
the Department of the Environment, with
special responsibility for Urban Affairs and
Housing, 1982–83. He was Labour's
spokesperson for Enterprise, Trade and
Employment in the last Dáil.

He was first elected to the Dáil in Dublin
South-East in 1977 but lost his seat in the
1981 general election. He regained his seat in
February 1982, having served as a Senator,
Industrial and Commercial panel, August
1981–February 1982. He was also a Senator
in 1976–77 when selected to fill a vacancy in
the Taoiseach's nominees.

Chair of the Holocaust Educational Trust of
Ireland; Chair of European Movement Ireland.

Member, Dublin City Council 1974–77 and
1991–93 (Leader, Labour group; Leader, Civic
Alliance).

John Gormley (GP)

Home Address
119 Ringsend, Dublin 4
Business Address
Department of the Environment, Heritage and
Local Government, Custom House, Dublin 1
Telephone
Home (01) 281 5134; *Office* (01) 888 2403;
Email minister@environ.ie
Website www.johngormley.com
Birth Place/Date
Dublin. 4 August 1959
Married
Penny Stuart. 1 son, 1 daughter
Education
St Munchin's College, Limerick; University
College, Dublin; Freiburg University, Germany
(BA)
Occupation
Government Minister. Formerly director of
Academy of European Languages

John Gormley was appointed Minister for the
Environment, Heritage and Local Government,
on 14 June 2007, and elected Leader of the
Green Party on 17 July 2007, by 478 votes out
of 775 cast by party members.

He was the first Cathaoirleach of the Green
Party and was first elected to the Dáil in June
1997. Party spokesperson on Foreign Affairs,
Health and Defence in the last Dáil. He
contested the Dublin South-East constituency
in 1992 and 1989.

Member of Dublin City Council 1991–98. He
was Lord Mayor, 1994–95.

Author of the *Green Guide for Ireland* (1990).
Member of Earthwatch, Amnesty
International and the Chartered Institute of
Water Management. His hobbies are reading
and computers.

Dublin South-East

Seats 4 Quota 6,769	1st Count	2nd Count	3rd Count	4th Count	5th Count
		Transfer of **Hearne, Ivory, O'Sullivan, Tierney Uzell, O'Gara** Votes	Transfer of **Doolan** Votes	Transfer of **Andrews** Surplus	Transfer of **O'Callaghan** Votes
ANDREWS, Chris (FF)	6,600	*(+166)* 6,766	*(+354)* 7,120		
CREIGHTON, Lucinda (FG)	6,311	*(+166)* 6,477	*(+118)* 6,595	*(+24)* 6,619	*(+306)* 6,925
DOOLAN, Daithí (SF)	1,599	*(+117)* 1,716	1,716		
GORMLEY, John* (GP)	4,685	*(+420)* 5,105	*(+611)* 5,716	*(+80)* 5,796	*(+599)* 6,395
HEARNE, Rory (Ind)	591				
IVORY, Noel (Ind)	84				
McDOWELL, Michael* (PD)	4,450	*(+116)* 4,566	*(+35)* 4,601	*(+13)* 4,614	*(+1,477)* 6,091
O'CALLAGHAN, Jim (FF)	3,120	*(+78)* 3,198	*(+112)* 3,310	*(+140)* 3,450	
O'GARA, Noel (Ind)	27				
O'SULLIVAN, Peter (Ind)	34				
QUINN, Ruairí* (Lab)	5,636	*(+311)* 5,947	*(+305)* 6,252	*(+51)* 6,303	*(+558)* 6,861
TIERNEY, Eoin (Ind)	102				
UZELL, Esther (Ind)	603				
NON-TRANSFERABLE		67	181	43	510

Outgoing Tánaiste Michael McDowell (PD) and John Gormley (GP) in the campaign confrontation which became known as the 'Rumble in Ranelagh'.

Dublin South-West

Elected

Conor Lenihan (FF)*	1st Count
Brian Hayes (FG)	1st Count
Pat Rabbitte (Lab)*	2nd Count
Charlie O'Connor (FF)*	6th Count

Party Share of Vote

1st Preferences	Number	%	Gain/Loss
Fianna Fáil	16,355	39.27	0.59%
Fine Gael	8,346	20.04	7.39%
Labour	8,325	19.99	0.19%
Green Party	1,546	3.71	0.57%
Sinn Féin	5,066	12.16	-8.12%
Others	2,014	4.84	-0.61%

Statistics

Electorate	67,148	
Total Poll	42,022	62.58
Spoiled	370	0.88
Total Valid Poll	41,652	62.03
Seats	4	
Quota	8,331	
Candidates	8	

	Quotas	Seats
FF	1.96	2
FG	1.00	1
Lab	1.00	1
FG gain from SF		

Conor Lenihan (FF)

Home Address
44 Templeogue Village, Dublin 6W
Constituency Office
Above First Active House, Tallaght Village
Telephone
Constituency office (01) 459 6285;
Fax (01) 244 3363
Birth Place/Date
Dublin. 3 March 1963
Married
Denise Russell. 3 children
Education
Belvedere College, Dublin; University College, Dublin (BA); Dublin City University (Diploma in Journalism); European Business School, INSEAD
Occupation
Minister of State. Formerly radio journalist, political correspondent

Conor Lenihan was appointed Minister of State at the Department of Community, Rural and Gaeltacht Affairs and the Department of Education and Science, and the Department of Justice, Equality and Law Reform, with special responsibility for Integration Policy, on 20 June 2007. He was previously Minister of State at the Department of Foreign Affairs, with responsibility for Overseas Development and Human Rights, 2004–07.

He was elected to the Dáil in 1997 on his first attempt. Member, Committee of Public Accounts 1997–2004 and Joint Committee on Enterprise and Small Business. Member of British–Irish Inter-Parliamentary Body.

He is a son of Brian Lenihan, a former Tánaiste, Minister for Foreign Affairs; Minister for Agriculture; Minister for Defence; Minister for Forestry and Fisheries; Minister for Transport and Power; Minister for Education; Minister for Justice; and a Dáil deputy for Roscommon–Leitrim 1961–73 and Dublin West 1977–95. He is a brother of Brian Lenihan, Minister for Justice and Dáil deputy for Dublin West since 1996. He is a nephew of Mary O'Rourke, a Dáil deputy 1982–2002 and re-elected 2007, and a former Minister in various portfolios. He is grandson of Patrick Lenihan, Dáil deputy 1965–70.

Brian Hayes (FG)

Home Address
48 Dunmore Park, Kingswood Heights, Tallaght, Dublin 24
Telephone
Home (01) 462 6545
Birth Place/Date
Dublin. 23 August 1969
Married
Genevieve Deering. 2 sons, 1 daughter
Education
St Joseph's College, Garbally Park, Ballinasloe, Co Galway; NUI Maynooth (BA); Trinity College Dublin (HDipEd)
Occupation
Full-time public representative. Formerly secondary school teacher

Brian Hayes was first elected to the Dáil in 1997 but lost his seat in 2002. Interim party spokesperson on Health and Children following the 2007 election, he was appointed party spokesperson on Education and Science in September 2007.

He was Fine Gael Leader in the Seanad, 2002–07, where he was elected on the Cultural and Educational panel, and Fine Gael front bench spokesperson for Dublin since 2003. Fine Gael spokesperson on Defence and Northern Ireland in Seanad.

Front bench Spokesperson on Social and Community Affairs 2001–02, on Northern Ireland 2000–01. Vice-Chairman of the Oireachtas All-Party Committee on Strategic Management Initiative 1999. Taoiseach's nominee to the Seanad 1995–97. Party spokesperson on Housing, House Prices and Urban Renewal in 28th Dáil.

Candidate in Dublin South-Central by-election in 1994. Former National Youth and Education Officer with Fine Gael.

Member, South Dublin County Council 1995–2003. Member, Irish Council for European Movement.

Pat Rabbitte (Lab)

Home Address
56 Monastery Drive, Clondalkin, Dublin 22
Telephone
Home (01) 459 3191; *Office* (01) 618 3772
Birth Place/Date
Claremorris, Co Mayo. 18 May 1949
Married
Derry McDermott. 3 daughters
Education
St Colman's College, Claremorris, Co Mayo;
University College, Galway (BA, HDipEd, LLB)
Occupation
Full-time public representative. Formerly trade
union official

Pat Rabbitte was Leader of the Labour Party,
from 25 October 2002 until 23 August 2007.
He was appointed party spokesperson on
Justice in September 2007.

He was first elected to the Dáil in 1989 for the
Workers' Party. During the 26th Dáil, six of
the party's TDs formed the Democratic Left
Party. During the 28th Dáil in 1999,
Democratic Left merged with the Labour
Party and the four DL deputies became part of
the Labour group. In 2002, Pat Rabbitte who
had been a member of the Labour Party until
1976, was re-elected in Dublin South-West as
a Labour deputy.

He was Minister of State to the Government
and at the Department of Enterprise and
Employment, with special responsibility for
Commerce, Science and Technology and
Consumer Affairs, 1994–97. As the so-called
'Super Minister of State', he also had the right
to attend Cabinet meetings.

Member, Dublin County Council 1985–95.
Elected to South Dublin County Council 1999.

Member, Irish Transport and General
Workers' Union (now SIPTU). Formerly
National Secretary. President, UCG Students'
Union 1970–71. President, Union of Students
in Ireland 1972–74.

Charlie O'Connor (FF)

Home Address
622 Virginia Heights, Springfield, Tallaght,
Dublin 24
Constituency Office
1 Main Street, Tallaght
Telephone
Office (01) 461 0715; *Fax* (01) 461 0766
Birth Place/Date
Dublin. 9 April 1946
Marital Status
Separated. 3 sons
Education
Synge Street CBS; Drimnagh Castle CBS;
Irish Marketing Institute; Industrial Relations
Institute
Occupation
Full-time public representative. Formerly
Press Officer for National Youth Federation

Charlie O'Connor was first elected in 2002.
Member of the Joint Oireachtas Committees
on Justice, Equality, Law Reform, Defence,
Women's Rights and Social and Family Affairs
during 29th Dáil. Government convenor on
Joint Oireachtas Committee on Health and
Children.

Chairman, Parliamentary Friendship group
with Ukraine. Treasurer, Inter-Parliamentary
Association.

Member, Dublin County Council 1991–94;
South Dublin County Council 1994–2003
(Chairperson, 1999–2000). Former member,
Dublin Vocational Education Committee.
Member, Tallaght Hospital Board. Founder
Chairman of the South-Western Area Health
Board. Member, Tallaght Welfare Society,
Tallaght Community Arts Group, Tallaght
Centre for the Unemployed, and PARTAS
(formerly Get Tallaght Working).

Dublin South-West

Seats 4 Quota 8,331	1st Count	2nd Count Transfer of **Lenihan** Surplus	3rd Count Transfer of **Kelly** Votes	4th Count Transfer of **Hayes** Surplus	5th Count Transfer of **Rabbitte** Surplus	6th Count Transfer of **Murphy** Votes
CROWE, Seán* (SF)	5,066	*(+10)* 5,076	*(+107)* 5,183	*(+2)* 5,185	*(+4)* 5,189	*(+577)* 5,766
DAVIDSON, Elizabeth (GP)	1,546	*(+6)* 1,552	*(+103)* 1,655	*(+7)* 1,662	*(+4)* 1,666	*(+568)* 2,234
HAYES, Brian (FG)	8,346					
KELLY, Ray (Ind)	434	*(+2)* 436				
LENIHAN, Conor* (FF)	8,542					
MURPHY, Mick (Soc)	1,580	*(+4)* 1,584	*(+75)* 1,659	*(+2)* 1,661	*(+)* 1,661	
O'CONNOR, Charlie* (FF)	7,813	*(+172)* 7,985	*(+117)* 8,102	*(+4)* 8,106	*(+3)* 8,109	*(+330)* 8,439
RABBITTE, Pat* (Lab)	8,325	*(+17)* 8,342				
NON-TRANSFERABLE			34			186

Is your garden soaking up Dublin's drinking water?

www.taptips.ie

WATER IS PRECIOUS
LET'S CONSERVE IT

Sponsored by Dublin Region Local Authorities & Supported by Department of the Environment, Heritage & Local Government

Dublin West

Elected

Party Share of Vote

1st Preferences	Number	%	Gain/Loss
Fianna Fáil	12,726	37.45	2.82%
Fine Gael	6,928	20.39	8.07%
Labour	5,799	17.06	4.36%
Prog Democrats	553	1.63	-6.28%
Green Party	1,286	3.78	1.29%
Sinn Féin	1,624	4.78	-3.24%
Others	5,066	14.91	-7.02%

Statistics

Electorate	52,193	
Total Poll	34,188	65.50
Spoiled	206	0.60
Total Valid Poll	33,982	65.11
Seats	3	
Quota	8,496	
Candidates	8	

	Quotas	Seats
FF	1.50	1
FG	0.82	1
Lab	0.68	1
FG gain from Ind		

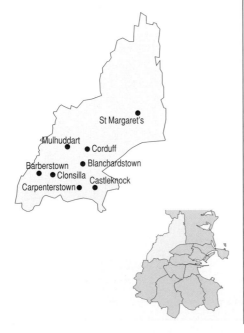

Brian Lenihan (FF)

Home Address
Longwood, Somerton Road, Strawberry Beds, Dublin 20
Business Address and Constituency Office
Department of Justice, Equality and Law Reform, 94 St Stephen's Green, Dublin 2
Local Office
Laurel Lodge Shopping Centre, Dublin 15
Telephone
Office (01) 602 8202; *Local office* (01) 822 0970
Birth Place/Date
Dublin. 21 May 1959
Married
Patricia Ryan. 1 son, 1 daughter
Education
Belvedere College, Dublin; Trinity College, Dublin (BA [Mod]); Cambridge University (LLB); King's Inns
Occupation
Government Minister. Senior Counsel

Brian Lenihan was appointed Minister for Justice, Equality and Law Reform, on 14 June 2007.

He was previously Minister of State, with responsibility for Children, at the Departments of Health and Children; Justice, Equality and Law Reform; and Education and Science, from 2002 to 2007. As Minister for Children, he attended Cabinet meetings.

He was first elected to the Dáil in April 1996 in the by-election caused by the death of his father, Brian, who had been a deputy in Dublin West since 1977. During the 28th Dáil, Brian Lenihan was Chairperson of the All-Party Oireachtas Committee on the Constitution which considered changes in the abortion laws.

He is a son of Brian Lenihan, former Tánaiste and a Minister in various portfolios, who was a Dáil deputy for Roscommon–Leitrim 1961–73 and for Dublin West 1977–95. He is a brother of Conor Lenihan, Minister of State and Dáil deputy for Dublin South-West, and a nephew of Mary O'Rourke, TD for Longford–Westmeath 2007 and 1982–2002, and who held various ministerial posts. He is a grandson of Patrick Lenihan, Dáil deputy 1965–70.

Leo Varadkar (FG)

Home Address
30 Rosehaven, Carpenterstown Road, Castleknock, Dublin 15
Constituency Office
37A Main Street, Ongar, Dublin 15
Telephone
Office (01) 640 3133
Birth Place/Date
Dublin. 18 January 1979
Marital Status
Single
Education
St Francis Xavier National School, Coolmine, Dublin 15; The King's Hospital, Palmerstown, Dublin 20; Trinity College, Dublin (BA, MB, BCh, BAO [2003]); Post-Graduate GP Training Programme attached to TCD
Occupation
General Practitioner

Leo Varadkar is a new TD, regaining the Fine Gael seat in Dublin West previously held by Austin Currie, Jim Mitchell and Dick Burke.

He was appointed Fine Gael spokesperson on Enterprise, Trade and Employment in September 2007. He was co-opted to Fingal County Council in November 2003 and was elected in his own right in June 2004 in the Castleknock electoral area, with the highest first preference vote in the country. Leas-Cathaoirleach 2004; Area Chairperson for Dublin 15 in 2006–07; member, Transport and Housing Strategic Policy committees. Member of the Institute of European Affairs and the European Movement.

Joan Burton (Lab)

Home Address
81 Old Cabra Road, Dublin 7
Telephone
Home (01) 838 8711;
Website www.joanburton.ie
Birth Place/Date
Dublin. 1 February 1949
Married
Pat Carroll. 1 daughter
Education
Sisters of Charity, Stanhope Street, Dublin;
University College, Dublin (BComm); Fellow
of Institute of Chartered Accountants
Occupation
Full-time public representative. Accountant
and formerly lecturer

Joan Burton was appointed party
spokesperson on Finance in September 2007.
She served in the same post in the latter half
of the 29th Dáil, having begun it as
spokesperson on Transport. She was first
elected to the Dáil in 1992 but lost her seat in
1997 and regained it in 2002.

Minister of State at the Department of Social
Welfare 1992–94; Minister of State at the
Department of Foreign Affairs, with
responsibility for Overseas Development, and
at the Department of Justice 1995–97.

She was an unsuccessful candidate for the
leadership of the Labour Party in 2002.

Member, Dublin County Council 1991–99,
Fingal County Council 1999-2003; Leader of
the Labour Party group.

Chair of Steering Committee of
Blanchardstown Women's Refuge. Board
member of Centre for Independent Living,
campaigning for transport rights of wheelchair
users.

Dublin West

Seats 3 Quota 8,496	1st Count	2nd Count Transfer of **Lenihan** Votes	3rd Count Transfer of **Murray** Votes	4th Count Transfer of **O'Gorman** Votes	5th Count Transfer of **Gallagher, Lynam** Votes
BURTON, Joan* (Lab)	5,799	*(+302)* 6,101	*(+114)* 6,215	*(+458)* 6,673	*(+1,232)* 7,905
GALLAGHER, Felix (SF)	1,624	*(+53)* 1,677	*(+6)* 1,683	*(+94)* 1,777	
HIGGINS, Joe* (Soc)	5,066	*(+204)* 5,270	*(+55)* 5,325	*(+282)* 5,607	*(+1,865)* 7,472
LENIHAN, Brian Jnr* (FF)	11,125				
LYNAM, Gerry (FF)	1,601	*(+1,613)* 3,214	*(+241)* 3,455	*(+132)* 3,587	
MURRAY, Mags (PD)	553	*(+123)* 676			
O'GORMAN, Roderic (GP)	1,286	*(+63)* 1,349	*(+68)* 1,417		
VARADKAR, Leo (FG)	6,928	*(+271)* 7,199	*(+161)* 7,360	*(+393)* 7,753	*(+957)* 8,710
NON-TRANSFERABLE			31	58	1,310

Trust your instincts.
Choose KPMG.

Ireland is widely regarded as the most dynamic economy in Europe and an ideal location to do business. It's no wonder so many successful Irish companies are making their mark at home and abroad.

It's also no surprise that so many of these companies choose KPMG to help them achieve their business objectives. We provide a wide choice of audit, tax and advisory services to a range of outstanding clients. We have many years' experience working closely with successful organisations ranging from fast growing privately owned Irish businesses to established multinational companies.

So if you're thinking about your next business challenge, you should be talking to KPMG. To find out more about how we can help contribute to your success story, call us today on + 353 (1) 410 1000.

kpmg.ie

AUDIT ▪ TAX ▪ ADVISORY

Dún Laoghaire

Dún Laoghaire

Elected

Mary Hanafin (FF)*	1st Count
Barry Andrews (FF)*	2nd Count
Eamon Gilmore (Lab)*	7th Count
Seán Barrett (FG)	9th Count
Ciaran Cuffe (GP)*	10th Count

Party Share of Vote

1st Preferences	Number	%	Gain/Loss
Fianna Fáil	20,471	34.87	4.58%
Fine Gael	13,832	23.56	8.51%
Labour	9,392	16.00	-6.68%
Prog Democrats	3,959	6.74	-6.62%
Green Party	4,534	7.72	-1.60%
Sinn Féin	1,292	2.20	-1.82%
Others	5,233	8.91	3.64%

Statistics

Electorate	89,035	
Total Poll	59,110	66.39
Spoiled	397	0.67
Total Valid Poll	58,713	65.94
Seats	5	
Quota	9,786	
Candidates	11	

	Quotas	Seats
FF	2.09	2
FG	1.41	1
Lab	0.96	1
GP	0.46	1
FG gain from PD		

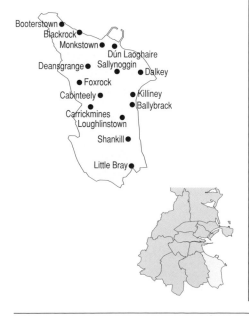

Mary Hanafin (FF)

Home Address
7 Oaklands Drive, Rathgar, Dublin 6
Business Address and Constituency Office
Department of Education and Science, Marlborough Street, Dublin 1
Telephone
Office (01) 878 8495
Email minister_hanafin@education.gov.ie
Birth Place/Date
Thurles, Co Tipperary. June 1959
Marital Status
Widowed
Education
Presentation Convent, Thurles; St Patrick's College, Maynooth (BA, HDipEd); Dublin Institute of Technology (Diploma in Legal Studies)
Occupation
Government Minister. Formerly secondary school teacher

Mary Hanafin was re-appointed Minister for Education and Science on 14 June 2007, having held the post since September 2004 following a Cabinet re-shuffle during the previous Dáil.

She was previously Government Chief Whip and Minister of State at the Department of the Taoiseach and at the Department of Defence from 2002 to September 2004.

She served as Minister of State at the Departments of Health and Children; Justice, Equality and Law Reform; and Education and Science, with special responsibility for Children, 2000–02.

She was first elected to the Dáil in 1997, having been a candidate in Dublin South-East constituency in the 1989 general election.

Joint Honorary Treasurer of Fianna Fáil since 1993. Awarded Stagiaire scholarship to European Parliament and Robert Schuman silver medal for services towards European unity.

She is daughter of Des Hanafin, Senator 1969–93 and 1997–2002, and sister of Senator John Hanafin, elected in 2002.

Barry Andrews (FF)

Home Address
73 Castlebyrne Park, Blackrock, Co Dublin
Constituency Office
56 Temple Road, Blackrock, Co Dublin
Telephone
Home (01) 288 0099 *Office* (01) 618 3856
Birth Place/Date
Dublin. 16 May 1967
Married
Sinéad McGrath. 2 sons
Education
Willow Park, Blackrock College, Co Dublin; University College, Dublin (MA History); King's Inns, Dublin (Barrister-at-Law)
Occupation
Public Representative. Barrister, formerly teacher

Barry Andrews was first elected to Dáil Éireann in 2002. He was Vice-Chairman of the Oireachtas Committee on European Affairs and member of Oireachtas Committees on the Constitution, and on Education and Science, in the last Dáil.

Member of Dún Laoghaire–Rathdown County Council 1999–2003. He is a Governor of the Board of the Royal Irish Academy of Music and a member of the Holocaust Educational Trust.

He is son of David Andrews who was a TD for Dún Laoghaire 1965–2002 and Minister for Foreign Affairs 1992–93 and 1997–2000, Minister for the Marine 1993–94. He is a cousin of Chris Andrews, TD for Dublin South-East since 2007, and a nephew of the late Niall Andrews, TD from 1977 to 1987 and MEP from 1984 to 2004. He is a grandson of Todd Andrews, former chairman of RTÉ and CIÉ and first managing director of Bord na Móna.

Eamon Gilmore (Lab)

Home Address
1 Corbawn Close, Shankill, Co Dublin
Telephone
Office (01) 618 3566; *Mobile* 087 220 0495;
Website www.gilmore.ie
Birth Place/Date
Galway. 24 April 1955
Married
Carol Hanney. 2 sons, 1 daughter
Education
Garbally College, Ballinasloe, Co Galway;
University College, Galway (BA)
Occupation
Full-time public representative. Formerly trade
union official

Eamon Gilmore was elected leader of the
Labour Party in September 2007. He was party
spokesperson on Environment, Heritage and
Local Government and on Communications and
Natural Resources in 29th Dáil. Member of
Labour's national executive committee;
Chairperson, Labour Party Policy Committee.
He helped negotiate the merger of Democratic
Left with the Labour Party during the 28th Dáil.
He was Minister of State at the Department of
the Marine 1994–97.

He was first elected to the Dáil in 1989 as a
Workers' Party deputy. He had contested the
general elections in November 1982 and 1987
for the Workers' Party, six of whose seven
deputies in the 26th Dáil formed Democratic
Left. He was Democratic Left spokesperson on
Education, Environment, Justice, Transport,
Energy and Communications 1993–94. He was
spokesperson on the Environment, Marine,
Agriculture and Public Enterprise 1997–2002.

Represents Ireland on the Parliamentary
Assembly of Council of Europe. Member, Dublin
County Council and Dún Laoghaire Borough
Corporation 1985–95. Member, Dún Laoghaire–
Rathdown County Council 1999–2004.

President, UCG Students' Union 1974–75;
President, Union of Students in Ireland
1976–78. Member, Irish Transport and General
Workers' Union (now SIPTU) since 1978. Union
official 1978–89.

Member, CND; Greenpeace; Irish Council
Against Blood Sports.

Seán Barrett (FG)

Home Address
Avondale, Ballinclea Road, Killiney, Co Dublin
Constituency Office
6 Rogan's Court, Patrick Street,
Dún Laoghaire
Telephone
Office (01) 284 5333; *Mobile* 087 285 5848
Birth Place/Date
Dublin. 9 August 1944
Married
Sheila Hyde. 2 sons, 3 daughters
Education
CBC Monkstown, Co Dublin; Presentation
College, Glasthule, Co Dublin; College of
Commerce, Rathmines
Occupation
Public representative. Insurance broker

Seán Barrett was first elected to the Dáil in
1981 and at every subsequent election until
he retired at the 2002 general election. He
was asked to run again in 2007.

He was Minister for Defence and Minister for
the Marine 1995–97. Minister of State at the
Department of the Taoiseach and
Government Chief Whip 1994–95. Minister of
State at the Department of the Taoiseach and
Minister of State at the Department of
Education and Leader of the House with
responsibility for Dáil Reform 1986–87.
Government Chief Whip and Minister of State
at the Department of the Taoiseach and
Department of Defence 1982–86.

Fine Gael Chief Whip 1997–2002; front bench
spokesperson on Defence and Marine
1993–94; Environment 1994; Industry and
Commerce 1989–91; Justice 1987–89.

Member, Dublin County Council 1974–82
(Chairman, 1981–82). Member, Board of
Management, Cabinteely School from 1975,
and Chairman 1977 and 1980.

Ciarán Cuffe (GP)

Home Address
Quarry Road, Shankill, Co Dublin
Constituency Office
96 Patrick Street, Dún Laoghaire
Telephone
Office (01) 284 6060; *Mobile* 087 265 2075;
Website www.CiaranCuffe.com
Blog www.CuffeStreet.Blogspot.com
Birth Place/Date
Dublin. 3 April 1963
Marital Status
Living with partner. 2 sons
Education
Gonzaga College, Dublin; University College,
Dublin (BArch 1989, MRUP 1996); School of
Architecture, University of Venice, Italy
Occupation
Public representative. Architect, urban planner

Ciarán Cuffe was first elected to the Dáil in
2002. Green Party spokesperson for the
Environment, Heritage and Local Government;
Justice, Equality and Law Reform in last Dáil.

Member of Dublin City Council 1991–2003.
Former Commissioner of Irish Lights. Former
member, Council of Dublin Docklands
Authority; Dublin Transportation Initiative's
Local Authority Committee. Member,
Amnesty International and An Taisce.

Dún Laoghaire

	1st Count	2nd Count	3rd Count	4th Count
Seats 5 Quota 9,786		Transfer of **Hanafin** Surplus	Transfer of **Ó Broin** Votes	Transfer of **Andrews** Surplus
ANDREWS, Barry* (FF)	8,587	*(+1,390)* 9,977		
BAILEY, John (FG)	4,309	*(+50)* 4,359	*(+47)* 4,406	*(+9)* 4,415
BARRETT, Seán (FG)	5,361	*(+57)* 5,418	*(+38)* 5,456	*(+9)* 5,465
BOYD BARRETT, Richard (Ind)	5,233	*(+61)* 5,294	*(+504)* 5,798	*(+15)* 5,813
CUFFE, Ciarán* (GP)	4,534	*(+92)* 4,626	*(+239)* 4,865	*(+21)* 4,886
GILMORE, Eamon* (Lab)	7,127	*(+127)* 7,254	*(+238)* 7,492	*(+22)* 7,514
HANAFIN, Mary* (FF)	11,884			
Ó BROIN, Eoin (SF)	1,292	*(+17)* 1,309		
O'MALLEY, Fiona* (PD)	3,959	*(+206)* 4,165	*(+47)* 4,212	*(+97)* 4,309
QUINN, Oisín (Lab)	2,265	*(+51)* 2,316	*(+50)* 2,366	*(+11)* 2,377
REGAN, Eugene (FG)	4,162	*(+47)* 4,209	*(+21)* 4,230	*(+7)* 4,237
NON-TRANSFERABLE		125		59

5th Count	6th Count	7th Count	8th Count	9th Count	10th Count
Transfer of **Quinn** Votes	Transfer of **O'Malley** Votes	Transfer of **Bailey** Votes	Transfer of **Gilmore** Surplus	Transfer of **Regan** Votes	Transfer of **Barrett** Surplus
(+132) 4,547	*(+385)* 4,932				
(+175) 5,640	*(+634)* 6,274	*(+2,307)* 8,581	*(+52)* 8,633	*(+4,457)* 13,090	
(+130) 5,943	*(+419)* 6,362	*(+343)* 6,705	*(+27)* 6,732	*(+407)* 7,139	*(+751)* 7,890
(+287) 5,173	*(+872)* 6,045	*(+323)* 6,368	*(+31)* 6,399	*(+958)* 7,357	*(+2,553)* 9,910
(+1,206) 8,720	*(+505)* 9,225	*(+712)* 9,937			
(+128) 4,437					
(+260) 4,497	*(+689)* 5,186	*(+1,062)* 6,248	*(+41)* 6,289		
59	933	185	467		

Galway East

Elected

Party Share of Vote

1st Preferences	Number	%	Gain/Loss
Fianna Fáil	22,137	39.68	-7.10%
Fine Gael	21,832	39.13	7.61%
Labour	1,747	3.13	3.13%
Prog Democrats	3,321	5.95	5.95%
Green Party	1,057	1.89	-0.17%
Sinn Féin	1,789	3.21	-0.49%
Others	3,911	7.01	-8.93%

Statistics

Electorate	81,864	
Total Poll	56,274	68.74
Spoiled	480	0.85
Total Valid Poll	55,794	68.15
Seats	4	
Quota	11,159	
Candidates	14	

	Quotas	Seats
FF	1.98	2
FG	1.96	2
FG gain from Ind		

Paul Connaughton (FG)

Home Address
Mount Bellew, Ballinasloe, Co Galway
Telephone
Home (090) 967 9249
Birth Place/Date
Mount Bellew. 6 June 1944
Married
Bernadette Keating. 2 sons, 5 daughters
Education
St Mary's Secondary School, Ballygar, Co Galway; St Jarlath's Vocational School, Mount Bellew; Mount Bellew Agricultural College; Athenry Agricultural College; IMI Management Course
Occupation
Public representative. Farmer. Formerly general manager, Tuam Livestock Mart

Paul Connaughton was Fine Gael spokesperson on Regional Development and Emigrant Affairs in the last Dáil.

He was first elected to the Dáil in 1981, having contested the 1977 general election as a Fine Gael candidate in Galway East and a by-election in the old Galway North-East constituency in 1975. Senator, Agricultural panel, 1977–81. Minister of State at the Department of Agriculture, with special responsibility for Land Structure and Development, 1982–87. Party spokesperson on Energy and Western Development 1993–94. Also served as spokesperson on Agriculture, Social Welfare, Regional Development, Defence, and as deputy spokesperson on Tourism.

Member, Galway County Council 1979–85 and 1991–2003; Galway County Committee of Agriculture 1979–85.

Member, Macra na Feirme; Irish Farmers' Association; Mount Bellew Town Development Association; Tuam Chamber of Commerce; Gaelic Athletic Association.

Michael P. Kitt (FF)

Home Address
Castleblakeney, Ballinasloe, Co Galway
Telephone
Home (090) 967 8147; *Fax* (090) 967 8148
Birth Place/Date
Tuam, Co Galway. 17 May 1950
Married
Catherine Mannion. 3 sons, 1 daughter
Education
St Jarlath's College, Tuam; University College Galway; St Patrick's Training College, Drumcondra, Dublin; University College, Dublin (BA, HDipEd)
Occupation
Minister of State. Formerly primary school teacher

Michael Kitt was appointed Minister of State at the Department of Foreign Affairs, with special responsibility for Overseas Development, on 20 June 2007.

He was first elected to the Dáil in 1975 at a by-election caused by the death of his father. He was defeated in the subsequent general election in 1977 but won the seat back in 1981 after a spell in the Seanad (1977–81). He lost his seat again in 2002 but regained it in 2007 at the expense of party colleague Joe Callanan. He was a Taoiseach's nominee to the Seanad 2002–07 and Chairman of the Committee on Development and Co-Operation.

Minister of State at the Department of the Taoiseach 1991–92. Chairman of Education and Science Committee in the 28th Dáil, 1997–2002.

Member, Galway County Council 1975–91 (Chairman, 1985–86). Member, Irish National Teachers' Organisation; Caltra GAA; Comhaltas Ceoltóirí Éireann.

He is son of Michael F. Kitt, Dáil deputy for Galway East constituencies 1948–51, 1957–75, and brother of Tom Kitt, Government Chief Whip and Minister of State at the Department of Defence since 2007 and TD, Dublin South, since 1987. Their sister, Áine Brady, was elected TD for Kildare North in 2007.

Ulick Burke (FG)

Home Address
Eagle Hill, Abbey, Loughrea, Co Galway
Constituency Office
Kelly Street, Loughrea, Co Galway
Telephone
Home (090) 974 5218; *Office* (091) 847 437,
Fax (091) 847 438; *Mobile* 087 285 5863
Birth Place/Date
Loughrea. 19 November 1943
Married
Maeve Naughton. 5 sons, 2 daughters
Education
St Molaise's College, Portumna, Co Galway;
University College, Galway (BA, HDipEd)
Occupation
Full-time public representative. Formerly
teacher

Ulick Burke was first elected to the Dáil in
1997. He lost his seat in 2002 and regained it
in 2007.

He was a member of the Seanad 1981–82
(Taoiseach's nominee); 1983–87 and 2002–07
(Agricultural panel). He stood in the 1987 Dáil
election but did not contest the Seanad
election that year

Member of Galway County Council
1974–2003. Former member, central
executive, Association of Secondary School
Teachers of Ireland.

Noel Treacy (FF)

Home Address
Gurteen, Ballinasloe, Co Galway
Constituency Office
Cross Street, Athenry, Co Galway
Telephone
Home (090) 967 7094;
Constituency office (091) 844 360
Birth Place/Date
Ballinasloe. 18 December 1951
Married
Mary Cloonan. 3 daughters, 1 son
Education
St Joseph's College, Garbally Park, Ballinasloe
Occupation
Public representative. Formerly auctioneer

Noel Treacy has been a TD since he was first
elected in a by-election in 1982, and a junior
minister in every subsequent Fianna Fáil-led
administration up to 2007.

He was Minister of State at the Department of
Agriculture and Food from 2002 to 2007, and at
the Department of the Taoiseach and
Department of Foreign Affairs, with
responsibility for European Affairs, from 2004 to
14 June 2007. Minister of State at the
Department of Enterprise, Trade and
Employment and at the Department of
Education, with special responsibility for
Science and Technology, 1997–2002. Minister
of State at the Departments of the Taoiseach,
Finance and Transport, Energy and
Communications, with special responsibility for
Energy, 1993–94. Minister of State at the
Department of Finance, with special
responsibility for the Office of Public Works and
the Central Development Committee, 1992–93.
Minister of State at the Department of Health
1989–91 and at the Department of Justice
1990. Minister of State at the Department of
Finance 1987–89, with responsibility for the
Office of Public Works, and Minister of State at
the Department of the Taoiseach, 1988–89,
with responsibility for Heritage Affairs.

Former member of Galway County Council
1985–91 and its Chairman in 1986–87.
Chairman, Galway/Mayo Regional Development
Organisation 1986–87.

Galway East

Seats 4 Quota 11,159	1st Count	2nd Count Transfer of **Feeney, Flynn, Ní Chróinín** Votes	3rd Count Transfer of **Devlin** Votes	4th Count Transfer of **Keaveney** Votes
BARTON, John (FG)	4,916	*(+163)* 5,079	*(+356)* 5,435	*(+228)* 5,663
BURKE, Ulick (FG)	5,149	*(+169)* 5,318	*(+125)* 5,443	*(+202)* 5,645
CALLANAN, Joe* (FF)	5,817	*(+105)* 5,922	*(+213)* 6,135	*(+49)* 6,184
CANNON, Ciarán (PD)	3,321	*(+126)* 3,447	*(+60)* 3,507	*(+92)* 3,599
CONNAUGHTON, Paul* (FG)	6,886	*(+103)* 6,989	*(+124)* 7,113	*(+285)* 7,398
DEVLIN, Jason (SF)	1,789	*(+164)* 1,953		
FEENEY, Adrian (Ind)	397			
FLYNN, Clare (Ind)	290			
KEAVENEY, Colm (Lab)	1,747	*(+373)* 2,120	*(+251)* 2,371	
KITT, Michael (FF)	8,796	*(+115)* 8,911	*(+210)* 9,121	*(+206)* 9,327
McHUGH, Paddy* (Ind)	3,224	*(+158)* 3,382	*(+220)* 3,602	*(+449)* 4,051
McHUGH, Tom (FG)	4,881	*(+77)* 4,958	*(+61)* 5,019	*(+510)* 5,529
NÍ CHRÓINÍN, Mairéad (GP)	1,057			
TREACY, Noel* (FF)	7,524	*(+144)* 7,668	*(+149)* 7,817	*(+126)* 7,943
NON-TRANSFERABLE		47	184	224

5th Count	6th Count	7th Count	8th Count	9th Count
Transfer of **Cannon** Votes	Transfer of **McHugh, P** Votes	Transfer of **Barton** Votes	Transfer of **McHugh, T** Votes	Transfer of **Connaughton** Surplus
(+387) 6,050	*(+168)* 6,218			
(+549) 6,194	*(+122)* 6,316	*(+2,296)* 8,612	*(+1,029)* 9,641	*(+1,542)* 11,183
(+618) 6,802	*(+148)* 6,950	*(+759)* 7,709	*(+141)* 7,850	*(+82)* 7,932
(+300) 7,698	*(+617)* 8,315	*(+1,612)* 9,927	*(+3,131)* 13,058	
(+393) 9,720	*(+917)* 10,637	*(+440)* 11,077	*(+1,148)* 12,225	
(+161) 4,212				
(+55) 5,584	*(+1,126)* 6,710	*(+226)* 6,936		
(+952) 8,895	*(+504)* 9,399	*(+406)* 9,805	*(+511)* 10,316	*(+275)* 10,591
184	610	479	976	

Galway West

Elected

Party Share of Vote

1st Preferences	Number	%	Gain/Loss
Fianna Fáil	20,468	37.15	-4.18%
Fine Gael	11,235	20.39	3.49%
Labour	6,086	11.05	0.51%
Prog Democrats	8,868	16.10	3.58%
Green Party	3,026	5.49	1.06%
Sinn Féin	1,629	2.96	-2.66%
Others	3,784	6.87	-1.80%

Statistics

Electorate	86,602	
Total Poll	55,023	64.24
Spoiled	533	0.01
Total Valid Poll	55,096	63.61
Seats	5	
Quota	9,183	
Candidates	15	

	Quotas	Seats
FF	2.23	2
FG	1.22	1
Lab	0.66	1
PD	0.97	1
No change		

Éamon Ó Cuív (FF)

Home Address
Corr na Móna, Co na Gaillimhe
Business Address
Department of Community, Rural and Gaeltacht Affairs, Dún Aimhirgin, 43–49 Mespil Road, Dublin 4
Constituency Office
Teach Kirwan, Sráid Thobar an Iarla, Gaillimh
Telephone
Home (094) 954 8021; *Constituency office* (091) 562 846; *Fax* (091) 562 844; *Office* (01) 647 3000; *Fax* (01) 647 3101
Birth Place/Date
Dublin. 1 June 1950
Married
Áine Ní Choincheannain. 3 sons, 1 daughter
Education
Oatlands College, Mount Merrion, Dublin; University College, Dublin (BSc)
Occupation
Government Minister. Formerly Gaeltacht co-operative manager

Éamon Ó Cuív was re-appointed Minister for Community, Rural and Gaeltacht Affairs on 14 June 2007, having held the portfolio throughout the previous Dáil from 2002 to 2007.

First elected to the Dáil in 1992, he was Minister of State at the Department of Agriculture, Food and Rural Development, with responsibility for Rural Development, 2001–02. Minister of State at the Department of Arts, Heritage, Gaeltacht and the Islands, with responsibility for the Gaeltacht areas, the Irish Language and for Island Development, 1997–2001. He was party spokesperson for Rural Development and the Islands 1995–97. Senator, Cultural and Educational panel, 1989–92. Member of Forum for Peace and Reconciliation.

Member, Galway County Council 1991–97 and of a number of subsidiary committees.

He is grandson of Éamon de Valera, President 1959–73; Taoiseach 1937–48, 1951–54, 1957–59; President of Executive Council, Irish Free State, 1932–37; President, First Dáil, 1919–21; President, Second Dáil, 1921–January 1922.

Michael D. Higgins (Lab)

Home Address
Letteragh, Circular Road, Rahoon, Galway
Telephone
Constituency office (091) 524 513; *Fax* (091) 528 501
Birth Place/Date
Limerick. 18 April 1941
Married
Sabina Coyne. 3 sons, 1 daughter
Education
St Flannan's College, Ennis, Co Clare; University College, Galway (BA, BComm); Indiana University (MA); Manchester University
Occupation
Public representative. University lecturer

Michael D. Higgins is President of the Labour Party, elected in 2003, and was party spokesperson on Foreign Affairs in the last Dáil.

He was appointed party spokesperson on Foreign Affairs in September 2007. Minister for Arts, Culture and the Gaeltacht 1993–97. Member of the Committee on Foreign Affairs and the Committee on Heritage and the Irish Language.

He was first elected to the Dáil in 1981. He lost his seat in the general election of November 1982 and regained it in 1987. Senator, NUI constituency, 1982–87, and Taoiseach's nominee 1973–77. Labour Party candidate in Galway West in the general elections of 1969, 1973 and 1977. He also contested the European Parliament elections in the Connacht–Ulster constituency in 1979 and 1985.

Member of the Parliamentary Assembly of the Council of Europe 2000–02.

Member, Galway City Council 1974–93 (Mayor 1982–83 and 1991–92). Member, Galway County Council 1974–85; Governing Body, University College, Galway.

Chairman of the Labour Party 1978–87. First recipient of the MacBride International Peace Prize 1992.

Author of several collections of poems; his latest collection of essays, *Causes for Concern*, was published in 2006. Writer and presenter of TV documentaries on Montserrat and Dr Noël Browne.

Padraic McCormack (FG)

Home Address
3 Renmore Park, Galway
Constituency Office
114 Bohermore, Galway
Telephone
Home (091) 753 992; *Office* (091) 568 688;
Fax (091) 569 204
Birth Place/Date
Longford. 16 May 1942
Married
Eilish King. 2 sons, 2 daughters
Education
Ballymahon Secondary School; Multyfarnham
Agricultural College (DipAgrSc)
Occupation
Full-time public representative. Formerly
auctioneer and company director

Padraic McCormack was Fine Gael's Deputy
Spokesperson on Environment and Local
Government, with special responsibility for
Urban Renewal and Housing Policy, in the
29th Dáil.

He has been a Dáil deputy since 1989, having
contested the general elections of 1977, 1981
and February 1982. Senator, Agricultural panel
1987–89. Chairman of Fine Gael Parliamentary
Party 2001–02. Former Member, Public
Accounts Committee and Environment
Committee.

Member of Galway County Council 1974–99;
Galway City Council since 1985; He was the
first Fine Gael councillor elected on the same
day to a county and a county borough council.
Mayor of Galway 1992–93. Member of
Galway Harbour Board 1979–95 (Chairman,
1990). General Council of County Councils
1979–87 (Vice-Chairman, 1984–85).

Member, Gaelic Athletic Association.

Noel Grealish (PD)

Home Address
Carnmore, Oranmore, Co Galway
Constituency Office
Unit 14, Briarhill Business Park, Briarhill,
Galway
Telephone
Constituency office (091) 764 807;
Fax (091) 764 974; *Mobile* 087 264 8607
Birth Place/Date
Carnmore. 16 December 1965
Marital Status
Single
Education
Carnmore National School; St Mary's College,
Galway
Occupation
Public representative. Company director

Noel Grealish was first elected to the Dáil in
2002 when he won the Progressive Democrat
seat in Galway West, vacated by the senior
party figure, Bobby Molloy, on the eve of the
general election. He was one of the two PD
deputies to survive the 2007 election.

Party spokesperson on Rural Planning in 29th
Dáil. Member, Oireachtas Committee for the
Environment and Local Government;
Oireachtas Committee for Members'
Interests and Procedures and Privileges.
Chairman, PD Parliamentary Party 2004.

Member, Galway County Council 1999–2003.

Member, Carnmore Hurling Club.

Frank Fahey (FF)

Home Address
4 Carraig Bán, Menlo, Co Galway
Constituency Office
Ballybane Industrial Estate, Galway
Telephone
Constituency office (091) 771 020;
Fax (091) 771 040;
Email frank@frankfahey.ie
Website www.frankfahey.ie
Birth Place/Date
Dublin. 6 June 1951
Married
Ethelle Griffin. 2 sons, 1 daughter
Education
St Mary's College, Galway; Our Lady's
College, Gort; University College, Galway
(BA, HDipEd)
Occupation
Public representative. Formerly secondary
school teacher

Frank Fahey was one of two Ministers of
State not re-appointed after the 2007 election.
He had been Minister of State at the
Department of Justice, Equality and Law
Reform, with responsibility for Equality,
2004–07, and at the Department of Enterprise
Trade and Employment, with responsibility for
Labour Affairs, 2002–04.

He was Minister for the Marine and Natural
Resources, January 2000–June 2002. Minister
of State at the Department of Health and
Children, with special responsibility for
Children, 1997–2000. Minister of State at the
Department of Education, with special
responsibility for Youth and Sport, 1987–92,
and also at the Department of Tourism,
Transport and Communications, with special
responsibility for Sports Tourism.

He was first elected to the Dáil in February
1982, and continued until he lost his seat in
1992 and regained it in 1997. Senator, Labour
panel, 1993–97.

He was Fianna Fáil deputy spokesperson on
Youth Affairs and Sport 1982–87.

Former member, Galway County Council;
Galway County Vocational Education
Committee; Western Health Board; Galway
Regional Development Organisation.

Galway West

Seats 5 Quota 10,308	1st Count	2nd Count Transfer of **King** Votes	3rd Count Transfer of **Lyons** Votes	4th Count Transfer of **Ó Cuív** Surplus	5th Count Transfer of **Carroll** Votes	6th Count Transfer of **Cox** Votes
CARROLL, Ann Marie (SF)	1,629	*(+8)* 1,637	*(+4)* 1,641	*(+11)* 1,652		
CONNOLLY, Catherine (Ind)	2,006	*(+8)* 2,014	*(+41)* 2,055	*(+11)* 2,066	*(+241)* 2,307	*(+273)* 2,580
COX, Margaret (Ind)	1,718	*(+5)* 1,723	*(+72)* 1,795	*(+13)* 1,808	*(+124)* 1,932	
CROWE, Michael (FF)	4,969	*(+7)* 4,976	*(+139)* 5,115	*(+118)* 5,233	*(+131)* 5,364	*(+288)* 5,652
FAHEY, Frank* (FF)	5,854	*(+1)* 5,855	*(+110)* 5,965	*(+185)* 6,150	*(+150)* 6,300	*(+181)* 6,481
GREALISH, Noel* (PD)	5,806	*(+6)* 5,812	*(+310)* 6,122	*(+19)* 6,141	*(+55)* 6,196	*(+117)* 6,313
HEALY EAMES, Fidelma (FG)	3,904	*(+)* 3,904	*(+56)* 3,960	*(+6)* 3,966	*(+56)* 4,022	*(+227)* 4,249
HIGGINS, Michael D.* (Lab)	6,086	*(+4)* 6,090	*(+172)* 6,262	*(+34)* 6,296	*(+313)* 6,609	*(+338)* 6,947
KING, Thomas (Ind)	60					
KYNE, Seán (FG)	1,912	*(+2)* 1,914	*(+15)* 1,929	*(+10)* 1,939	*(+31)* 1,970	*(+63)* 2,033
LYONS, Donal (PD)	1,168	*(+1)* 1,169				
McCORMACK, Padraic (FG)	5,419	*(+6)* 5,425	*(+72)* 5,497	*(+16)* 5,513	*(+68)* 5,581	*(+138)* 5,719
Ó BROLCHÁIN, Niall (GP)	3,026	*(+6)* 3,032	*(+81)* 3,113	*(+11)* 3,124	*(+333)* 3,457	*(+201)* 3,658
Ó CUÍV, Éamon* (FF)	9,645					
WELBY, Tom (PD)	1,894	*(+3)* 1,897	*(+89)* 1,986	*(+28)* 2,014	*(+61)* 2,075	*(+44)* 2,119
NON-TRANSFERABLE		3	8		11	89

7th Count	8th Count	9th Count	10th Count	11th Count	12th Count	13th Count
Transfer of **Kyne** Votes	Transfer of **Welby** Votes	Transfer of **Connolly** Votes	Transfer of **Ó Brolcháin** Votes	Transfer of **Higgins** Surplus	Transfer of **Healy Eames** Votes	Transfer of **McCormack** Surplus
(+51) 2,631	(+53) 2,684					
(+56) 5,708	(+155) 5,863	(+254) 6,117	(+221) 6,338	(+169) 6,507	(+335) 6,842	(+317) 7,159
(+68) 6,549	(+487) 7,036	(+198) 7,234	(+187) 7,421	(+115) 7,536	(+378) 7,914	(+225) 8,139
(+53) 6,366	(+574) 6,940	(+125) 7,065	(+176) 7,241	(+136) 7,377	(+739) 8,116	(+918) 9,034
(+456) 4,705	(+126) 4,831	(+220) 5,051	(+445) 5,496	(+674) 6,170		
(+242) 7,189	(+258) 7,447	(+937) 8,384	(+2,532) 10,916			
(+755) 6,474	(+360) 6,834)	(+234 7,068	(+302) 7,370	(+489) 7,859	(+3,733) 11,592	
(+96) 3,754	(+80) 3,834	(+498) 4,332				
(+210) 2,329						
46	236	218	469	150	985	949

Kerry North

Elected

Jimmy Deenihan (FG)*	1st Count
Tom McEllistrim (FF)*	4th Count
Martin Ferris (SF)*	4th Count

Party Share of Vote

1st Preferences	Number	%	Gain/Loss
Fianna Fáil	12,304	31.30	1.15%
Fine Gael	12,697	32.30	10.21%
Labour	4,287	10.90	-11.49%
Green Party	747	1.90	1.90%
Sinn Féin	8,030	20.43	-3.82%
Others	1,248	3.17	2.05%

Statistics

Electorate	55,862	
Total Poll	39,647	70.97
Spoiled	334	0.84
Total Valid Poll	39,313	70.38
Seats	3	
Quota	9,829	
Candidates	10	

	Quotas	Seats
FF	1.25	1
FG	1.29	1
SF	0.82	1
No change		

Jimmy Deenihan (FG)

Home Address
Finuge, Lixnaw, Co Kerry
Telephone
Home (068) 40235/40154
Birth Place/Date
Listowel, Co Kerry. 11 September 1952
Married
Mary Dowling
Education
St Michael's College, Listowel; National College of Physical Education, Limerick (BEd)
Occupation
Full-time public representative. Formerly teacher

Jimmy Deenihan was appointed party spokesperson on Defence in September 2007. He was party spokesperson on Arts, Sport and Tourism in the 29th Dáil.

He has been a TD since 1987. He was Minister of State at the Department of Agriculture, Food and Forestry, with special responsibility for Rural Development, the LEADER programme and monitoring the activities of An Bord Bia and the food industry 1994–97. He was a candidate in the general election of November 1982 and a Senator, Taoiseach's nominee, 1982–87. Spokesperson on the Office of Public Works 1997–2002.

Member, Kerry County Council 1985–94; Kerry County Vocational Educational Committee; Library Committee 1985–94.

Member, Gaelic Athletic Association. He won All-Ireland football medals in 1975, 1978, 1979, 1980 and 1981 and was captain of the 1981 team. He also won four National League medals and five Railway Cup medals. GAA All-Star Award 1981.

Tom McEllistrim (FF)

Home Address
Ahane, Ballymacelligott, Tralee, Co Kerry
Telephone
Home/Office (066) 713 7127
Birth Place/Date
Tralee. 24 October 1968
Marital Status
Single
Education
Presentation Convent, Tralee; St Patrick's College, Castleisland, Co Kerry; St Brendan's College, Killarney; St Patrick's College, Maynooth (BA, HDipEd)
Occupation
Public representative. Formerly secondary school teacher

Tom McEllistrim was first elected to the Dáil in 2002, re-instating in the Oireachtas, after a ten-year gap, a family dynasty going back to 1923. He was an unsuccessful candidate in the 1997 general election.

Member of Joint Oireachtas Committees on Education and Science, and Communications, Marine and Natural Resources. Member of Kerry County Council 1999–2003, where he became the youngest councillor and the fourth generation of the family to serve in local politics.

Member, Kerry County Enterprise Board; Fenit Harbour Board; Partnership Tra Lí; Ballyseedy Wood Committee; Kerry County Rural Water Company; Housing and Social Support Strategic Policy Committee.

His father, Tom McEllistrim, was a TD for Kerry North from 1969 to 1987 and from 1989 to 1992; he was a Taoiseach's nominee to the Seanad from 1987 to 1989. His grandfather, also Tom McEllistrim, was TD for Kerry and subsequently Kerry North from 1923 to 1969; he did not take his seat until 1927.

Martin Ferris (SF)

Home Address
18 Casement View, Ardfert, Co Kerry
Constituency Office
2 Moyderwell, Tralee, Co Kerry; Market
Street, Listowel, Co Kerry
Telephone
Constituency office (066) 712 9545; *Fax* (066)
712 9572 (Tralee); (068) 24949 (Listowel)
Birth Place/Date
Tralee. 28 March 1952
Married
Marie Hoare. 3 sons, 3 daughters, 4
grandchildren
Education
Barrow National School, Ardfert; Tralee CBS
(The Green)
Occupation
Full-time public representative. Formerly
fisherman

Martin Ferris was first elected in 2002, having
been a candidate in the general election of 1997.

He first became a member of the Sinn Féin Ard-
Comhairle in 1983. He was arrested on board
the *Marita Ann* in 1984, attempting to import
arms for the IRA. Imprisoned in Portlaoise
Prison, 1984–94, for possession of explosive
substances for unlawful purpose and for
possession of firearms and ammunition with
intent to endanger life. Also served prison
sentences in 1970s and spent 47 days on
hunger strike in Portlaoise Prison in 1976.

Member, Sinn Féin Ard-Comhairle since 1995;
Sinn Féin delegation to the Forum for Peace
and Reconciliation; party delegation in direct
talks with the British Prime Minister, Tony
Blair, in 1997; negotiating team for Good
Friday Agreement 1998. Member, Sinn Féin
delegation to Leeds Castle talks 2004 and St
Andrews talks 2006.

In the last Dáil, he was party spokesperson on
Agriculture, Rural Affairs, the Marine and
Natural Resources. Member, Joint Oireachtas
Committee on Agriculture and Food and
Committee on Communications, Marine and
Natural Resources.

Member of Kerry County Council 1999–2003.
Member, Joint Community Policing
Committee in Tralee.

Seats 3 Quota 9,829	1st Count	2nd Count Transfer of **Deenihan** Surplus	3rd Count Transfer of **Dineen, Donovan, Grey, Locke, O'Connor** Votes	4th Count Transfer of **Foley** Votes
DEENIHAN, Jimmy* (FG)	12,697			
DINEEN, Anthony (Ind)	689	*(+114)* 803		
DONOVAN, Tom (Ind)	111	*(+23)* 134		
FERRIS, Martin* (SF)	8,030	*(+601)* 8,631	*(+653)* 9,284	*(+912)* 10,196
FOLEY, Norma (FF)	4,937	*(+320)* 5,257	*(+278)* 5,535	
GREY, David (GP)	747	*(+146)* 893		
LOCKE, Sam (Ind)	397	*(+20)* 417		
McELLISTRIM, Tom* (FF)	7,367	*(+335)* 7,702	*(+338)* 8,040	*(+3,207)* 11,247
O'BRIEN, Terry (Lab)	4,287	*(+1,302)* 5,589	*(+743)* 6,332	*(+950)* 7,282
O'CONNOR, Michael (Ind)	51	*(+7)* 58		
NON-TRANSFERABLE			293	466

Kerry South

Kerry South

Elected

John O'Donoghue (FF)*	3rd Count
Tom Sheahan (FG)	5th Count
Jackie Healy-Rae (Ind)*	6th Count

Party Share of Vote

1st Preferences	Number	%	Gain/ Loss
Fianna Fáil	15,868	40.65	-3.98%
Fine Gael	9,795	25.09	7.43%
Labour	5,263	13.48	-1.00%
Green Party	738	1.89	1.89%
Sinn Féin	1,375	3.52	3.52%
Others	5,993	15.35	-7.87%

Statistics

Electorate	53,660	
Total Poll	39,325	73.29
Spoiled	293	0.75
Total Valid Poll	39,032	72.74
Seats	3	
Quota	9,759	
Candidates	8	

	Quotas	Seats
FF	1.63	1
FG	1.00	1
Ind	0.61	1
FG gain from Lab		

John O'Donoghue (FF)

Home Address
Garranearagh, Cahirciveen, Co Kerry
Business Address
Office of the Ceann Comhairle, Dáil Éireann, Leinster House, Dublin 2
Telephone
Home (066) 947 2413/2631;
Fax (066) 947 2667; *Office* (01) 618 3343
Email Ceann.Comhairle@oireachtas.ie
Website www.johnodonoghue.ie
Birth Place/Date
Cahirciveen. 28 May 1956
Married
Kate Ann Murphy. 2 sons, 1 daughter
Education
CBS, Cahirciveen; University College, Cork (BCL, LLB); Incorporated Law Society of Ireland, Dublin
Occupation
Ceann Comhairle. Formerly Government Minister and solicitor

John O'Donoghue was elected Ceann Comhairle of the 30th Dáil on 14 June 2007.

First elected to the Dáil in 1987, he was previously Minister for the Arts, Sport and Tourism from 2002 to 2007; Minister for Justice, Equality and Law Reform 1997–2002; Minister of State at the Department of Finance, with special responsibility for the Office of Public Works, November 1991–February 1992.

He was party spokesperson on Justice 1995–97. Member, British–Irish Inter-Parliamentary Body 1993–97.

Member, Kerry County Council 1985–91 (Chairperson, 1990–91) and 1993–97; Southern Health Board and the Psychiatric Services Committee 1982–97 (Chairperson, 1992–93); Kerry County Committee of Agriculture (1985–88); Kerry County Fisheries Committee 1989–91 (Chairperson, 1989–90); Kerry County Library Committee 1991–97.

Member, St Mary's Gaelic Athletic Association Club and Cahirciveen Social Services Committee.

Tom Sheahan (FG)

Home Address
Rathbeg, Rathmore, Co Kerry
Constituency Office
31 College Street, Killarney, Co Kerry
Telephone
Home (064) 58102; *Office* (064) 22420 (Killarney), (01) 618 3333 (Dáil);
Mobile (087) 202 1661
Birth Place/Date
Glenbeigh, Co Kerry. 5 September 1968
Married
Mary Lenihan. 2 daughters, 1 son
Education
Glenbeigh National School; De La Salle Brothers; Coláiste Iosagáin, Ballyvourney, Co Cork.
Occupation
Public representative. Businessman

First Fine Gael deputy elected in Kerry South for 18 years.

Former member of Kerry County Council. Member HSE (South), Kerry Mental Health Association, Rathmore Community Council. Played rugby and gaelic football and represented Munster in basketball.

Jackie Healy-Rae (Ind)

Home Address
Main Street, Kilgarvan, Co Kerry
Business Address
Main Street, Kilgarvan
Telephone
Home (064) 85315;
Constituency office (064) 37376
Birth Place/Date
Kilgarvan. March 1931
Marital Status
Separated. 4 sons, 2 daughters
Occupation
Full-time public representative. Formerly
farmer, publican, plant-hire business

Jackie Healy-Rae was first elected to the Dáil
in 1997 when he stood as an Independent
after he failed to get a Fianna Fáil nomination.
He voted for Bertie Ahern as Taoiseach in
1997 and 2007 and supported the Fianna
Fáil–Green Party–Progressive Democrat
coalition in the 30th Dáil.

Vice-Chairman of the Joint Committee on
Environment and Local Government in the last
Dáil and Chairman of the Committee in the
28th Dáil. Fianna Fáil member of Kerry County
Council 1974–97, and 1997–2003 as
Independent. Chairman of County Council
1995–96. Served for many years on the
Southern Health Board (Chairperson,
1981–82).

Chairperson for seven years of Comhaltas
Ceoltóirí Chiarraí.

Kerry South

Seats 3 Quota 9,759	1st Count	2nd Count Transfer of **Hickey, Ní Bhaoigheallháin** Votes	3rd Count Transfer of **Fitzgerald** Votes	4th Count Transfer of **O'Donoghue** Surplus	5th Count Transfer of **Moynihan- Cronin** Votes	6th Count Transfer of **Sheahan** Surplus
FITZGERALD, Seamus (FG)	4,195	*(+224)* 4,419				
FLEMING, Tom (FF)	6,740	*(+232)* 6,972	*(+249)* 7,221	*(+57)* 7,278	*(+1,115)* 8,393	*(+462)* 8,855
HEALY-RAE, Jackie* (Ind)	5,993	*(+363)* 6,356	*(+472)* 6,828	*(+54)* 6,882	*(+1,644)* 8,526	*(+789)* 9,315
HICKEY, John (GP)	738					
MOYNIHAN-CRONIN, Breeda* (Lab)	5,263	*(+641)* 5,904	*(+870)* 6,774	*(+53)* 6,827		
NÍ BHAOIGHEALLÁIN, Lynn (SF)	1,375					
O'DONOGHUE, John* (FF)	9,128	*(+279)* 9,407	*(+549)* 9,956			
SHEAHAN, Tom (FG)	5,600	*(+219)* 5,819	*(+2,108)* 7,927	*(+33)* 7,960	*(+3,050)* 11,010	
NON-TRANSFERABLE		155	177		1,018	

Gerry Adams and Mary Lou McDonald arriving at the Dublin Central count to learn that she has not won a seat.

Kildare North

Kildare North

Elected

Áine Brady (FF)	1st Count
Emmet Stagg (Lab)*	5th Count
Michael Fitzpatrick (FF)	5th Count
Bernard Durkan (FG)*	6th Count

Party Share of Vote

1st Preferences	Number	%	Gain/Loss
Fianna Fáil	17,851	39.50	-3.71%
Fine Gael	9,590	21.22	3.68%
Labour	7,882	17.44	-3.94%
Prog Democrats	983	2.18	-9.71%
Green Party	2,215	4.90	-1.08%
Sinn Féin	1,103	2.44	2.44%
Others	5,567	12.32	12.32%

Statistics

Electorate	71,311	
Total Poll	45,423	63.70
Spoiled	232	0.51
Total Valid Poll	45,191	63.37
Seats	4	
Quota	9,039	
Candidates	11	

	Quotas	Seats
FF	1.97	2
FG	1.06	1
Lab	0.87	1

Extra seat in constituency, won by FF

Áine Brady (FF)

Home Address
28 Clonwood Heights, Clane, Co Kildare
Constituency Office
Main Street, Naas; 4 Centre Point Mall, Maynooth, Co Kildare
Telephone
Home (045) 868 531; *Office* (045) 873 666 (Naas), (01) 628 5269 (Maynooth); *Mobile* 087 288 1000
Birth Place/Date
Tuam, Co Galway. 8 September 1954
Married
Gerry Brady. 2 sons, 2 daughters
Education
Killasolan NS, Caltra, Ballinasloe, Co Galway; Presentation Convent, Tuam; Carysfort College of Education; St Patrick's College of Education
Occupation
Full-time public representative. Formerly teacher

Áine Brady is a new TD. She contested the by-election in Kildare in 2005 caused by the appointment of former Minister Charlie McCreevy as an EU Commissioner.

She was the first youth representative on the Fianna Fáil's National Executive; member of the National Executive for many years in the 1980s, topping the poll in the 'Committee of 15' elections at the party's Ard-Fheiseanna. Member, Fianna Fáil strategic national general election team in the 1980s.

Two of her brothers are also members of the 30th Dáil: Tom Kitt who is Government Chief Whip and Minister of State and TD for Dublin South, and Michael Kitt, Minister of State and TD for Galway East. Their father, Michael F. Kitt, was Dáil deputy for Galway East constituencies 1948–51, 1957–75.

Áine Brady's husband, Gerry Brady, was TD for Kildare in the 24th Dáil, March–November 1982.

Emmet Stagg (Lab)

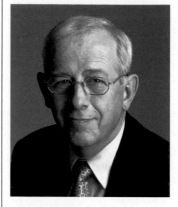

Home Address
736 Lodge Park, Straffan, Co Kildare
Telephone
Home (01) 627 2149; *Office* (01) 618 3797
Birth Place/Date
Mayo. October 1944
Married
Mary Morris. 1 son, 1 daughter
Education
Ballinrobe CBS; College of Technology, Kevin Street, Dublin; Member, Institute of Medical Laboratory Sciences
Occupation
Full-time public representative. Formerly medical laboratory technologist

Emmet Stagg was appointed the Labour Party's Chief Whip in September 2007. He was Minister of State at the Department of the Environment, with special responsibility for Housing and Urban Renewal, 1993–94; Minister of State at the Department of Transport, Energy and Communications, with special responsibility for Nuclear Safety, Renewable Energy, Gas and Oil Industry, Air Safety, Road Haulage and Bus Regulation, 1994–97. He was first elected to the Dáil in 1987.

Labour Party spokesperson on Public Enterprise since 1997; on Social Welfare 1989–92; on Agriculture 1987–89. Vice-Chairman of the Labour Party 1987–89.

Member, Kildare County Council 1978–93 and 1999–2003 (Chairperson, 1981–82); Kildare County Vocational Education Committee 1985–93; Eastern Health Board 1978–85; Kildare County Library Committee 1975–89.

Member, SIPTU.

Member, Gaelic Athletic Association and President of Celbridge Soccer Club. President, Maynooth Soccer Club.

Michael Fitzpatrick (FF)

Home Address
Áit Bhride, Allenwood, Naas, Co Kildare
Constituency Office
South Main Street, Naas, Co Kildare
Telephone
Office (045) 888 438; *Mobile* 086 270 6150
Birth Place/Date
Cavan. 12 October 1942
Married
Maureen Roche. 1 son
Education
St Michael's College, Cootehill, Co Cavan
Occupation
Public representative. Auctioneer and
assurance agent; formerly garda

Michael Fitzpatrick is a new member of the
Dáil.

A former adviser and constituency manager
for Charlie McCreevy, former Minister and TD
for Kildare from 1977 to 2004, he was elected
to Kildare County Council in 1999 and re-
elected in 2004. Mayor of Kildare, 2003–04.
Leader of the Fianna Fáil grouping in Kildare
County Council.

Former member of Fianna Fáil's National
Executive, Comhairle Dáil Ceanntair Chairman,
and director of European, Dáil and local
elections in constituency.

Member of second-level school boards in
North Kildare including Scoil Mhuire, Clane.
Chairman of Maynooth Post-Primary School.
Member and former Chairman, St Wolstan's
Community School, Celbridge.

Bernard Durkan (FG)

Home Address
Timard, Maynooth, Co Kildare
Telephone
Home (01) 628 6063/5215
Birth Place/Date
Killasser, Swinford, Co Mayo. 26 March 1945
Married
Hilary Spence. 2 sons
Education
St John's National School, Carramore,
Co Mayo
Occupation
Full-time public representative. Formerly
agricultural contractor

Bernard Durkan was Fine Gael front bench
spokesperson for Communications and
Natural Resources in the last Dáil and former
Chief Whip of the party.

He was first elected to the Dáil in 1981, lost
his seat in February 1982 and regained it in
November 1982. He has since been re-
elected in successive general elections.

Minister of State at the Department of Social
Welfare, with special responsibility for
Information and Customer Services and the
Integration of the Tax and Social Welfare
Codes, 1994–97. Spokesperson on Overseas
Development Assistance and Human Rights
in 28th Dáil. Spokesperson on Health 1994; on
the Office of the Tánaiste and on the National
Development Plan 1993–94; on the Insurance
Industry 1991–92; on Trade and Marketing
1989–91; on the Food Industry 1987–89.
Assistant Whip 1986–87.

Member, Kildare County Council 1976–94
(Chairperson, 1986–87). He has served on the
Eastern Regional Development Organisation
and various Dáil committees including Public
Accounts and Foreign Affairs.

Kildare North

Seats 4 Quota 9,039	1st Count	2nd Count Transfer of **Brady** Surplus	3rd Count Transfer of **Browne, Corish** Votes	4th Count Transfer of **Aherne, McCauley** Votes	5th Count Transfer of **Fitzgerald** Votes	6th Count Transfer of **Scully** Votes
AHERNE, Jeff (PD)	983	*(+100)* 1,083	*(+20)* 1,103			
BRADY, Áine (FF)	11,245					
BROWNE, Gerry (Ind)	145	*(+8)* 153				
CORISH, Dr John F. (Ind)	234	*(+10)* 244				
DURKAN, Bernard* (FG)	5,340	*(+87)* 5,427	*(+44)* 5,471	*(+192)* 5,663	*(+249)* 5,912	*(+3,317)* 9,229
FITZGERALD, Shane (GP)	2,215	*(+74)* 2,289	*(+53)* 2,342	*(+326)* 2,668		
FITZPATRICK, Michael (FF)	6,606	*(+1,507)* 8,113	*(+38)* 8,151	*(+666)* 8,817	*(+280)* 9,097	
McCAULEY, Cristin (SF)	1,103	*(+32)* 1,135	*(+19)* 1,154			
MURPHY, Catherine* (Ind)	5,188	*(+151)* 5,339	*(+135)* 5,474	*(+407)* 5,881	*(+852)* 6,733	*(+919)* 7,652
SCULLY, Darren (FG)	4,250	*(+56)* 4,306	*(+26)* 4,332	*(+157)* 4,489	*(+343)* 4,832	
STAGG, Emmet* (Lab)	7,882	*(+181)* 8,063	*(+44)* 8,107	*(+361)* 8,468	*(+752)* 9,220	
NON-TRANSFERABLE			18	148	192	596

Dublin City
Baile Átha Cliath

DUBLIN CITY COUNCIL
First Local Authority to Buy
Eco-friendly Biofuel Cars

Dublin City Council has accepted
delivery of 18 Ford Focus flexi-fuel cars.
It is the first Local Authority in Ireland to choose vehicles
that run on environmentally friendly bioethanol .

The fleet is for frontline staff delivering
Housing, Drainage and Waste Management Services
to residents and customers.
The fleet represents 10% of the Council's car fleet.

For further information contact:
DUBLIN CITY COUNCIL
CIVIC OFFICES
WOOD QUAY
DUBLIN 8
Tel: 222 2222
Email: info@dublincity.ie

www.dublincity.ie

DUBLIN CITY COUNCIL LEADING THE WAY TO A CLEANER ENVIRONMENT

Kildare South

Elected

Party Share of Vote

1st Preferences	Number	%	Gain/Loss
Fianna Fáil	17,425	50.37	3.94%
Fine Gael	5,939	17.17	-0.59%
Labour	7,154	20.68	2.16%
Prog Democrats	1,513	4.37	-7.54%
Green Party	2,136	6.18	2.47%
Others	424	1.23	-0.45%

Statistics

Electorate	56,670	
Total Poll	34,938	61.65
Spoiled	347	0.99
Total Valid Poll	34,591	61.04
Seats	3	
Quota	8,648	
Candidates	8	

	Quotas	Seats
FF	2.01	2
Lab	0.83	1
No change		

Seán Ó Fearghail (FF)

Home Address
Fennor House, Kildare
Constituency Office
4 Offaly Street, Athy, Co Kildare
Telephone
Home (045) 522966; *Office* (059) 863 4805;
Mobile 087 236 7155
Birth Place/Date
Dublin. 17 April 1960
Married
Mary Clare Meaney. 1 son, 3 daughters
Education
De La Salle primary school, Kildare;
St Joseph's Academy, Kildare
Occupation
Public representative. Farmer

Seán Ó Fearghail was first elected in 2002,
having contested the previous four general
elections in 1987, 1989, 1992 and 1997.

In the last Dáil, he was a member of the Joint
Oireachtas Committee on Justice, Equality,
Defence and Women's Rights; Committee on
Procedure and Privileges; and the sub-
committee on the Barron Report into the
Murder of Seamus Ludlow. He was convenor
of the Joint Oireachtas Committee on
Agriculture and Food. He was a Senator on
the Agricultural panel 1997–2002.

Member, Kildare County Council 1985–2003.

Seán Power (FF)

Home Address
Caragh, Naas, Co Kildare
Business Address
Main Street, Newbridge, Co Kildare
Telephone
Office (045) 432 289; *Fax* (045) 435 380
Birth Place/Date
Caragh, Naas. 14 October 1960
Married
Deirdre Malone. 3 sons, 1 daughter
Education
Caragh National School; Naas CBS
Occupation
Minister of State. Publican

Seán Power was appointed Minister of State
at the Department of Justice, Equality and
Law Reform, with special responsibility for
Equality Issues, on 20 June 2007. He was
Minister of State at the Department of Health
and Children 2004–June 2007. Chairman of
the Environment and Local Government
Committee in the 29th Dáil.

He was first elected to the Dáil in 1989, and
was Assistant Government Whip in the last
Dáil. He served on the following committees:
Environment and Local Government;
European Affairs; Public Enterprise and
Transport.

Member of Raheen and Éire Óg Gaelic
Football Clubs.

Son of Paddy Power, Dáil deputy for Kildare
1969–89; Minister for Defence
March–December 1982; Minister for Fisheries
1979–81; Member of European Parliament
1977–79.

Jack Wall (Lab)

Home Address
Castlemitchell, Athy, Co Kildare
Constituency Office
15 Leinster Street, Athy, Co Kildare
Telephone
Home (059) 863 1495; *Office* (059) 863 2874; *Fax* (059) 863 3157; *Mobile* 087 257 0275
Birth Place/Date
Castledermot, Co Kildare. 1 July 1945
Married
Ann Byrne. 2 sons, 2 daughters
Education
Castledermot Vocational School; Kevin Street College of Technology, Dublin
Occupation
Full-time public representative. Formerly electrician

Jack Wall was first elected to the Dáil in 1997.

He was appointed party spokesperson on Community and Rural Affairs in September 2007. He was party spokesperson on Arts, Sport and Tourism in the last Dáil, previously spokesperson on Agriculture and Defence. Member, Joint Oireachtas Committee on Arts, Sport and Tourism. Party spokesperson on Defence in 28th Dáil. Senator (Taoiseach's nominee) 1993–97. Spokesperson in the Seanad on Social Welfare.

Member, Kildare County Council 1999–2003. Member, Athy Urban District Council since 1991 (Chairperson, 1996). Former member Eastern Regional Health Authority.

Chairperson, Kildare GAA County Board 1989–1999. Director, Athy Credit Union.

Seats 3 Quota 8,648	1st Count	2nd Count Transfer of **Doyle, Mullins** Votes	3rd Count Transfer of **Power, J. J.** Votes
DALY, Richard (FG)	3,353	*(+301)* 3,654	*(+385)* 4,039
DOYLE, Tom (Ind)	424		
GILLIS, Allan (FG)	2,586	*(+275)* 2,861	*(+317)* 3,178
MULLINS, Jane (PD)	1,513		
Ó FEARGHAIL, Seán* (FF)	8,731		
POWER, J.J. (GP)	2,136	*(+522)* 2,658	
POWER, Seán* (FF)	8,694		
WALL, Jack* (Lab)	7,154	*(+558)* 7,712	*(+1,433)* 9,145
NON-TRANSFERABLE		281	523

Laois–Offaly

Elected

Brian Cowen (FF)*	1st Count
Olwyn Enright (FG)*	8th Count
Seán Fleming (FF)*	9th Count
Charles Flanagan (FG)	9th Count
John Moloney (FF)*	11th Count

Party Share of Vote

1st Preferences	Number	%	Gain/Loss
Fianna Fáil	40,307	56.38	5.08%
Fine Gael	19,560	27.36	4.34%
Labour	1,703	2.38	-0.15%
Prog Democrats	4,233	5.92	-8.45%
Green Party	812	1.14	0.31%
Sinn Féin	3,656	5.11	1.00%
Others	1,220	1.71	-2.13%

Statistics

Electorate	103,673	
Total Poll	72,153	69.60
Spoiled	662	0.92
Total Valid Poll	71,491	68.96
Seats	5	
Quota	11,916	
Candidates	16	

	Quotas	Seats
FF	3.38	3
FG	1.64	2
FG gain from PD		

Brian Cowen (FF)

Home Address
Ballard, Tullamore, Co Offaly
Business Address
Department of Finance, Merrion Street, Dublin 2
Constituency Office
O'Connor Street, Tullamore, Co Offaly
Telephone
Home (057) 935 2047; *Business* (01) 676 7571; *Constituency office* (057) 932 1976; *Fax* (057) 932 1910
Birth Place/Date
Tullamore. January 1960
Married
Mary Molloy. 2 daughters
Education
Ardscoil Naomh Ciarán, Clara, Co Offaly; Mount St Joseph's College, Roscrea, Co Tipperary; University College, Dublin (BCL); Incorporated Law Society of Ireland, Dublin
Occupation
Government Minister. Formerly solicitor

Brian Cowen was appointed Tánaiste and re-appointed Minster for Finance on 14 June 2007. Deputy Leader of Fianna Fáil.

He was first appointed Minister for Finance in September 2004, succeeding Charlie McCreevy, who was appointed to the European Commission. He was Minister of Foreign Affairs from January 2000 to September 2004. Minister for Health and Children, June 1997–January 2000; Minister for Transport, Energy and Communications, January 1993–December 1994; Minister for Labour, February 1992–January 1993.

He was first elected to the Dáil in a by-election in June 1984, caused by the death of his father, Bernard Cowen. Party front bench spokesperson on Agriculture, Food and Forestry, December 1994–March 1997 and on Health, March to June 1997.

He is a son of the late Bernard Cowen, Fianna Fáil deputy for Laois–Offaly 1969–73 and 1977–84; Senator 1973–77; and Minister of State at the Department of Agriculture March–December 1982.

Olwyn Enright (FG)

Home Address
31 Meadowville, Birr, Co Offaly
Constituency Office
1 John's Place, Birr; 2 Cormac Street, Tullamore
Telephone
Home (0506) 29870; *Birr office* (057) 912 2326; *Tullamore office* (057) 932 9870; *Website* www.olwynenright.com
Birth Place/Date
Birr. 1 July 1974
Married
Joe McHugh
Education
St Brendan's Community School, Birr; University College, Dublin (BCL); Law Society of Ireland; University College, Galway (Dip Community Development Practice)
Occupation
Public representative. Solicitor

Olwyn Enright was first elected to the Dáil in 2002. She was appointed party spokesperson on Social and Family Affairs in September 2007. She was Fine Gael front bench spokesperson for Education and Science in the 29th Dáil.

Member of Offaly County Council 1999–2004. Member, Midland Regional Authority. Chairperson, Birr Vintage Week.

She is married to Joe McHugh, new Fine Gael TD for Donegal North East; they are the first married couple to sit in the Dáil at the same time since Fine Gael TDs Alexis Fitzgerald (1982) and Mary Flaherty (1981–97). She is a daughter of Tom Enright, Dáil deputy 1969–92 and 1997–2002; Senator 1993–97.

Seán Fleming (FF)

Home Address
Silveracre, Castletown, Portlaoise, Co Laois
Telephone
Home (057) 873 2692
Birth Place/Date
The Swan, Co Laois. 1 February 1958
Married
Mary O'Gorman. 1 son
Education
Salesian College, Ballinakill; University College, Dublin (BComm); Fellow of the Institute of Chartered Accountants
Occupation
Full-time public representative. Formerly accountant and Financial Director of Fianna Fáil at national level

Seán Fleming was first elected to the Dáil in 1997. He was chairperson of the Oireachtas Committee on Finance and a member of the Public Accounts Committee in the 29th Dáil.

Member, Laois County Council 1999–2003.

Charles Flanagan (FG)

Home Address
Glenlahan, Portlaoise, Co Laois
Office
Lismard Court, Portlaoise, Co Laois
Telephone
Home (057) 866 0707; *Office* (057) 862 0232; *Fax* (057) 862 1590
Birth Place/Date
Dublin. November 1956
Married
Mary McCormack. 2 daughters
Education
Coláiste na Rinne, Waterford; Knockbeg College, Carlow; University College, Dublin; Law School of the Incorporated Law Society.
Occupation
Public representative. Solicitor

Charles Flanagan was first elected in 1987 but lost his seat in 2002 and was re-elected in 2007. He was appointed party spokesperson on Justice, Equality and Law Reform in September 2007.

Member of the Fine Gael front bench from 1997 to 2002, first as Chief Whip (1997–2001) under John Bruton's leadership, and then as spokesman on Enterprise, Trade and Employment under Michael Noonan's leadership. Member of the National Forum on Europe from 2002.

Previously Fine Gael spokesperson on Criminal Law Reform and Northern Ireland 1997–2002; Health 1993–94; Transport and Tourism 1992–93; Law Reform 1988–90. Fine Gael Chief Whip 1990–92; Assistant Whip 1987–88. Chairman, Select Committee on Legislation and Security 1995–97; Vice-Chair, Joint Committee on Women's Rights 1995–97.

Member of Laois County Council 1984–2004, and former member Mountmellick Town Commissioners. Founder member of Young Fine Gael.

He is son of Oliver J. Flanagan, Dáil deputy for Laois–Offaly 1943–87, Minister for Defence 1976–77, Parliamentary Secretary to the Minister for Local Government 1975–76, and to Minister for Agriculture and Fisheries 1954–57.

John Moloney (FF)

Home Address
27 Patrick Street, Mountmellick, Co Laois
Constituency Office
26 Patrick Street, Mountmellick, Co Laois
Telephone
Home/Office (057) 862 4391; *Mobile* 087 277 0147
Birth Place/Date
Portlaoise, Co Laois. 12 June 1953
Married
Patricia McEvoy. 2 sons, 1 daughter
Education
Patrician Brothers, Ballyfin, Co Laois
Occupation
Full-time public representative. Formerly air traffic controller, publican and undertaker

John Moloney was first elected to the Dáil in June 1997. In the 29th Dáil he was Chairman of the Joint Committee on Health and Children (November 2004 to April 2007). In the previous Dáil, he was Government Whip on the Oireachtas Committee on Education and Science; member of Committees on Tourism, Sport and Recreation and Family, Community and Social Affairs.

Member, Laois County Council 1981–2003 (Chairperson, 1989–90). Chairperson, Mountmellick Community Employment Scheme; Mountmellick Tidy Towns Committee; Kyletelisha Environmental Group.

John Moloney became the third generation of his family to serve on Laois County Council.

Laois–Offaly

	1st Count	2nd Count	3rd Count	4th Count	5th Count
Seats 5 **Quota 11,916**		Transfer of **Cowen** Surplus	Transfer of **Callanan, McCormack, O'Gara, Whelan** Votes	Transfer of **McKay** Votes	Transfer of **Bracken** Votes
BRACKEN, John (Ind)	934	(+210) 1,144	(+60) 1,204	(+48) 1,252	
BUCKLEY, Molly (FG)	2,196	(+337) 2,533	(+62) 2,595	(+77) 2,672	(+201) 2,873
CALLANAN, Colm (CSP)	156	(+5) 161			
COWEN, Brian* (FF)	19,102				
ENRIGHT, Olwyn* (FG)	8,297	(+794) 9,091	(+104) 9,195	(+159) 9,354	(+319) 9,673
FLANAGAN, Charles (FG)	9,067	(+143) 9,210	(+49) 9,259	(+67) 9,326	(+54) 9,380
FLEMING, Seán* (FF)	8,064	(+2,025) 10,089	(+42) 10,131	(+69) 10,200	(+113) 10,313
FOLEY, John (FF)	5,899	(+2,025) 7,924	(+34) 7,958	(+32) 7,990	(+124) 8,114
McCORMACK, Joseph (Ind)	85	(+3) 88			
McKAY, Maire (GP)	812	(+49) 861	(+41) 902		
MOLONEY, John* (FF)	7,242	(+768) 8,010	(+32) 8,042	(+33) 8,075	(+41) 8,116
O'BRIEN, Jim (Lab)	1,278	(+32) 1,310	(+220) 1,530	(+181) 1,711	(+35) 1,746
O'GARA, Noel (Ind)	45	(+3) 48			
PARLON, Tom* (PD)	4,233	(+596) 4,829	(+38) 4,867	(+66) 4,933	(+87) 5,020
STANLEY, Brian (SF)	3,656	(+146) 3,802	(+60) 3,862	(+113) 3,975	(+145) 4,120
WHELAN, David (Lab)	425	(+50) 475			
NON-TRANSFERABLE			30	57	133

6th Count	7th Count	8th Count	9th Count	10th Count	11th Count
Transfer of **O'Brien** Votes	Transfer of **Buckley** Votes	Transfer of **Stanley** Votes	Transfer of **Parlon** Votes	Transfer of **Enright** Surplus	Transfer of **Fleming** Surplus
(+122) 2,995					
(+365) 10,038	*(+1,770)* 11,808	*(+736)* 12,544			
(+454) 9,834	*(+381)* 10,215	*(+750)* 10,965	*(+1,143)* 12,108		
(+124) 10,437	*(+124)* 10,561	*(+670)* 11,231	*(+1,302)* 12,533		
(+27) 8,141	*(+169)* 8,310	*(+309)* 8,619	*(+861)* 9,480	*(+138)* 9,618	*(+348)* 9,966
(+119) 8,235	*(+63)* 8,298	*(+669)* 8,967	*(+928)* 9,895	*(+113)* 10,008	*(+269)* 10,277
(+73) 5,093	*(+156)* 5,249	*(+265)* 5,514			
(+253) 4,373	*(+104)* 4,477				
209	228	1,078	1,280	377	

Limerick East

Elected

Party Share of Vote

1st Preferences	Number	%	Gain/Loss
Fianna Fáil	24,042	48.69	8.75%
Fine Gael	12,601	25.52	-2.32%
Labour	5,098	10.33	1.07%
Prog Democrats	3,354	6.79	-2.98%
Green Party	1,296	2.62	0.79%
Sinn Féin	2,081	4.21	4.21%
Others	903	1.83	-9.53%

Statistics

Electorate	76,874	
Total Poll	49,806	64.79
Spoiled	431	0.87
Total Valid Poll	49,375	64.23
Seats	5	
Quota	8,230	
Candidates	14	

	Quotas	Seats
FF	2.92	2
FG	1.53	2
Lab	0.62	1
FG gain from PD		

Willie O'Dea (FF)

Home Address
Milltown, Kilteely, Co Limerick
Business Address
Office of The Minister for Defence,
Department of Defence, Infirmary Road,
Dublin 7
Constituency Office
2 Glenview Gardens, Farranshore, Limerick
Telephone
Home (061) 454 488; Business (01) 804 2105
Birth Place/Date
Limerick. November 1952
Married
Geraldine Kennedy
Education
Patrician Brothers, Ballyfin, Co Laois;
University College, Dublin; King's Inns, Dublin;
Institute of Certified Accountants (BCL, LLM,
BL, Certified Accountant)
Occupation
Government Minister. Formerly barrister and
accountant

Willie O'Dea was appointed Minister for
Defence on 14 June 2007, the Cabinet
position which he had held since September
2004.

He was Minister of State at the Department
of Justice, Equality and Law Reform, with
responsibility for equality issues including
disability issues, 2002–04; Minister of State at
the Department of Education, Science and
Technology, with special responsibility for
Adult Education, Youth Affairs and School
Transport, 1997–2002; Minister of State at the
Departments of Justice and Health 1993–94;
Minister of State at the Department of
Justice, February 1992–January 1993.

He was first elected to the Dáil in February
1982. He contested Limerick East
unsuccessfully in the 1981 general election.

Peter Power (FF)

Home Address
Kilfeara, Ennis Road, Limerick
Constituency Office
78 O'Connell Street, Limerick
Telephone
Office (061) 317 106
Birth Place/Date
Limerick. 26 January 1966
Married
Lorraine Power. 4 children
Education
John F. Kennedy, Ennis Road, Limerick; Ard
Scoil Rís, Ennis Road; University College, Cork
(BCL); Blackhall Place (Diploma in Property
Taxation)
Occupation
Public representative

Peter Power was first elected in 2002, having
previously contested the 1997 general
election.

During the 29th Dáil he was Chairman of the
Joint Oireachtas Committee on Child
Protection; Vice-Chairman, Joint Oireachtas
Committee on Transport; member, Justice
Committee, Constitution Committee.

Member, Fianna Fáil National Executive
1989–91.

Elected as Alderman to Limerick Corporation
1999–2003. Deputy Mayor 2000–01.
Chairperson, Limerick Inner City Renewal
Committee. Member, Limerick City Enterprise
Board. Member of numerous community,
cultural and sporting organisations.

Michael Noonan (FG)

Home Address
18 Gouldavoher Estate, Father Russell Road, Limerick
Telephone
Home (061) 229 350
Birth Place/Date
Limerick. 21 May 1943
Married
Florence Knightly. 3 sons, 2 daughters
Education
St Patrick's Secondary School, Glin, Co Limerick; St Patrick's Teachers' Training College, Drumcondra, Dublin; University College, Dublin (BA, HDipEd)
Occupation
Full-time public representative. Formerly teacher

Michael Noonan was elected leader of Fine Gael in February 2001 but resigned in June 2002 after what was regarded as a disastrous general election for the party, with a loss of 23 seats. He was party spokesperson for Northern Ireland while leader.

He was Chairman of the Public Accounts Committee 2004–07 when he was also appointed to the Fine Gael front bench without portfolio. He was first elected to the Dáil in 1981 and was Minister for Justice 1982–86, Minister for Industry and Commerce 1986–87, and Minister for Energy, January–March 1987. He was party spokesperson on Finance 1987–93, Minister for Health 1994–97, and party spokesperson on Finance again 1997–2001.

Member, Limerick County Council 1974–82 and 1991–94; Mid-Western Health Board, 1974–82 and 1991–94.

Member, Association of Secondary Teachers of Ireland (ASTI).

Jan O'Sullivan (Lab)

Home Address
7 Lanahone Avenue, Corbally, Limerick
Constituency Office
Mechanics' Institute, Hartstonge Street, Limerick
Telephone
Home (061) 346 522; *Constituency office* (061) 312 316; *Fax* (061) 313 707; *Mobile* 087 243 0299
Birth Place/Date
Limerick. 6 December 1950
Married
Dr Paul O'Sullivan. 1 son, 1 daughter
Education
Villiers School, Limerick. Trinity College, Dublin
Occupation
Full-time public representative. Formerly pre-school teacher

Jan O'Sullivan was appointed party spokesperson on Health in September 2007. She was first elected to the Dáil in 1998 in a by-election caused by the death of Jim Kemmy. Party spokesperson on Education and Science and Vice-Chairperson of Oireachtas Committee on Education and Science and member, All-Party Committee on the Constitution in last Dáil. Previously member, Oireachtas Committee on Justice, Equality, Defence and Women's Rights.

She was elected to the Seanad in 1993 and was leader of the Labour group there 1993–97. Member of Forum for Peace and Reconciliation and the National Economic and Social Forum.

Member, Democratic Socialist Party until it merged with the Labour Party.

Member, Limerick City Council 1985–2003. Mayor of Limerick 1993–94. Former member, Mid-Western Health Board. Former member of City of Limerick Vocational Education Committee.

Member of Board of the Island Theatre Company. Chairperson CARA (Ireland) Housing Association; Chairperson, Limerick-Quimper Twinning Committee; on the Board of Rape Crisis Centre, Red Ribbon Project. Member of Amnesty International.

Kieran O'Donnell (FG)

Home Address
8 Milltown Manor, Monaleen, Castletroy, Limerick
Constituency Office
27 William Street, Limerick
Telephone
Home (061) 330 652; *Office* (061) 204 040; *Fax* (061) 204 057; *Mobile* 086 843 0202
Birth Place/Date
Limerick. 8 May 1963
Married
Phil FitzGerald. 2 sons, 2 daughters
Education
Ard Scoil Mhuire, Bruff, Co Limerick; University of Limerick BBS (honours), Fellow of the Institute of Chartered Accountants in Ireland (FCA)
Occupation
Full-time public representative. Chartered accountant

Kieran O'Donnell is a new TD, elected to the Dáil at his first attempt.

He was elected to Limerick County Council, representing the Castleconnell Electoral Area, in June 2004. Member, Mid-West Regional Authority and Limerick Market Trustees, Planning and Transport Strategic Policy Committees of Limerick County Council, June 2004 to May 2007.

An active local community worker, he has served as Chairperson of the Castleconnell Electoral Area and Community and Voluntary Forum (2001–03) and is involved in various local community and sports organisations. He has a special interest in the disabled and has campaigned on their behalf

He is a nephew of Tom O'Donnell, TD for Limerick East 1961–87, Minister for the Gaeltacht 1973–77, and MEP for Munster 1979–89.

Limerick East

128

Seats 5

Quota 8,230

	1st Count	2nd Count Transfer of **O'Dea** Surplus	3rd Count Transfer of **Power** Surplus
DEVANE, John (Ind)	330	*(+127)* 457	*(+4)* 461
FORDE BRENNAN, Trish (GP)	1,296	*(+124)* 1,420	*(+5)* 1,425
McCARTHY, Cathal (Ind)	188	*(+44)* 232	*(+1)* 233
MOORE, Patrick Mary (Ind)	28	*(+10)* 38	
NOONAN, Michael* (FG)	7,507	*(+977)* 8,484	
O'DEA, Willie* (FF)	19,082		
O'DONNELL, Kieran (FG)	5,094	*(+472)* 5,566	*(+18)* 5,584
O'DONOGHUE, Conor (CSP)	171	*(+31)* 202	*(+1)* 203
O'MALLEY, Tim* (PD)	3,354	*(+857)* 4,211	*(+57)* 4,268
O'SULLIVAN, Jan* (Lab)	5,098	*(+1,138)* 6,236	*(+35)* 6,271
POWER, Peter* (FF)	3,569	*(+5,100)* 8,669	
QUINLIVAN, Maurice (SF)	2,081	*(+399)* 2,480	*(+14)* 2,494
RIORDAN, Denis (Ind)	186	*(+21)* 207	*(+2)* 209
RYAN, Noreen (FF)	1,391	*(+1,552)* 2,943	*(+302)* 3,245
NON-TRANSFERABLE			

4th Count	5th Count	6th Count	7th Count	8th Count
Transfer of **Noonan** Surplus	Transfer of **Devane, McCarthy, Moore, O'Donoghue, Riordan** Votes	Transfer of **Forde Brennan** Votes	Transfer of **Quinlivan** Votes	Transfer of **Ryan** Votes
(+8) 469				
(+7) 1,432	*(+187)* 1,619			
(+3) 236				
(+60) 5,644	*(+172)* 5,816	*(+332)* 6,148	*(+350)* 6,498	*(+468)* 6,966
(+2) 205				
(+40) 4,308	*(+79)* 4,387	*(+139)* 4,526	*(+144)* 4,670	*(+1,106)* 5,776
(+81) 6,352	*(+204)* 6,556	*(+680)* 7,236	*(+878)* 8,114	*(+937)* 9,051
(+19) 2,513	*(+173)* 2,686	*(+153)* 2,839		
(+1) 210				
(+33) 3,278	*(+141)* 3,419	*(+117)* 3,536	*(+574)* 4,110	
	202	198	893	1,599

Limerick West

Elected

Niall Collins (FF)	1st Count
John Cregan (FF)*	3rd Count
Dan Neville (FG)*	3rd Count

Party Share of Vote

1st Preferences	Number	%	Gain/Loss
Fianna Fáil	19,097	47.23	-6.20%
Fine Gael	16,153	39.95	-1.70%
Labour	2,277	5.63	5.63%
Prog Democrats	1,935	4.79	4.79%
Green Party	969	2.40	-0.26%
Others	0	0.00	-2.26%

Statistics

Electorate	58,712	
Total Poll	40,812	69.51
Spoiled	381	0.93
Total Valid Poll	40,431	68.86
Seats	3	
Quota	10,108	
Candidates	7	

	Quotas	Seats
FF	1.89	2
FG	1.60	1
No change		

Niall Collins (FF)

Home Address
Red House Hill, Patrickswell, Co Limerick
Telephone
Home (061) 355 219; *Fax* (061) 300 985
Birth Place/Date
Limerick. 30 March 1973
Married
Eimear O'Connor. 1 son
Education
St Munchin's College, Limerick
Occupation
Public representative. Accountant, former lecturer at Limerick Institute of Technology, and Shannon Regional Fisheries Board employee

Niall Collins is a new TD.

He was elected to Limerick County Council in June 2004 at his first attempt, receiving 1,600 first preference votes.

He is a grandson of Jimmy Collins, TD for Limerick West from 1948 to 1967. He is a nephew of Gerard Collins, TD for Limerick West 1967–97, Cabinet Minister 1970–73, 1977–81, 1982, 1987–92, MEP 1994–2004. He is also a nephew of Michael Collins, TD for Limerick West 1997–2007.

John Cregan (FF)

Home Address
Church Street, Drumcollogher, Co Limerick
Constituency Office
St Mary's Road, Newcastle West, Co Limerick
Telephone
Constituency office (069) 77671;
Fax (069) 77672; *Mobile* 087 267 9453
Birth Place/Date
Drumcollogher. 21 May 1961
Married
Patsy Breen. 1 son, 2 daughters
Education
St Joseph's National School; St Mary's Secondary School, Drumcollogher
Occupation
Public representative. Formerly Telecom Éireann employee

John Cregan was first elected in 2002. Chairman, Joint Oireachtas Committee on the Environment and Local Government; member, Joint Oireachtas Committee on Finance and Public Service in last Dáil.

He was a Senator, Labour panel, 1998–2002. Member, Oireachtas Committee on Justice, Equality and Law Reform in 28th Dáil.

Member, Limerick County Council 1991–2003. Member, Mid-Western Health Board; Association of Health Boards in Ireland.

Dan Neville (FG)

Home Address
Kiltannan, Croagh, Co Limerick
Constituency Office
Main St, Rathkeale, Co Limerick
Telephone
Home/Constituency office/Fax (061) 396 351;
Mobile 086 243 5536;
Website www.danneville.ie
Birth Place/Date
Croagh. 12 December 1946
Married
Goretti O'Callaghan. 2 sons, 2 daughters
Education
Adare CBS, Co Limerick; University of
Limerick, School of Management Studies;
University College, Cork (Industrial
Engineering, Personnel Management, Social
Science)
Occupation
Full-time public representative. Formerly
personnel manager

Dan Neville was Fine Gael's deputy
spokesperson on Health, with special
responsibility for Children and Mental Health,
in the last Dáil. He was also Fine Gael
Assistant Whip.

He was a member of the Oireachtas
Committee on Health and Children and of the
Dáil Committee on Procedure and Privileges in
the 29th Dáil.

He was first elected to the Dáil in 1997 when
Fine Gael took two seats in Limerick West for
the first time, defeating his running mate
Michael Finucane by only one vote. Dan Neville
was a candidate in the general elections of
1987 and 1992. He was a Senator, Labour
panel, 1989–97; Deputy Leader of Fine Gael in
the Seanad and spokesperson on Justice and
Law Reform 1992–97.

Member, Limerick County Council 1985–2003.

President of the Irish Association of
Suicidology and a director of the Irish Palatine
Association.

Seats 3 Quota 10,108	1st Count	2nd Count Transfer of **Nix** Votes	3rd Count Transfer of **Brennan,** **Heffernan** Votes
BRENNAN, Michael (PD)	1,935	*(+58)* 1,993	
COLLINS, Niall (FF)	10,396		
CREGAN, John* (FF)	8,701	*(+122)* 8,823	*(+1,532)* 10,355
FINUCANE, Michael (FG)	7,839	*(+136)* 7,975	*(+1,052)* 9,027
HEFFERNAN, James (Lab)	2,277	*(+410)* 2,687	
NEVILLE, Dan* (FG)	8,314	*(+190)* 8,504	*(+1,514)* 10,018
NIX, James (GP)	969		
NON-TRANSFERABLE		53	582

Longford–Westmeath

Elected

Willie Penrose (Lab)*	5th Count
Mary O'Rourke (FF)	7th Count
Peter Kelly (FF)*	7th Count
James Bannon (FG)	7th Count

Party Share of Vote

1st Preferences	Number	%	Gain/Loss
Fianna Fáil	22,599	41.15	
Fine Gael	16,999	30.95	
Labour	9,692	17.65	
Prog Democrats	2,298	4.18	
Green Party	960	1.75	
Sinn Féin	2,136	3.89	
Others	232	0.42	

Statistics

Electorate	83,980	
Total Poll	55,529	66.12
Spoiled	613	1.10
Total Valid Poll	54,916	65.39
Seats	4	
Quota	10,984	
Candidates	13	

	Quotas	Seats
FF	2.06	2
FG	1.55	1
Lab	0.88	1

New constituency: FG gain from PD

Willie Penrose (Lab)

Home Address
Ballintue, Ballynacargy, Co Westmeath
Constituency Office
Convent Lane, Bishopgate Street, Mullingar, Co Westmeath
Telephone
Home (044) 73264; *Constituency office* (044) 43966; *Mobile* 087 824 1933
Birth Place/Date
Mullingar, Co Westmeath. August 1956
Married
Anne Fitzsimons. 3 daughters
Education
St Mary's CBS, Mullingar; Multyfarnham Agricultural College, Co Westmeath; University College, Dublin (BAgrSc, MAgrSc [Economics]); King's Inns, Dublin (Diploma in Legal Studies, Barrister-at-Law)
Occupation
Public representative. Barrister

Willie Penrose was first elected to the Dáil in 1992. He was appointed party spokesperson on Enterprise, Trade and Employment in September 2007. Chairman of the Joint Oireachtas Committee on Social and Family Affairs 2002–07, he was spokesperson on Agriculture 1997–2002 and Social and Family Affairs from 2002-07.

Member, Westmeath County Council 1984–2003 and the Council's Planning and Environmental Committee, Agricultural Committee and Coiste Gaeilge.

Member, Ballynacargy GAA Club; Cullion Hurling Club; GAA County Board Committee on Cusack Park, Mullingar Development. Member, Royal Canal Development Group. Director, Ballynacargy Community Childcare Ltd, and Westmeath County Childcare Committee Ltd.

Mary O'Rourke (FF)

Home Address
Aisling, Arcadia, Athlone, Co Westmeath
Constituency Office
St Mary's Square, Athlone
Telephone
Home (090) 647 2313; *Office* (090) 647 5000; *Mobile* 087 280 2806
Birth Place/Date
Athlone. 31 May 1937
Marital Status
Widowed. 2 sons
Education
Loreto Convent, Bray, Co Wicklow; University College, Dublin; Maynooth College (BA, HDipEd)
Occupation
Public representative. Formerly secondary school teacher

Mary O'Rourke was a member of the Dáil from 1982 to 2002 and was re-elected in May 2007 after five years in the Seanad as a Taoiseach's nominee. Leader of the Seanad 1997–2002.

She was Minister for Public Enterprise from June 1997 to June 2002; Minister for Health 1991–92; Minister for Education 1987–91. Minister of State at the Department of Enterprise and Employment 1993–94; Minister of State at the Department of Industry and Commerce 1992–93.

She is a former Deputy Leader of Fianna Fáil, Senator on the Cultural and Educational panel 1981–82. She was a member of Westmeath County Council 1979–87.

She and her late brother Brian Lenihan (TD 1961–73 and 1977–95) were the first brother and sister to be members of the same Cabinet. She is a daughter of the late Paddy Lenihan, TD for Longford–Westmeath 1965–70, and aunt of two members of the 30th Dáil, Brian and Conor Lenihan.

Peter Kelly (FF)

Home Address
Lanherne, Battery Road, Longford
Constituency Office
Dublin Road, Longford
Telephone
Home (043) 46304; *Office* (043) 45070;
Fax (043) 41996;
Email deputypeterkelly@eircom.ie
Website www.peterkelly.ie
Birth Place/Date
Longford. 17 August 1944
Married
Maura Hester. 2 sons, 1 daughter
Education
St Michael's Boys' School, Longford;
St Mary's College, Dundalk, Co Louth
Occupation
Full-time public representative. Formerly
funeral director and publican

Peter Kelly was first elected to the Dáil in
2002

Member, Longford County Council 1985–2003
and a former Chairperson. Member, County
Longford Tourism; Midland Regional
Authority.

James Bannon (FG)

Home Address
Newtown, Legan, Co Longford
Constituency Office
Richmond Street, Longford
Telephone
Home (044) 935 7575; *Office* (043) 36185;
Mobile 087 203 1816
Birth Place/Date
Longford, 26 March 1953
Marital Status
Single
Education
Our Lady's Secondary School, Ballymahon,
Co Longford
Occupation
Public representative. Farmer and auctioneer

James Bannon is a new deputy.

He was a member of the Seanad on the
Industrial and Commercial panel 2002–07
where he was Fine Gael spokesperson on the
Environment and Local Government.

Member of Longford County Council
1985–2003 (Chairman, 1991–92). Former
General Secretary of LAMA, the Local
Authorities' Members' Association.

Longford–Westmeath

Seats 4 Quota 10,984	1st Count	2nd Count Transfer of **Callanan, Cunningham, Doran, O'Gara** Votes	3rd Count Transfer of **Hogan** Votes
BANNON, James (FG)	7,652	*(+71)* 7,723	*(+220)* 7,943
BURKE, Peter (FG)	3,988	*(+152)* 4,140	*(+105)* 4,245
CALLANAN, Colm (CSP)	124		
CASSIDY, Donie* (FF)	6,664	*(+76)* 6,740	*(+218)* 6,958
CUNNINGHAM, Séamus (Ind)	24		
DORAN, Betty (GP)	960		
HOGAN, Paul (SF)	2,136	*(+144)* 2,280	
KELLY, Peter* (FF)	7,720	*(+45)* 7,765	*(+227)* 7,992
McFADDEN, Nicky (FG)	5,359	*(+117)* 5,476	*(+322)* 5,798
O'GARA, Noel (Ind)	84		
O'ROURKE, Mary (FF)	8,215	*(+96)* 8,311	*(+335)* 8,646
PENROSE, Willie* (Lab)	9,692	*(+363)* 10,055	*(+468)* 10,523
SEXTON, Mae* (PD)	2,298	*(+52)* 2,350	*(+70)* 2,420
NON-TRANSFERABLE		76	315

4th Count	5th Count	6th Count	7th Count
Transfer of **Sexton** Votes	Transfer of **Burke** Votes	Transfer of **Penrose** Surplus	Transfer of **Cassidy** Votes
(+668) 8,611	(+856) 9,467	(+378) 9,845	(+313) 10,158
(+42) 4,287			
(+102) 7,060	(+270) 7,330	(+225) 7,555	
(+975) 8,967	(+39) 9,006	(+20) 9,026	(+2,006) 11,032
(+96) 5,894	(+1,359) 7,253	(+489) 7,742	(+534) 8,276
(+226) 8,872	(+93) 8,965	(+118) 9,083	(+3,594) 12,677
(+193) 10,716	(+1,560) 12,276		
118	110	62	1,108

Louth

Elected

Séamus Kirk (FF)*	5th Count
Dermot Ahern (FF)*	5th Count
Fergus O'Dowd (FG)*	5th Count
Arthur Morgan (SF)*	6th Count

Party Share of Vote

1st Preferences	Number	%	Gain/Loss
Fianna Fáil	23,181	42.14	-1.44%
Fine Gael	16,159	29.37	9.14%
Labour	2,739	4.98	-1.71%
Green Party	4,172	7.58	3.43%
Sinn Féin	8,274	15.04	0.09%
Others	489	0.89	-9.51%

Statistics

Electorate	86,007	
Total Poll	55,606	64.65
Spoiled	592	1.06
Total Valid Poll	55,014	63.96
Seats	4	
Quota	11,003	
Candidates	12	

	Quotas	Seats
FF	2.11	2
FG	1.47	1
SF	0.75	1
No change		

Séamus Kirk (FF)

Home Address
Rathiddy, Knockbridge, Co Louth
Telephone
Home (042) 933 1032
Birth Place/Date
Drumkeith, Co Louth. 26 April 1945
Married
Mary McGeough. 3 sons, 1 daughter
Education
Dundalk CBS
Occupation
Full-time public representative. Farmer

Séamus Kirk was appointed Chairman of the Fianna Fáil Parliamentary Party in 2002. He was first elected to the Dáil in November 1982. Minister of State at the Department of Agriculture and Food, with special responsibility for Horticulture, March 1987–February 1992.

During the 28th Dáil he was Chairman of the European Affairs Committee, a member of the All-Party Committee on the Constitution and the Oireachtas Committee on Local Government.

Member, Forum for Peace and Reconciliation 1994–96. Member of the British–Irish Inter-Parliamentary Body.

Member, Louth County Council 1974–85; Louth County Health Committee 1974–85; Louth County Committee of Agriculture 1974–85; East Border Region Committee 1974–85.

Member, Gaelic Athletic Association since 1958. Member, Tidy Towns Committee.

Dermot Ahern (FF)

Home Address
Hill Cottage, The Crescent, Blackrock, Co Louth
Business Address
Department of Foreign Affairs, Iveagh House, 79–80 St Stephen's Green, Dublin 2
Constituency Office
18 Francis Street, Dundalk, Co Louth
Telephone
Constituency office (042) 933 9609 / 932 9016; *Ministerial office* (01) 408 2000; *Fax* (01) 408 2400
Birth Place/Date
Drogheda. 2 February 1955
Married
Maeve Coleman. 2 daughters
Education
St Mary's College, Dundalk; University College, Dublin (BCL); Incorporated Law Society of Ireland
Occupation
Government Minister. Formerly solicitor

Dermot Ahern was appointed Minister for Foreign Affairs on 14 June 2007, the portfolio he held in the 29th Dáil from September 2004. From June 2002 to September 2004, he was Minister for Communications, the Marine and Natural Resources.

He was Minister for Social, Community and Family Affairs 1997–2002. Minister of State at the Department of the Taoiseach, with special responsibility as Government Chief Whip, and Minister of State at the Department of Defence, November 1991–February 1992. He was Assistant Government Chief Whip 1988–91. He was first elected to the Dáil in 1987.

He was Fianna Fáil Chief Whip, Leader of the House in Opposition and in charge of party parliamentary strategy and legislative proposals in the Dáil 1995–97. Member of the British–Irish Inter-Parliamentary Body 1991–97 (Co-Chairman, 1993–95).

Member of Louth County Council 1979–91.

Fergus O'Dowd (FG)

Arthur Morgan (SF)

Home Address
24 St Mary's Villas, Drogheda, Co Louth
Constituency Office
10 Boyne Shopping Centre, Drogheda,
Co Louth
Telephone
Home (041) 983 3392; *Office* (041) 984 2275;
Fax (041) 987 0282
Birth Place/Date
Thurles, Co Tipperary. September 1948
Married
Margaret Thornton. 3 sons
Education
Drogheda CBS; Diploma in General and Rural
Science
Occupation
Full-time public representative. Formerly
teacher

Fergus O'Dowd was appointed party
spokesperson on Transport and the Marine in
September 2007. He was first elected in
2002. He was Fine Gael front bench
spokesperson on Environment, Heritage and
Local Government from 2004 and previously
spokesperson on Community, Rural and
Gaeltacht Affairs in the 29th Dáil.

He was a Senator on the Administrative panel
from 1997 to 2002.

Member, Louth County Council 1979–2003.
Member, Drogheda Corporation 1974–2003.
Served three terms as Mayor (1977–78,
1981–82, 1994–95). Member, North Eastern
Health Board. Campaigned for closure of
Sellafield nuclear re-processing plant and
against a local incinerator.

Founding Chairman of the Droichead Arts
Centre, Drogheda.

Home Address
Omeath, Co Louth
Constituency Office
7 Williamson's Place, Dundalk; 46 Magdalene
Street, Drogheda
Telephone
Office (042) 932 8859 (Dundalk);
(041) 987 3823 (Drogheda)
Birth Place/Date
Omeath. 23 July 1954
Married
Marion Traynor
Education
St Brigid's National School, Omeath;
St Michael's College, Omeath
Occupation
Full-time public representative. Company
director

Arthur Morgan was first elected in 2002,
having contested the general elections in
Louth in 1987 and 1989 and the European
elections in 1999.

He is a former member of the Sinn Féin Ard-
Comhairle 1997–2001. He was a member of
the party's background team in the
negotiation of the Good Friday Agreement
1998. He was convicted for the possession of
explosives and weapons and imprisoned in
the H-Blocks in the Maze Prison 1977–84. He
took part in the H-Block protest in the early
1980s. He made the case in 1986 to the
Louth Comhairle Ceanntair that Sinn Féin
should abandon its abstentionist policy.

Member, Louth County Council 1999–2003.

Louth

Seats 4 Quota 11,003	1st Count	2nd Count Transfer of **Duke, Martin, Short** Votes	3rd Count Transfer of **D'Arcy** Votes	4th Count Transfer of **Nash** Votes	5th Count Transfer of **Maher** Votes	6th Count Transfer of **Dearey** Votes
AHERN, Dermot* (FF)	9,982	(+38) 10,020	(+355) 10,375	(+125) 10,500	(+821) 11,321	
D'ARCY, Jim (FG)	2,573	(+23) 2,596				
DEAREY, Mark (GP)	4,172	(+124) 4,296	(+415) 4,711	(+407) 5,118	(+107) 5,225	
DUKE, Dermot (Ind)	127					
KIRK, Séamus* (FF)	10,190	(+35) 10,225	(+175) 10,400	(+57) 10,457	(+1,239) 11,696	
MAHER, Frank (FF)	3,009	(+22) 3,031	(+14) 3,045	(+242) 3,287		
MARTIN, Luke (Ind)	169					
McGUINNESS, Mairead (FG)	5,199	(+29) 5,228	(+1,012) 6,240	(+263) 6,503	(+47) 6,550	(+2,297) 8,847
MORGAN, Arthur* (SF)	8,274	(+111) 8,385	(+211) 8,596	(+240) 8,836	(+153) 8,989	(+1,567) 10,556
NASH, Gerald (Lab)	2,739	(+47) 2,786	(+70) 2,856			
O'DOWD, Fergus* (FG)	8,387	(+34) 8,421	(+317) 8,738	(+1,470) 10,208	(+828) 11,036	
SHORT, Peter (Ind)	193					
NON-TRANSFERABLE		26	27	52	92	1,361

Make the right choice*

PricewaterhouseCoopers recognises that public sector organisations are faced with many complex issues which impact their ability to deliver effective and responsive services.

We combine a broad understanding of regulatory and economic conditions with the functional skills of our public sector specialists, to deliver innovative solutions.

We aim to contribute to advancing public sector priorities while delivering value for money.

To discuss how we can help your organisation, please contact:

Paul Tuite, Advisory Leader
T: (01) 792 6502
E: paul.tuite@ie.pwc.com

Kevin Egan, Assurance Leader
T: (01) 792 6069
E: kevin.egan@ie.pwc.com

Colm Kelly, Tax and Legal Services Leader
T: (01) 792 6866
E: colm.r.kelly@ie.pwc.com

www.pwc.com/ie

*connectedthinking

Mayo

Elected

Enda Kenny (FG)*	1st Count
Michael Ring (FG)*	2nd Count
John O'Mahony (FG)	8th Count
Dara Calleary (FF)	8th Count
Beverley Flynn (Ind)*	8th Count

Party Share of Vote

1st Preferences	Number	%	Gain/Loss
Fianna Fáil	17,459	24.46	-15.52%
Fine Gael	38,426	53.83	16.24%
Labour	831	1.16	1.16%
Prog Democrats	296	0.41	-1.03%
Green Party	580	0.81	-0.24%
Sinn Féin	3,608	5.05	1.77%
Others	10,186	14.27	-2.37%

Statistics

Electorate	98,696	
Total Poll	72,086	73.04
Spoiled	700	0.97
Total Valid Poll	71,386	72.33
Seats	5	
Quota	11,898	
Candidates	13	

	Quotas	Seats
FF	1.47	1
FG	3.23	3
Ind	0.57	1

FG gain from Ind; Ind gain from FF

Enda Kenny (FG)

Home Address
Hawthorn Avenue, Lightfort, Castlebar, Co Mayo
Constituency Office
Tucker Street, Castlebar, Co Mayo
Telephone
Office (094) 902 5600; *Fax* (094) 902 6554
Birth Place/Date
Castlebar. 24 April 1951
Married
Fionnuala O'Kelly. 2 sons, 1 daughter
Education
St Gerald's Secondary School, Castlebar; St Patrick's Training College, Drumcondra, Dublin; University College, Galway
Occupation
Leader of Fine Gael. Formerly national school teacher

Enda Kenny was elected Leader of Fine Gael in June 2002 following the resignation of Michael Noonan after that year's general election. He had been defeated by Mr Noonan in the contest for the leadership in January 2001.

He was Minister for Tourism and Trade 1994–97; Minister of State at the Department of Education and at the Department of Labour, with special responsibility for Youth Affairs, February 1986–March 1987. He was first elected to the Dáil in November 1975, at a by-election caused by his father's death.

He served as party spokesperson on Arts, Heritage, Gaeltacht and the Islands 1997–2002, Fine Gael Chief Whip 1992–94, and spokesperson on Regional Development 1994. Spokesperson on the Gaeltacht 1987–88 and in 1982; on Western Development 1982; on Youth Affairs and Sport 1977-80. Chairperson, Fine Gael Economic Affairs Committee 1991–92. Member, New Ireland Forum; British–Irish Inter-Parliamentary Body 1991–92.

Member, Mayo County Council 1975–95; former chairperson, Mayo Vocational Education Committee, Western Health Board.

He is a son of Henry Kenny, Dáil deputy for Mayo South 1954–69 and for Mayo West 1969–75, and Parliamentary Secretary to the Minister for Finance 1973–75.

Michael Ring (FG)

Home Address
The Paddock, Westport, Co Mayo
Constituency Office
Quay Street, Westport
Telephone
Home (098) 25734; *Constituency office* (098) 27012; *Fax* (098) 27644;
Website www.michaelringtd.com
Birth Place/Date
Westport. 24 December 1953
Married
Ann Fitzgerald. 1 son, 2 daughters
Education
Westport Vocational School
Occupation
Full-time public representative. Former auctioneer

Michael Ring was appointed party spokesperson on Community, Rural & Gaeltacht Affairs in September 2007. He was first elected to the Dáil in a by-election in June 1994 in the old Mayo-West constituency, following the resignation of Deputy Pádraig Flynn (FF) to become an EU Commissioner. Party spokesperson on Social and Family Affairs 2002–04; Agriculture — Livestock, Breeding and Horticulture 1997–2000; deputy spokesperson on Health 2000–02.

Member of Joint Committee on Health and Children in 28th Dáil. Member British–Irish Inter-Parliamentary Body.

Member, Mayo County Council 1991–2003, Westport Urban District Council 1979–2003 (Chairman, 1982–83 and 1988–89).

John O'Mahony (FG)

Home Address
'Tower House', Charlestown Road,
Ballaghaderreen, Co Mayo
Constituency Office
D'Alton Street, Claremorris, Co Mayo
Telephone
Office (094) 9373560; *Dáil office*
(01) 618 3706; *Fax* (01) 618 4595;
Mobile 086 833 8017
Birth Place/Date
Kilmovee, Co Mayo. 8 June 1953
Married
Gerardine Towey. 5 daughters
Education
Magheraboy NS; St Nathy's College,
Ballaghaderreen, Co Mayo; St Patrick's
College Maynooth, Co Kildare (BA); National
University of Ireland, Galway (HDipEd)
Occupation
Public representative. Formerly secondary
school teacher

John O'Mahony is a new deputy, elected to
the Dáil in 2007 on his first attempt.

He became manager of the Mayo senior
football team in November 2006 after seven
years as manager of the Galway senior
football team, during which it won two All-
Ireland championships in 1998 and 2001. He
previously managed the Leitrim team, taking it
to its first Connacht title in 1994.

A teacher in St Nathy's College,
Ballaghaderreen, Co Mayo, from 1974 to
2006, he won All-Ireland football medals with
Mayo minors (1971) and under-21s (1974).

Dara Calleary (FF)

Home Address
8 Quignalecka, Sligo Road, Ballina, Co Mayo
Constituency Office
Pearse Street, Ballina, Co Mayo
Telephone
Office (096) 777 613 (Ballina), (01) 618 3331
(Dublin); *Mobile* (086) 223 8810;
Email daracalleary@ireland.com
Website www.daracalleary.ie
Birth Place/Date
Mayo. 10 May 1973
Marital Status
Single
Education
St Oliver Plunkett NS (The Quay), Ballina; St
Muredach's College, Ballina; Trinity College,
Dublin (BA Hons in Business and Politics)
Occupation
Full-time public representative. Former
Manager, Chamber Development & BMW
Regional Co-ordinator Chambers Ireland)

Dara Calleary is a new Dáil deputy, having won
a seat in his first election. He is the third
generation of his family to represent Mayo in
the Dáil.

He was a Member of Fianna Fáil Ard-
Chomhairle from 1997 to 2007. Member of the
Fianna Fáil National Youth Committee 1994–96,
1998–2003, 2006–07 and secretary to the Ard-
Comhairle Committee on Enterprise.

Member, Irish European Movement, Ballina
Rugby Club, Ballina Stephanites GAA Club, and
the committee of the Ballina Salmon Festival.

He is the son of Seán Calleary, TD for East
Mayo 1973–1992 and Minister of State at the
Department of the Public Service 1979–1981,
Department of Industry and Commerce 1982,
and the Department of Foreign Affairs
1987–1992. He is the grandson of P.A.
Calleary, TD for North Mayo 1952–1969.

Beverley Flynn (Ind)

Home Address
2 The Manor Village, Westport Road,
Castlebar, Co Mayo
Constituency Office
Newtown, Castlebar
Telephone
Home (094) 26800; *Constituency office*
(094) 27035; *Mobile* 087 256 0229
Birth Place/Date
Tuam, Co Galway. 9 June 1966
Marital Status
Separated. Current partner, Tony Gaughan.
2 children.
Education
St Joseph's Secondary School, Castlebar;
University College, Dublin (BComm), IPM, ACII
Occupation
Full-time public representative

Beverley Flynn was first elected to the Dáil in
1997 as a Fianna Fáil TD, having been a by-
election candidate in Mayo-West in June 1994
to fill the seat vacated by her father, Pádraig
Flynn, when he was appointed an EU
Commissioner in 1993.

She was expelled twice from the Fianna Fáil
Parliamentary Party during the 28th Dáil and a
third time in 2004 during the 29th Dáil. Her
first expulsion, in February 1999, was for
voting against a Dáil motion asking her father
to clarify his position on allegations that he
received a financial contribution. The second
expulsion, in April 2001, followed a failed libel
action against RTÉ. Having been re-elected in
2002, with Fianna Fáil backing, she was
expelled again in 2004 when the Supreme
Court upheld the High Court libel judgment.

She supported Bertie Ahern's election as
Taoiseach and his coalition Government on 14
June 2007. She settled a court case with RTÉ
over the €2.4 million costs of her
unsuccessful libel action against the station.

Member of Mayo County Council 1996–2003.

She is a daughter of Pádraig Flynn, Fianna Fáil
TD for Mayo West 1977–93, a former Minister
for Justice, Industry and Commerce,
Environment, Trade, Commerce, and Tourism
and the Gaeltacht. EU Commissioner
1993–2000.

Mayo

	1st Count	2nd Count	3rd Count
Seats 5 **Quota 11,898**		Transfer of **Kenny** Surplus	Transfer of **Ring** Surplus
BARRETT, Harry (Lab)	831	(+65) 896	(+21) 917
CALLEARY, Dara (FF)	7,225	(+23) 7,248	(+3) 7,251
CARTY, John* (FF)	5,889	(+37) 5,926	(+11) 5,937
CHAMBERS, Frank (FF)	4,345	(+41) 4,386	(+20) 4,406
COOKE, Tommy (PD)	296	(+2) 298	(+) 298
COWLEY, Jerry* (Ind)	3,407	(+80) 3,487	(+42) 3,529
ENRIGHT, Peter (GP)	580	(+14) 594	(+3) 597
FLYNN, Beverley* (Ind)	6,779	(+352) 7,131	(+81) 7,212
KENNY, Enda* (FG)	14,717		
MULHERIN, Michelle (FG)	5,428	(+449) 5,877	(+139) 6,016
MURRAY, Gerry (SF)	3,608	(+52) 3,660	(+8) 3,668
O'MAHONY, John (FG)	6,869	(+675) 7,544	(+215) 7,759
RING, Michael* (FG)	11,412	(+1,029) 12,441	
NON-TRANSFERABLE			

4th Count	5th Count	6th Count	7th Count	8th Count
Transfer of **Barrett, Cooke, Enright** Votes	Transfer of **Murray** Votes	Transfer of **Chambers** Votes	Transfer of **Cowley** Votes	Transfer of **Mulherin** Votes
(+187) 7,438	*(+261)* 7,699	*(+1,104)* 8,803	*(+542)* 9,345	*(+1,924)* 11,269
(+54) 5,991	*(+528)* 6,519	*(+1,306)* 7,825	*(+389)* 8,214	*(+89)* 8,303
(+93) 4,499	*(+206)* 4,705			
(+381) 3,910	*(+874)* 4,784	*(+558)* 5,342		
(+175) 7,387	*(+656)* 8,043	*(+1,279)* 9,322	*(+1,362)* 10,684	*(+566)* 11,250
(+400) 6,416	*(+265)* 6,681	*(+82)* 6,763	*(+881)* 7,644	
(+177) 3,845				
(+244) 8,003	*(+714)* 8,717	*(+138)* 8,855	*(+732)* 9,587)	*(+4,149)* 13,736
101	341	238	1,436	916

Meath East

Elected

Party Share of Vote

1st Preferences	Number	%	Gain/Loss
Fianna Fáil	18,735	43.56	
Fine Gael	11,129	25.88	
Labour	5,136	11.94	
Prog Democrats	957	2.23	
Green Party	1,330	3.09	
Sinn Féin	1,695	3.94	
Others	4,025	9.36	

Statistics

Electorate	67,443	
Total Poll	43,366	64.30
Spoiled	359	0.83
Total Valid Poll	43,007	63.77
Seats	3	
Quota	10,752	
Candidates	11	

	Quotas	Seats
FF	1.74	2
FG	1.04	1

New constituency

Mary Wallace (FF)

Home Address
Fairyhouse Road, Ratoath, Co Meath
Telephone
Home (01) 825 6259
Birth Place/Date
Dublin. 13 June 1959
Married
Declan Gannon. 1 son
Education
Loreto Convent, Balbriggan, Co Dublin; Loreto Convent, North Great George's Street, Dublin; Rathmines College of Commerce, Dublin (Dip Hospital and Health Services Administration)
Occupation
Public representative. Formerly personnel executive

Mary Wallace was re-appointed Minister of State at the Department of Agriculture and Food, with special responsibility for Forestry, on 20 June 2007. She was first appointed to the post in February 2006. She was previously Minister of State at the Department of Justice, Equality and Law Reform, with special responsibility for Equality and Disabilities, 1997–2002.

She was first elected to the Dáil in 1989. Senator, Administrative panel, 1987–89. Party spokesperson for People with Disabilities, and Carers, 1995–97. Chairperson, Oireachtas Joint Committee on Women's Rights 1995–97 (Vice-Chairperson 1989–92).

Chairperson of Fianna Fáil National Women's Committee 1992–94. Chairperson of the National Steering Committee on Violence Against Women 1998–2002.

Member, Meath County Council 1982–97; North-Eastern Health Board 1985–89; Meath Vocational Education Committee 1991–95; Meath County Committee of Agriculture 1982–87 (Chairperson 1986–87); Blanchardstown Hospital 1977–87.

Shane McEntee (FG)

Home Address
Castletown Kilpatrick, Navan, Co Meath
Constituency Office
Copper Beech, Duleek, Co Meath; Main Street, Nobber, Co Meath
Telephone
Office (Duleek) (041) 988 2727;
Fax (041) 988 2477; (Nobber) (046) 905 2653;
Fax (046) 905 2561
Birth Place and Date
Nobber. 19 December 1956
Married
Kathleen Corbally, 3 children.
Education
St Finian's College, Mullingar
Occupation.
Public Representative. Publican; formerly farmer and agricultural sales representative

Shane McEntee was first elected in March 2005 in the former constituency of Meath, in a by-election which was caused by the resignation from the Dáil of former Taoiseach John Bruton, to take up an appointment as EU Ambassador to the US.

He is deeply involved in the GAA and has trained the Meath minor football team.

Thomas Byrne (FF)

Home Address
42 The Boulevard, Grange Rath, Colpe,
Co Meath
Constituency Office
Donacarney, Co Meath
Telephone
Home (041) 981 8435; *Mobile* 087 694 3942;
Website www.thomasbyrne.blogspot.com
Birth Place/Date
Drogheda. 1 June 1977
Married
Ann Hunt
Education
Scoil Aonghusa, Drogheda, Co Louth;
St Mary's Diocesan School, Drogheda; Trinity
College, Dublin (LLB); Law Society of Ireland
(qualified as solicitor 2001); Bar of the State of
New York (qualified as Attorney and
Counselor-at-Law 2003)
Occupation
Public Representative, Solicitor, Attorney-at-
Law

Thomas Byrne was elected to Dáil Éireann in
2007 in his first electoral outing.

He is a cousin of Colm Hilliard, Dáil deputy for
Meath 1982–97, and of Michael Hilliard, Dáil
deputy 1943–73, Minister for Posts and
Telegraphs 1959–65 and Minister for Defence
1965–69.

Meath East

Seats 3	1st Count	2nd Count	3rd Count
Quota 10,752		Transfer of **Cahill** Votes	Transfer of **Campbell** Votes
BONNER, Joseph (Ind)	1,170	*(+25)* 1,195	*(+28)* 1,223
BYRNE, Thomas (FF)	7,834	*(+32)* 7,866	*(+401)* 8,267
CAHILL, A J (Ind)	269		
CAMPBELL, Sirena (PD)	957	*(+26)* 983	
DOHERTY, Regina (FG)	4,363	*(+14)* 4,377	*(+131)* 4,508
FINNEGAN, Joanne (SF)	1,695	*(+28)* 1,723	*(+39)* 1,762
FITZGERALD, Brian (Ind)	2,586	*(+31)* 2,617	*(+42)* 2,659
HANNIGAN, Dominic (Lab)	5,136	*(+57)* 5,193	*(+144)* 5,337
McENTEE, Shane* (FG)	6,766	*(+23)* 6,789	*(+88)* 6,877
Ó BUACHALLA, Seán (GP)	1,330	*(+25)* 1,355	*(+62)* 1,417
WALLACE, Mary* (FF)	10,901		
NON-TRANSFERABLE		8	48

4th Count	5th Count	6th Count	7th Count	8th Count
Transfer of **Bonner** Votes	Transfer of **Ó Buachalla** Votes	Transfer of **Finnegan** Votes	Transfer of **Fitzgerald** Votes	Transfer of **Doherty** Votes
(+202) 8,469	*(+159)* 8,628	*(+451)* 9,079	*(+691)* 9,770	*(+307)* 10,077
(+256) 4,764	*(+228)* 4,992	*(+172)* 5,164	*(+808)* 5,972	
(+97) 1,859	*(+149)* 2,008			
(+157) 2,816	*(+192)* 3,008	*(+326)* 3,334		
(+238) 5,575	*(+520)* 6,095	*(+459)* 6,554	*(+693)* 7,247	*(+1,349)* 8,596
(+64) 6,941	*(+165)* 7,106	*(+245)* 7,351	*(+519)* 7,870	*(+3,749)* 11,619
(+130) 1,547				
79	134	355	623	567

Meath West

Elected

Noel Dempsey (FF)*	1st Count
Johnny Brady (FF)*	2nd Count
Damien English (FG)*	7th Count

Party Share of Vote

1st Preferences	Number	%	Gain/Loss
Fianna Fáil	20,874	51.59	
Fine Gael	11,745	29.03	
Labour	1,634	4.04	
Green Party	1,011	2.50	
Sinn Féin	4,567	11.29	
Others	633	1.56	

Statistics

Electorate	56,267	
Total Poll	40,852	72.60
Spoiled	388	0.95
Total Valid Poll	40,464	71.91
Seats	3	
Quota	10,117	
Candidates	10	

	Quotas	Seats
FF	2.06	2
FG	1.16	1

New constituency

Noel Dempsey (FF)

Home Address
Newtown, Trim, Co Meath
Business Address
The Department of Transport, Transport House, Kildare Street, Dublin 2
Telephone
Home/Constituency office (046) 943 1146; *Fax* (046) 943 6643; *Office* (01) 670 7444
Birth Place/Date
Trim. 6 January 1953
Married
Bernadette Rattigan. 2 sons, 2 daughters
Education
St Michael's CBS, Trim; University College, Dublin; St Patrick's College, Maynooth (BA, HDipEd); Diploma in Career Guidance; Diploma in Youth Leadership
Occupation
Government Minister. Formerly career guidance counsellor

Noel Dempsey was appointed Minister for Transport and the Marine, on 14 June 2007. He was Minister for Communications, Marine and Natural Resources from September 2004 to June 2007, and previously Minister for Education and Science from June 2002.

He was Minister for the Environment and Local Government 1997–2002. Minister of State at the Department of the Taoiseach, with special responsibility as Government Chief Whip, and at the Department of Finance, with special responsibility for the Office of Public Works, and at the Department of Defence, 1993–94. Minister of State at the Departments of the Taoiseach and Defence (Chief Whip), February 1992–January 1993. He has been a Dáil deputy since 1987.

Party spokesperson on the Environment 1995–97. Party convenor on Forum for Peace and Reconciliation.

Former member, Meath County Council 1977–92 (Chairman, 1986–87); Trim Urban District Council (Chairman, 1981–82, 1985–86 and 1991–92).

Johnny Brady (FF)

Home Address
Springville, Kilskyre, Kells, Co Meath
Constituency Office
John Street, Kells, Co Meath
Telephone
Constituency office (046) 924 0852; *Fax* (046) 924 9566; *Dáil office* (01) 618 359; *Website* www.johnnybrady.ie
Birth Place/Date
Meath. 1 January 1948
Married
Kathleen Clarke. 1 son
Education
Kells Vocational School
Occupation
Full-time public representative. Farmer

Johnny Brady was elected to the Dáil in 1997 in his first general election.

Chairman, Joint Oireachtas Committee on Agriculture and Food in last Dáil. Member, British–Irish Inter-Parliamentary Body.

Member of Meath County Council 1974–2003 (Chairman, 1995–96). Former member of Meath County Committee of Agriculture and of the North-Eastern Health Board.

He served as chairman of Meath Juvenile GAA Hurling Board for six years and with local youth organisations.

Damien English (FG)

Home Address
40 Watergate Street, Navan, Co Meath
Constituency Office
16 Bridge Street, Navan
Telephone
Office (046) 907 1667; *Fax* 046 907 2225;
Mobile 086 814 3495;
Website homepage.eircom.net\~denglish
Birth Place/Date
Drogheda, Co Louth. 21 February 1978
Married
Laura Kenny
Education
Kells Community School; Chartered Institute
of Management Accountants
Occupation
Full-time public representative

Damien English was first elected to the Dáil in 2002 as the youngest TD returned at that election. In the last Dáil, he was Fine Gael's deputy spokesperson on Justice and Community Affairs, with special responsibility for Drugs, Alcohol and Crime Prevention. He was previously deputy spokesperson on Arts, Sport and Tourism.

He was elected secretary to the Fine Gael Parliamentary Party in September 2002.

He was a member of Meath County Council from 1999 to 2003. Member of the Meath County Development Board and of the Navan Shamrock Festival Board.

Meath West

Seats 3	1st Count	2nd Count	3rd Count
Quota 10,117		Transfer of **Dempsey** Surplus	Transfer of **Cantwell, Coleman** Votes
BRADY, Johnny* (FF)	8,868	*(+1,310)* 10,178	
CANTWELL, Phil (Ind)	506	*(+38)* 544	
COLEMAN, Paul (Ind)	127	*(+3)* 130	
COLLINS, Brian (Lab)	1,634	*(+29)* 1,663	*(+71)* 1,734
DEMPSEY, Noel* (FF)	12,006		
ENGLISH, Damien* (FG)	7,227	*(+200)* 7,427	*(+139)* 7,566
FLANAGAN, Brian (GP)	1,011	*(+36)* 1,047	*(+147)* 1,194
GERAGHTY, Graham (FG)	1,284	*(+42)* 1,326	*(+34)* 1,360
HIGGINS, Peter (FG)	3,234	*(+101)* 3,335	*(+89)* 3,424
REILLY, Joe (SF)	4,567	*(+130)* 4,697	*(+106)* 4,803
NON-TRANSFERABLE			88

4th Count	5th Count	6th Count	7th Count
Transfer of **Flanagan** Votes	Transfer of **Geraghty** Votes	Transfer of **Collins** Votes	Transfer of **Higgins** Votes
(+363) 2,097	*(+84)* 2,181		
(+290) 7,856	*(+671)* 8,527	*(+1,021)* 9,548	*(+3,386)* 12,934
(+60) 1,420			
(+110) 3,534	*(+426)* 3,960	*(+419)* 4,379	
(+221) 5,024	*(+163)* 5,187	*(+401)* 5,588	*(+427)* 6,015
150	76	340	566

Roscommon–South Leitrim

Elected

Frank Feighan (FG)	4th Count
Michael Finneran (FF)*	4th Count
Denis Naughten (FG)*	4th Count

Party Share of Vote

1st Preferences	Number	%	Gain/Loss
Fianna Fáil	17,897	38.84	
Fine Gael	18,031	39.13	
Labour	832	1.81	
Green Party	836	1.81	
Sinn Féin	3,876	8.41	
Others	4,605	9.99	

Statistics

Electorate	62,437	
Total Poll	46,470	74.43
Spoiled	393	0.85
Total Valid Poll	46,077	73.80
Seats	3	
Quota	11,520	
Candidates	9	

	Quotas	Seats
FF	1.55	1
FG	1.57	2

New constituency

Frank Feighan (FG)

Home Address
Bridge Street, Boyle, Co Roscommon
Constituency Office
Bridge Street, Boyle, Co Roscommon
Telephone
Home/Office (071) 966 2608/2115;
Fax (071) 966 3956; *Mobile* 086 833 1234
Birth Place/Date
Roscommon. 4 July 1962
Marital Status
Single
Education:
St Joseph's National School, Boyle; St Mary's College, Boyle
Occupation
Full-time public representative. Businessman

Frank Feighan is a new member of the Dáil. He was elected to Seanad Éireann on the Administrative panel in 2002. He was a member of the Oireachtas Committee on Health and Children's Affairs in the last Dáil.

He was elected to Roscommon County Council in 1999, topping the poll in the Boyle electoral area, and served on the Council until the ending of the dual mandate in 2003.

Chairman of Roscommon VEC for the periods 2000–01 and 2001–02. Member, West Region Authority, Roscommon County Enterprise Board, Roscommon GAA Supporters' Club. Chairman, Roscommon Adult Education Board, Lough Key Forest Park Action Group. President, North Roscommon Anglers' Association; past President, Boyle Chamber of Commerce.

Director, Boyle 2000.com non-profit organisation, Boyle Ledford Park Oval Car Racing Club. Member of the Irish Kidney Association.

Michael Finneran (FF)

Home Address
Riverside Avenue, Roscommon
Telephone
Mobile (087) 234 1017
Birth Place/Date
Roscommon. 10 September 1947
Married
Elizabeth Walsh. 2 sons, 2 daughters
Education
Fevagh National School, Co Roscommon; Summerhill College, Sligo
Occupation
Public representative. Formerly psychiatric nurse

Michael Finneran was first elected to the Dáil in 2002. Vice-Chairman of the Joint Oireachtas Committee on Finance and Public Service in last Dáil. Senator, Administrative panel, 1989–2002. Government spokesperson on Finance, in Seanad, 1997–2002.

One of two Irish representatives on the Consultative Council to the European Commission, 1988–92, forerunner to the Committee of the Regions.

Member, Roscommon County Council 1989–2003.

Denis Naughten (FG)

Home Address
Abbey Street, Roscommon
Constituency Offices
Abbey Street, Roscommon; Ardkeenan,
Drum, Co Roscommon
Telephone
Home (090) 662 7557; *Constituency offices*
(090) 662 7557; (090) 643 7324;
Fax (090) 662 7556;
Website www.naughten.ie
Birth Place/Date
Drum, Athlone. 23 June 1973
Marital Status
Single
Education
St Aloysius College, Athlone; University
College, Dublin (BSc); University College,
Cork (Researcher in Food Microbiology).
Occupation
Full-time public representative. Formerly
research scientist

Denis Naughten was appointed party
spokesperson on Immigration and Integration
in September 2007. He was first elected in
1997 for Longford–Roscommon as the
youngest TD in the 28th Dáil. Previously
Senator, Agricultural Panel, 1997.

He was Fine Gael front bench spokesperson
on Agriculture and Food, October 2004;
Transport 2002–04. Member of Joint
Oireachtas Committee on Agriculture and
Food 2004–07; Joint Oireachtas Committee
on Transport 2002–04. Co-author of Joint
Oireachtas Committee on Education and
Science reports on school transport and on
science and technology.

Member, Roscommon County Council
1997–2003; Western Health Board
1997–2003; Association of Health Boards
1997–99.

He is son of the late Liam Naughten, Dáil
deputy 1982–89; Senator, Agricultural panel
1981–82 and 1989–96; Leas-Chathaoirleach
of the Seanad 1989–95 and Cathaoirleach
1995–96.

Seats 3 Quota 11,520	1st Count	2nd Count Transfer of **Baxter, McDaid, O'Gara** Votes	3rd Count Transfer of **Kenny** Votes	4th Count Transfer of **Kelly** Votes
BAXTER, Hughie (Lab)	832			
ELLIS, John* (FF)	7,915	*(+145)* 8,060	*(+1,287)* 9,347	*(+303)* 9,650
FEIGHAN, Frank (FG)	9,103	*(+404)* 9,507	*(+914)* 10,421	*(+1,644)* 12,065
FINNERAN, Michael* (FF)	9,982	*(+153)* 10,135	*(+394)* 10,529	*(+1,488)* 12,017
KELLY, John (Ind)	4,539	*(+300)* 4,839	*(+683)* 5,522	
KENNY, Martin (SF)	3,876	*(+242)* 4,118		
McDAID, Garreth (GP)	836			
NAUGHTEN, Denis* (FG)	8,928	*(+426)* 9,354	*(+316)* 9,670	*(+1,378)* 11,048
O'GARA, Noel (Ind)	66			
NON-TRANSFERABLE		64	524	709

Sligo–North Leitrim

Elected

Eamon Scanlon (FF)	5th Count
John Perry (FG)*	5th Count
Jimmy Devins (FF)*	5th Count

Party Share of Vote

1st Preferences	Number	%	Gain/Loss
Fianna Fáil	16,360	40.97	
Fine Gael	15,684	39.27	
Labour	1,555	3.89	
Green Party	1,209	3.03	
Sinn Féin	4,684	11.73	
Others	442	1.11	

Statistics

Electorate	57,517	
Total Poll	40,330	70.12
Spoiled	396	0.98
Total Valid Poll	39,934	69.43
Seats	3	
Quota	9,984	
Candidates	10	

	Quotas	Seats
FF	1.64	2
FG	1.57	1

New constituency

Eamon Scanlon (FF)

Home Address
Keenaghan, Ballymote, Co Sligo
Telephone
Home (071) 83113; *Office* (071) 918 9224; *Fax* (071) 918 9339
Birth Place/Date
Ballymote, Co Sligo. 20 September 1954
Married
Ann Killoran. 4 sons, 2 daughters
Education
Ballymote Corran College
Occupation
Auctioneer and butcher

Eamon Scanlon is a new deputy. He was elected to the Agricultural panel of the Seanad in 2002 having unsuccessfully contested that year's Dáil election.

Former member Fianna Fáil National Executive and director of elections for former TD Matt Brennan, 1981. Member, Governing Body of Letterkenny Institute of Technology, Sligo/Omagh Cross Border Partnership, Ballymote GAA Club, Ballymote Community Enterprise Board.

Member Sligo County Council 1991–2003.

John Perry (FG)

Home Address
Grianán Iuda, Carrownanty, Ballymote, Co Sligo
Constituency Offices
Teeling Street, Ballymote; Westward Town Centre, Bridge Street, Sligo
Telephone
Ballymote (071) 918 9333/9611; *Sligo* (071) 915 1011; *Fax* (071) 915 1119
Birth Place/Date
Ballymote. 15 August 1956
Married
Marie Mulvey. 1 son
Education
Corran College, Ballymote
Occupation
Full-time public representative.

John Perry was first elected to the Dáil in 1997.

In the 29th Dáil he was Vice-Chairman of the Oireachtas Joint Committee on Communications and Natural Resources and a member of the Audit Committee of the Houses of the Oireachtas Commission. Chairman of the Public Accounts Committee, September 2002–October 2004. Party spokesperson on the Marine 2004–07, on Science, Technology, Small Business and Enterprise, Border Counties 1997–2002.

Elected to Sligo County Council 1999. Chairman, Ballymote Community Enterprise. Chairman of Ballymote Cattle and Horse Show. Member of various community and development committees and organisations.

Irish Quality Business award in 1991 and 1992. Sligo Person of the Year award, 1993.

Jimmy Devins (FF)

Home Address
Lia Fáil, Calry Road, Co Sligo
Constituency Office
Mail Coach Road, Sligo
Telephone
Constituency office (071) 915 2970;
Fax (071) 915 2971
Birth Place/Date
Sligo. 20 September 1948
Married
Mary Tracey. 4 daughters
Education
St John's National School; Blackrock College,
Co Dublin; University College, Dublin (MB,
BCh, BAO); Trinity College, Dublin (MSc in
Family Medicine); DCH, D.Obst, MICGP
Occupation
Public representative. Medical doctor

Jimmy Devins was appointed Minister of
State, with responsibility for Disability and
Mental Health, at the Department of Health
and Children, in June 2007.

He was first elected to the Dáil in 2002. Vice-
Chairman of the Joint Committee on Health
and Children, from November 2004 to April
2007. Member, British–Irish Parliamentary
Body.

Member, Sligo County Council 1991–2003.
Former member, Border Regional Authority;
Border and Mid-West Assembly. Former
Chairperson of the Institute of Technology,
Sligo.

He is a grandson of James Devins, TD for
Sligo–Mayo East in 2nd and 3rd Dáil 1921–22,
and killed during the civil war in 1922.

Sligo–North Leitrim

Seats 3 Quota 9,984	1st Count	2nd Count Transfer of **Higgins, McSharry** Votes	3rd Count Transfer of **Scanlon** Votes	4th Count Transfer of **Henry, McGarry** Votes	5th Count Transfer of **MacManus** Votes
COMISKEY, Michael (FG)	4,937	*(+79)* 5,016	*(+155)* 5,171	*(+1,561)* 6,732	*(+1,025)* 7,757
DEVINS, Jimmy* (FF)	7,102	*(+66)* 7,168	*(+120)* 7,288	*(+616)* 7,904	*(+1,283)* 9,187
HENRY, Imelda (FG)	2,837	*(+26)* 2,863	*(+124)* 2,987		
HIGGINS, John Francis (Ind)	89				
MacMANUS, Seán (SF)	4,684	*(+100)* 4,784	*(+291)* 5,075	*(+694)* 5,769	
McGARRY, Jim (Lab)	1,555	*(+16)* 1,571	*(+258)* 1,829		
McSHARRY, Andrew (Ind)	353				
PERRY, John* (FG)	7,910	*(+42)* 7,952	*(+134)* 8,086	*(+1,407)* 9,493	*(+870)* 10,363
SCANLON, Brian (GP)	1,209	*(+31)* 1,240			
SCANLON, Eamon (FF)	9,258	*(+59)* 9,317	*(+73)* 9,390	*(+272)* 9,662	*(+1,109)* 10,771
NON-TRANSFERABLE		23	85	266	1,482

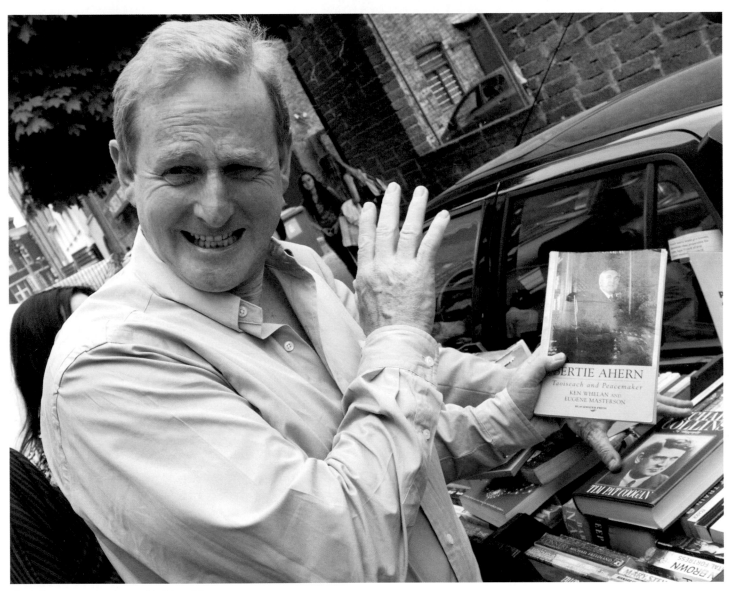

Enda Kenny on election trail in Limerick.

Tipperary North

Elected

Party Share of Vote

1st Preferences	Number	%	Gain/Loss
Fianna Fáil	15,245	34.31	-8.35%
Fine Gael	7,061	15.89	0.98%
Labour	4,561	10.27	-3.25%
Prog Democrats	634	1.43	-2.10%
Green Party	495	1.11	1.11%
Sinn Féin	1,672	3.76	3.76%
Others	14,763	33.23	7.84%

Statistics

Electorate	57,084	
Total Poll	44,783	78.45
Spoiled	352	0.79
Total Valid Poll	44,431	77.83
Seats	3	
Quota	11,108	
Candidates	9	

	Quotas	Seats
FF	1.37	1
FG	0.64	1
Ind	1.16	1
FG gain from FF		

Michael Lowry (Ind)

Home Address
Glenreigh, Holycross, Thurles, Co Tipperary
Business Address
Abbey Road, Thurles
Telephone
Business (0504) 22022; *Fax* (0504) 23349;
Website www.michaellowry.ie
Birth Place/Date
Holycross. 13 March 1954
Married
Catherine McGrath. 2 sons, 1 daughter
Education
Thurles CBS
Occupation
Public representative. Company director

Michael Lowry was first elected to the Dáil in 1987, for Fine Gael. He was Minister for Transport, Energy and Communications 1994–November 1996 when he resigned. He resigned from the Fine Gael Parliamentary Party in 1997. He has topped the poll and been elected on the first count in all subsequent general elections. He supported Bertie Ahern for election as Taoiseach in the 30th Dáil.

Chairman, Fine Gael Parliamentary Party 1993–94. Member of front bench 1993–94. Fine Gael leader of the British–Irish Inter-Parliamentary Body 1994.

Member, Tipperary North County Council 1979–95 and 1999–2003. He served on the County Development Team, Mid-Western Health Board and Association of Health Boards in Ireland.

Former Chairman, Semple Stadium Management Committee. Former Chairman, County Tipperary Gaelic Athletic Association Board and Mid-Tipperary GAA Board.

Noel Coonan (FG)

Home Address
Gortnagoona, Roscrea, Co Tipperary
Constituency Offices
Bank Street, Templemore, Co Tipperary;
Rosemount, Roscrea, Co Tipperary
Telephone
Constituency offices (0504) 32544
(Templemore); (0505) 31655 (Roscrea);
Mobile 086 242 7733;
Website www.noelcoonan.com
Birth Place/Date
Roscrea. 6 January 1951
Married
Education
CBS Templemore, Co Tipperary
Occupation
Full-time public representative

Noel Coonan is a new member of the Dáil. He contested Tipperary North unsuccessfully in the 2002 general election and was a Senator on the Cultural and Educational panel from 2002 to 2007. Party spokesperson on Agriculture and Food in the last Senate.

Member of North Tipperary County Council 1991–2003 and Templemore Town Council 1994–2003. Former member, Mid-Western Health Board. President, Collins22 Society, which commemorates Michael Collins.

Máire Hoctor (FF)

Home Address
Teach Ruadhain, 40 Melrose, Nenagh,
Co Tipperary
Constituency Office
3A Ormond Court, Ormond Street, Nenagh,
Co Tipperary
Telephone
Constituency office (067) 32943;
Fax (067) 50470
Birth Place/Date
Nenagh, Co Tipperary. 20 January 1963
Marital Status
Single
Education
St Mary's Secondary School, Nenagh; St
Patrick's College, Maynooth (BA Th., HDipEd)
Occupation
Full-time public representative. Formerly
secondary school teacher

Máire Hoctor was appointed Minister of State
at the Department of Health and Children,
with responsibility for Older People, in June
2007.

She was first elected to the Dáil in 2002. In
the last Dáil, she was Vice-Chairperson of
the Oireachtas Committee on Agriculture
and Food. Government Convener of Joint
Oireachtas Committee on Justice, Equality,
Defence and Women's Rights. Member
of Joint Oireachtas Committee on Education
and Science.

Member, Tipperary North County Council
1999–2003. Member, Nenagh Town Council
1994–2003.

Director of Nenagh Community Reparation
Project. Director of Young Nenagh Project.

Tipperary North

Seats 3
Quota 11,108

	1st Count	2nd Count Transfer of **Lowry** Surplus	3rd Count Transfer of **McNally, Sheary** Votes	4th Count Transfer of **Morris** Votes	5th Count Transfer of **Ryan** Votes	6th Count Transfer of **O'Meara** Votes
COONAN, Noel (FG)	7,061	*(+508)* 7,569	*(+194)* 7,763	*(+218)* 7,981	*(+459)* 8,440)	*(+3,059)* 11,499
HOCTOR, Máire* (FF)	7,374	*(+290)* 7,664	*(+241)* 7,905	*(+344)* 8,249	*(+544)* 8,793	*(+1,374)* 10,167
LOWRY, Michael * (Ind)	12,919					
McNALLY, Paul (GP)	495	*(+24)* 519				
MORRIS, Seamus (SF)	1,672	*(+82)* 1,754	*(+127)* 1,881			
O'MEARA, Kathleen (Lab)	4,561	*(+298)* 4,859	*(+359)* 5,218	*(+530)* 5,748	*(+563)* 6,311	
RYAN, Jim (Ind)	1,844	*(+349)* 2,193	*(+90)* 2,283	*(+281)* 2,564		
SHEARY, Tony (PD)	634	*(+24)* 658				
SMITH, Michael* (FF)	7,871	*(+236)* 8,107	*(+116)* 8,223	*(+257)* 8,480	*(+495)* 8,975	*(+632)* 9,607
NON-TRANSFERABLE			50	251	503	1,246

LET US TAKE THE HASSLE OUT OF LETTING YOUR PROPERTY.

Make the most of your property investment and let with RAS. We can guarantee your rent with no vacant periods for a minimum of four years, no advertising costs and no need for any rent collection on your part. We even screen your tenants as part of our service. It really is the smarter way to let. Call us on 222 5299 for details on how to let your properties the hassle-free way.

Dublin City Council
Comhairle Cathrach Bhaile Átha Cliath

Tipperary South

Elected

Tom Hayes (FG)*	5th Count
Mattie McGrath (FF)	6th Count
Dr Martin Mansergh (FF)	8th Count

Party Share of Vote

1st Preferences	Number	%	Gain/Loss
Fianna Fáil	18,004	46.42	7.91%
Fine Gael	8,200	21.14	-3.39%
Labour	3,400	8.77	-0.38%
Prog Democrats	541	1.39	1.39%
Green Party	591	1.52	1.52%
Sinn Féin	1,198	3.09	-0.21%
Others	6,848	17.66	-6.85%

Statistics

Electorate	54,637	
Total Poll	39,112	71.59
Spoiled	330	0.84
Total Valid Poll	38,782	70.98
Seats	3	
Quota	9,696	
Candidates	11	

	Quotas	Seats
FF	1.86	2
FG	0.85	1
FF gain from Ind		

Tom Hayes (FG)

Home Address
Cahervillahow, Golden, Co Tipperary
Constituency Office
The Green, Cashel, Co Tipperary; Kickham Street, Clonmel, Co Tipperary
Telephone
Home (062) 62892; *Fax* (062) 63595; *Office* (052) 80731; *Fax* (052) 82895; *Mobile* 087 810 5016
Birth Place/Date
Golden, Co Tipperary. 16 February 1952
Married
Marian Thornton. 3 sons
Education
Thomastown National School; Mount Mellary Secondary School; Vocational School, Tipperary Town; University College, Cork (Diploma in Public Administration)
Occupation
Public representative and farmer

Tom Hayes was first elected to the Dáil in July 2001 at a by-election caused by the death of Fine Gael colleague Theresa Ahearn. He had previously served in the Seanad (Agricultural panel) from 1997.

Elected Chairman of the Fine Gael Parliamentary Party in September 2002. Deputy party spokesperson for Environment, with special responsibility for Heritage and Rural Affairs, and member of the Committee of Public Accounts in the last Dáil.

Party spokesman on Agriculture, in the Seanad. Served on Agriculture and Strategic Management committees.

Member of Tipperary South Riding County Council 1991–2003. Served on Vocational Education Committee, County Enterprise Board, Cashel Heritage Committee.

Member of GAA, Macra na Feirme and IFA.

Mattie McGrath (FF)

Home Address
Garrancasey, Newcastle, Clonmel, Co Tipperary
Telephone
Home (052) 36352; *Fax* (052) 36825; *Office* (052) 29155
Birth Place/Date
Newcastle, Clonmel. September 1958
Married
Margaret Sherlock. 5 daughters, 3 sons
Education
St Joseph's College, Cahir; Kildalton Agricultural College, Co Kilkenny (1986); University College, Cork (diploma in communication skills).
Occupation
Plant-hire owner. Formerly agricultural salesman.

Mattie McGrath is a new TD.

He was a member of South Tipperary County Council for the Cahir electoral area from 1999 until his Dáil election. Chairperson of South Tipperary County Council 2004–05.

Director, Muintir na Tíre, Ring a Link transport service, Irish Council for Social Housing. Member, board of management of Naíonra Chaisleán Nua, South Tipperary Childcare Committee.

All-Ireland set dancer 1974.

Martin Mansergh (FF)

Home Address
Friarsfield, Tipperary, Co Tipperary
Telephone
Home (062) 51226; *Mobile* 087 223 9022
Birth Place/Date
England. 31 December 1946
Married
Elizabeth Young. 5 children
Education
King's School, Canterbury; Christ Church, Oxford (PPE) (MA [Politics, Philosophy and Economics], D Phil. [18th century Pre-Revolutionary French History])
Occupation
Full-time public representative. Formerly civil servant in Department of Foreign Affairs and government adviser

Martin Mansergh is a new member of the Dáil. He was elected on the Agricultural panel of the Seanad in 2002.

A former Head of Research with Fianna Fáil, he was Special Adviser on Northern Ireland to three Taoisigh, Charles J. Haughey, Albert Reynolds and Bertie Ahern. He was primarily responsible for dialogue with the Sinn Féin leadership and church intermediaries, which led to the IRA ceasefires during the 1990s. He worked on the text of what subsequently became known as Hume-Adams and the Downing Street Declarations. He was Co-chair of the British–Irish Constitutional Sub-Group 1994 and a member of the Delegation and Steering Group for the Good Friday Agreement. With Noel Dempsey he drafted the *Committee of Forum for Peace and Reconciliation* paper.

He was the author of the paper which formed the basis of negotiations leading to the Fianna Fáil–Labour coalition 1992–94 and was also a member of the four-person negotiating team to put together and later review the Fianna Fáil–Progressive Democrats Action Programme for the Millennium, in 1997.

Martin Mansergh is a member of the Council of State, appointed by President Mary McAleese in December 2004.

Tipperary South

Seats 3 Quota 9,696	1st Count	2nd Count Transfer of **Lennon, Molloy, O'Donnell** Votes	3rd Count Transfer of **Wood** Votes
AMBROSE, Siobhán (FF)	4,286	*(+128)* 4,414	*(+83)* 4,497
BROWNE, Liam (SF)	1,198	*(+68)* 1,266	*(+97)* 1,363
HAYES, Tom* (FG)	8,200	*(+186)* 8,386	*(+437)* 8,823
HEALY, Seamus* (Ind)	5,707	*(+177)* 5,884	*(+152)* 6,036
LENNON, Bernard (GP)	591		
MANSERGH, Martin (FF)	6,110	*(+151)* 6,261	*(+145)* 6,406
McGRATH, Mattie (FF)	7,608	*(+103)* 7,711	*(+100)* 7,811
MOLLOY, Richie (PD)	364		
O'DONNELL, Peadar (PD)	177		
PRENDERGAST, Phil (Lab)	3,400	*(+231)* 3,631	*(+121)* 3,752
WOOD, Tom (Ind)	1,141	*(+46)* 1,187	
NON-TRANSFERABLE		42	52

4th Count	5th Count	6th Count	7th Count	8th Count
Transfer of **Browne** Votes	Transfer of **Prendergast** Votes	Transfer of **Ambrose** Votes	Transfer of **Hayes** Surplus	Transfer of **McGrath** Surplus
(+152) 4,649	(+448) 5,097			
(+247) 9,070	(+1,448) 10,518			
(+420) 6,456	(+1,092) 7,548	(+1,043) 8,591	(+607) 9,198	(+84) 9,282
(+122) 6,528	(+224) 6,752	(+2,061) 8,813	(+215) 9,028	(+313) 9,341
(+183) 7,994	(+469) 8,463	(+1,630) 10,093		
(+155) 3,907				
84	226	363		

Waterford

Elected

Martin Cullen (FF)*	1st Count
John Deasy (FG)*	9th Count
Brian O'Shea (Lab)*	10th Count
Brendan Kenneally (FF)	11th Count

Party Share of Vote

1st Preferences	Number	%	Gain/Loss
Fianna Fáil	23,025	46.49	0.15%
Fine Gael	13,552	27.36	5.88%
Labour	5,610	11.33	-2.03%
Prog Democrats	0	0.00	-4.59%
Green Party	1,049	2.12	-0.80%
Sinn Féin	3,327	6.72	0.37%
Others	2,965	5.99	1.02%

Statistics

Electorate	73,434	
Total Poll	49,958	68.03
Spoiled	430	0.59
Total Valid Poll	49,528	67.45
Seats	4	
Quota	9,906	
Candidates	13	

	Quotas	Seats
FF	2.32	2
FG	1.37	1
Lab	0.57	1
No change		

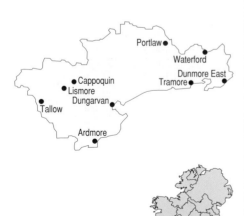

Martin Cullen (FF)

Home Address
Maritana Gate, Canada Street, Waterford
Business Address
Department of Social and Family Affairs, Áras Mhic Dhiarmada, Store Street, Dublin 1
Constituency Office
23 Catherine Street, Waterford
Telephone
Constituency office (051) 844860; *Fax* (051) 876943; *Ministerial office* (01) 704 3887; *Fax* (01) 704 3869
Birth Place/Date
Waterford. 2 November 1954
Married
1 daughter, 3 sons
Education
Waterpark College, Waterford; Waterford Regional Technical College
Occupation
Government Minister. Formerly Chief Executive of the Federation of Transport Operators

Martin Cullen was appointed Minister for Social and Family Affairs on 14 June 2007. He served as Minister for Transport from September 2004 to June 2007 and established Transport 21, the Government's 10-year €34.4 billion investment programme for transport development.

He was Minister for the Environment, Heritage and Local Government from June 2002 to September 2004. He served as Minister of State at the Department of Finance, with special responsibility for the Office of Public Works, 1997–2002.

He was first elected to the Dáil as a Progressive Democrat TD in 1987, lost his seat in the 1989 general election and regained it in 1992. During the 27th Dáil he joined Fianna Fáil. Senator, Taoiseach's nominee, 1989–92. Spokesperson on Enterprise and Employment 1993; Industry and Commerce 1988–89; Tourism, Transport and Communications 1987–88.

Member, Waterford City Council 1991–97; Mayor 1993–94 (his father and grandfather were both mayors of Waterford).

John Deasy (FG)

Home Address
Kilrush, Dungarvan, Co Waterford
Constituency Office
20 Grattan Square, Dungarvan
Telephone
Constituency office (058) 43003; *Fax* (058) 45315
Birth Place/Date
Abbeyside, Dungarvan. 8 October 1967
Married
Maura Derrane
Education
Coláiste na Rinne, Ring, Dungarvan; St Augustine's College, Dungarvan; Mercyhurst College, Erie, Pennsylvania, USA (BA History/Communications); University College, Cork (BCL)
Occupation
Public representative. Formerly US Congressional aide

John Deasy was first elected to the Dáil in 2002. He was Fine Gael's front bench spokesperson for Justice, Equality and Law Reform 2002–04. Chairman of the Dáil's European Affairs Committee and member of the Public Accounts Committee 2004–07.

Member of Waterford County Council 1999–2003. Member, Dungarvan Town Council 1999–2003. Board member, Waterford Regional Airport. Manager of public affairs for multinational waste-management company 1991–92. Legislative assistant to Senator John Heinz in US Senate, handling Trade and Foreign Affairs (1990–91); legislative assistant to Representative Ronald K. Machtley in US House of Representatives 1993–95.

He is son of Austin Deasy, Dáil deputy 1977–2002; Senator 1973–77.

Brian O'Shea (Lab)

Home Address
61 Sweetbriar Lawn, Tramore, Co Waterford
Telephone
Home (051) 381 913; *Fax* (051) 386 427;
Mobile 087 294 3292
Birth Place/Date
Waterford. 9 December 1944
Married
Eileen Walsh. 2 sons, 4 daughters
Education
Mount Sion CBS, Waterford; St Patrick's
Teachers' Training College, Dublin
Occupation
Full-time public representative. Formerly
national school teacher

Brian O'Shea was first elected to the Dáil in
1989. He was appointed party spokesperson
on Defence and the Irish language in
September 2007.

He was previously spokesperson on Arts,
Heritage, Gaeltacht and the Islands, and
Communications and Sport 1998–2002; on
Defence 1997–98. Member, Joint Committee
on Arts, Sport, Tourism, Community, Rural and
Gaeltacht Affairs, and of Dáil Select Committee
on Arts, Sport, Tourism, Community, Rural and
Gaeltacht Affairs 2002–07

Minister of State at the Department of Health,
with special responsibility for Mental Handicap,
Health Promotion, Food Safety and Public
Health 1994–97. Minister of State at the
Department of Agriculture, with special
responsibility for Food and Horticulture 1993–94.

Senator, Industrial and Commercial panel,
1987–89.

Member, Waterford County Council 1985–93;
Waterford City Council 1985–93; Tramore Town
Commissioners 1979–93.

Former Chairman, South-Eastern Airport
Company; former President of Waterford
Council of Trade Unions; former President of
Tramore Community Care Organisation; former
Chairman of Waterford City Branch of INTO.

Brendan Kenneally (FF)

Home Address
Hillside House, Dunmore Road, Waterford
Telephone
Home (051) 855 964;
Website
www.brendankenneally.blogspot.com
Birth Place/Date
Waterford. 28 April 1955
Married
Martina Crotty. 1 son, 3 daughters
Education
De La Salle College, Waterford; Waterford
Institute of Technology
Occupation
Full-time public representative. Formerly
accountant

Brendan Kenneally was first elected to the
Dáil in 1989 but lost his seat to a party
colleague in the 2002 election. He was a
Taoiseach's nominee to the Seanad in 2002.

He was Minister of State at the Department
of Tourism, Transport and Communications
1992–93. Vice-Chairman of the Heritage and
the Irish Language Committee in the 28th
Dáil. Fianna Fáil deputy spokesperson on
Equality and Law Reform 1994–97.

Member, Waterford Corporation 1985–92
(Mayor, 1988–89). Director, South-eastern
Airport Company 1985–92. Member,
Waterford Youth Committee 1987–91,
President, Waterford Area Basketball Board.

He is the son of Billy Kenneally, TD for
Waterford 1965–82 and Senator 1982. He is
grandson of William Kenneally, TD for
Waterford 1952–61.

Waterford

Seats 4 Quota 9,906	1st Count	2nd Count Transfer of **Cullen** Surplus	3rd Count Transfer of **Hennessy, Waters** Votes	4th Count Transfer of **Roche** Votes	5th Count Transfer of **McCann** Votes
COFFEY, Paudie (FG)	4,658	(+48) 4,706	(+26) 4,732	(+93) 4,825	(+110) 4,935
CULLEN, Martin* (FF)	11,438				
CULLINANE, David (SF)	3,327	(+63) 3,390	(+25) 3,415	(+72) 3,487	(+144) 3,631
DARCY, Jim (FG)	1,340	(+32) 1,372	(+6) 1,378	(+55) 1,433	(+86) 1,519
DEASY, John* (FG)	7,554	(+120) 7,674	(+38) 7,712	(+127) 7,839	(+167) 8,006
HALLIGAN, John (WP)	1,708	(+60) 1,768	(+16) 1,784	(+85) 1,869	(+132) 2,001
HENNESSY, Francis Joseph (Ind)	53	(+2) 55			
KENNEALLY, Brendan (FF)	5,624	(+760) 6,384	(+39) 6,423	(+138) 6,561	(+70) 6,631
McCANN, Brendan (GP)	1,049	(+13) 1,062	(+23) 1,085	(+121) 1,206	
O'SHEA, Brian* (Lab)	5,610	(+136) 5,746	(+28) 5,774	(+188) 5,962	(+364) 6,326
ROCHE, Mary (Ind)	934	(+39) 973	(+41) 1,014		
WATERS, Declan (Ind)	270	(+1) 271			
WILKINSON, Ollie* (FF)	5,963	(+258) 6,221	(+37) 6,258	(+61) 6,319	(+57) 6,376
NON-TRANSFERABLE			47	74	76

6th Count	7th Count	8th Count	9th Count	10th Count	11th Count
Transfer of **Darcy** Votes	Transfer of **Halligan** Votes	Transfer of **Cullinane** Votes	Transfer of **Coffey** Votes	Transfer of **Deasy** Surplus	Transfer of **O'Shea** Surplus
(+447) 5,382	*(+140)* 5,522	*(+372)* 5,894			
(+66) 3,697	*(+599)* 4,296				
(+540) 8,546	*(+232)* 8,778	*(+787)* 9,565	*(+3,616)* 13,181		
(+92) 2,093					
(+68) 6,699	*(+296)* 6,995	*(+668)* 7,663	*(+369)* 8,032	*(+440)* 8,472	*(+376)* 8,848
(+219) 6,545	*(+541)* 7,086	*(+1,112)* 8,198	*(+1,060)* 9,258	*(+1,959)* 11,217	
(+19) 6,395	*(+48)* 6,443	*(+323)* 6,766	*(+393)* 7,159	*(+390)* 7,549	*(+325)* 7,874
68	237	1,034	456	486	610

Wexford

Elected

Party Share of Vote

1st Preferences	Number	%	Gain/Loss
Fianna Fáil	28,949	42.19	2.10%
Fine Gael	21,658	31.56	5.83%
Labour	9,445	13.77	0.53%
Prog Democrats	2,162	3.15	3.15%
Green Party	802	1.17	1.17%
Sinn Féin	5,068	7.39	-0.83%
Others	532	0.78	-11.94%

Statistics

Electorate	103,562	
Total Poll	69,443	67.05
Spoiled	827	1.19
Total Valid Poll	68,616	66.26
Seats	5	
Quota	11,437	
Candidates	11	

	Quotas	Seats
FF	2.53	2
FG	1.89	2
Lab	0.83	1
FG gain from Ind		

John Browne (FF)

Home Address
34 Beechpark, Enniscorthy, Co Wexford
Constituency Office
6 Court Street, Enniscorthy, Co Wexford
Telephone
Home (053) 893 5089;
Constituency office (053) 923 5046
Birth Place/Date
Marshalstown, Enniscorthy, 1 August 1948
Married
Judy Doyle. 1 son, 3 daughters
Education
St Mary's CBS, Enniscorthy
Occupation
Full-time public representative

John Browne was Minister of State at the Department of Communications, the Marine and Natural Resources, 2002–04 and 2006–07; at the Department of Agriculture and Food 2004–06.

He was Chairman of the Oireachtas Committee on Agriculture, Food and the Marine 1997–2002. Minister of State at the Department of the Environment, with special responsibility for Environmental Protection, 1993–94; Minister of State at the Department of Agriculture and Food, with special responsibility for the Food Industry, 1992–93. He was first elected to the Dáil in November 1982 at his first attempt. Assistant Party Chief Whip 1982–87.

Former member, Wexford County Council; Enniscorthy Urban District Council; Wexford County Health Committee 1979–92.

Member, Gaelic Athletic Association, since 1965.

Brendan Howlin (Lab)

Home Address
Whiterock Hill, Wexford
Telephone
Constituency office (053) 912 4036;
Website www.brendanhowlin.ie
Birth Place/Date
Wexford. 9 May 1956
Marital Status
Single
Education
Wexford CBS; St Patrick's College, Drumcondra, Dublin
Occupation
Full-time public representative. Formerly national school teacher

Brendan Howlin was elected Leas-Cheann Comhairle of the Dáil in June 2007. He was appointed Labour Party spokesperson on Constitutional Matters and Law Reform in September 2007. He was first elected to the Dáil in 1987 and elected Deputy Leader of the Labour Party in 1997. He was party spokesperson on Justice and a member of the Houses of the Oireachtas Commission in the last Dáil.

He was spokesperson on Finance in 2002 and on Justice 1997–2002. He was Minister for the Environment 1994–97; Minister for Health 1993–94. He was a Taoiseach's nominee to the Seanad 1982–87. Party spokesperson on Health and Youth Affairs 1989–93; on Health and Women's Rights 1987–89. Spokesman on Education in Seanad 1983–87.

Member, Wexford County Council 1985–93; Wexford Borough Council 1981–93 (Alderman, 1985–93. Mayor, 1986–87). Former member of Town of Wexford Vocational Education Committee.

Former Chairman, Wexford Branch of INTO. Former Vice-Chairman of Wexford Council of Trade Unions.

Seán Connick (FF)

Home Address
Millbanks, Rosbercon, New Ross, Co Wexford
Business Address
Waterford Road Business Park, Waterford Road, New Ross, Co Wexford
Constituency Office
The Quay, New Ross, Co Wexford
Telephone
Mobile 087 256 4576;
Email seanconnick@eircom.net
Website www.seanconnick.ie
Birth Place/Date
New Ross, Co Wexford. 27 August 1963
Married
Lourde
Education
St Canice's Primary; CBS New Ross Primary and Secondary; Professional Certificate in Business Management
Occupation
Self-employed businessman, public representative

Sean Connick is a new deputy.

Elected to Wexford County Council in 2004, toping the poll in his electoral area. Member, New Ross Town Council from 1999 until his election to the Dáil. Chairman of New Ross Town Council 2001–02

A wheelchair user since a traffic accident in 1977, he was Junior Chamber Ireland's Outstanding Young Person of Ireland 1993 and Junior Chamber of New Ross Person of the Year 1986.

He has served on many boards, including Hook Lighthouse; JFK Trust (Dunbrody Famine Ship); Chairman of New Ross Marina Development Committee; President of the Association of Municipal Authorities of Ireland 2005; Director of New Ross Chamber of Commerce and New Ross Port Company; Chairman of JFK Dunbrody Festival; Chairman of County Wexford Network of the Status of People with Disabilities 1996–98; and Chairman New Ross Special Olympics Host Town for the World Games 2003.

Paul Kehoe (FG)

Home Address
Coolteigue, Bree, Enniscorthy, Co Wexford
Constituency Office
7 Weafer Street, Enniscorthy, Co Wexford
Telephone
Home/Office (053) 924 3558;
Fax (053) 923 9562; *Mobile* 087 202 1383
Birth Place/Date
Wexford. 11 January 1973
Married
Brigid O'Connor
Education
St Mary's CBS, Enniscorthy; Kildalton Agricultural College
Occupation
Full-time public representative. Farmer

Paul Kehoe was first elected in 2002 and was Fine Gael Chief Whip from 2004 in the last Dáil. He was reappointed as Chief Whip in September 2007. He was previously deputy spokesperson on Communications, Marine and Natural Resources.

Former County Youth Officer for Fine Gael. Former Youth Officer with Co Wexford GAA. Former Chairman Macra na Feirme. Winner of Macra National Leadership Award 2001.

Member, Fleadh Cheoil na hÉireann; Irish Handicapped Children's Pilgrimage Trust.

Michael W. D'Arcy (FG)

Home Address
Annagh, Gorey, Co Wexford
Constituency Office
Waygood, Dublin Road, Gorey
Telephone
Home (053) 942 8177; *Office* (053) 948 3966;
Mobile 087 990 1055
Birth Place/Date
Wexford. 26 February 1970
Married
Shelly Vaughan. 2 children
Education
Ballythomas NS; Gorey CBS; University of London
Occupation
Full-time public representative. Formerly farmer and teacher

Michael D'Arcy is a new deputy.

He was elected to Wexford County Council for the Gorey district in 2004 (Vice-Chairman, 2004–05). Former Chairman, Wexford VEC.

Director of Wexford County Enterprise Board (CEB), Wexford Organisation for Rural Development (WORD) and Courtown Water World Ltd. Member Amnesty International, IFA, ICMSA, Kilanerin/Ballyfad Community Development Association, Kilanerin/Ballyfad GAA Club.

He won an All-Ireland junior football title with Wexford in 1992, and was a Leinster U-21 runner-up in 1988. He has won five Wexford senior titles with Kilanerin. He also played U-16 and youths soccer with Wexford.

He is a son of Michael D'Arcy, TD for Wexford 1977–92 and 1997–2002; Senator 1992–97; Minister of State at the Department of Agriculture 1981–82, at the Department of Fisheries, Forestry and Department of the Gaeltacht 1982–86.

Wexford

	1st Count	2nd Count	3rd Count
Seats 5 Quota 11,437		Transfer of **Browne** Surplus	Transfer of **Harpur, McGuire** Votes
BROWNE, John* (FF)	12,768		
CONNICK, Seán (FF)	9,826	*(+570)* 10,396	*(+80)* 10,476
D'ARCY, Michael W. (FG)	7,692	*(+64)* 7,756	*(+105)* 7,861
DWYER, John (SF)	5,068	*(+57)* 5,125	*(+177)* 5,302
HARPUR, Tom (GP)	802	*(+5)* 807	
HOWLIN, Brendan (Lab)	9,445	*(+95)* 9,540	*(+468)* 10,008
KEHOE, Paul* (FG)	8,459	*(+169)* 8,628	*(+100)* 8,728
McDONALD, Lisa (FF)	6,355	*(+314)* 6,669	*(+88)* 6,757
McGUIRE, Alan (Ind)	532	*(+7)* 539	
O'GORMAN, Colm (PD)	2,162	*(+26)* 2,188	*(+134)* 2,322
TWOMEY, Liam* (FG)	5,507	*(+24)* 5,531	*(+147)* 5,678
NON-TRANSFERABLE			47

4th Count	5th Count	6th Count	7th Count
Transfer of **O'Gorman** Votes	Transfer of **Dwyer** Votes	Transfer of **Twomey** Votes	Transfer of **Kehoe** Surplus
(+386) 10,862	(+988) 11,850		
(+413) 8,274	(+456) 8,730	(+1,643) 10,373	(+1,300) 11,673
(+129) 5,431			
(+405) 10,413	(+1,439) 11,852		
(+203) 8,931	(+636) 9,567	(+3,312) 12,879	
(+432) 7,189	(+563) 7,752	(+678) 8,430	(+142) 8,572
(+249) 5,927	(+381) 6,308		
105	968	675	

Wicklow

Elected

Party Share of Vote

1st Preferences	Number	%	Gain/Loss
Fianna Fáil	24,706	38.05	6.80%
Fine Gael	15,033	23.15	7.20%
Labour	10,608	16.34	-13.27%
Prog Democrats	903	1.39	1.39%
Green Party	4,790	7.38	1.50%
Sinn Féin	3,234	4.98	2.18%
Others	5,651	8.70	-5.81%

Statistics

Electorate	91,492	
Total Poll	65,479	71.57
Spoiled	554	0.85
Total Valid Poll	64,925	70.96
Seats	5	
Quota	10,821	
Candidates	15	

	Quotas	Seats
FF	2.28	2
FG	1.39	2
Lab	0.98	1
FG gain from Ind		

Dick Roche (FF)

Home Address/Constituency Office
2 Herbert Terrace, Herbert Road, Bray,
Co Wicklow
Business Address
Department of Foreign Affairs, Iveagh House,
79–80 St Stephen's Green, Dublin 2
Telephone
Home (01) 286 3211; *Fax* (01) 286 7666;
Office (01) 408 2000;
Website www.dickroche.com
Birth Place/Date
Wexford. 30 March 1947
Married
Eleanor Griffin. 3 sons, 1 daughter
Education
Wexford CBS; University College, Dublin
(BComm, DPA, MPA)
Occupation
Public representative. University lecturer

Dick Roche was appointed Minister of State
for European Affairs on 14 June 2007. He was
a member of the Cabinet as Minister for the
Environment, Heritage and Local Government
from September 2004 to 14 June 2007.

He was previously Minister of State at the
Departments of the Taoiseach and Foreign
Affairs, 2002 to September 2004. He was first
elected to the Dáil in 1987, defeated in 1992
and re-elected in 1997. Having lost his seat in
the 1992 general election, he was elected to
the Seanad, Administrative panel, during
1993–97. He was Taoiseach's nominee,
November 1992–February 1993.

Chairman, Oireachtas Joint Committee on the
Strategic Management Initiative 1997–2002.
Party spokesperson on Public Finance in
Seanad 1992–97, and on Public Service
Reform 1994–97. Chairman, Oireachtas Joint
Committee on State-Sponsored Bodies
1989–92.

Member, Wicklow County Council 1985–2002.

Member, Institute of Public Administration;
International Ombudsman Institute; Associate
of Graduates in Public Administration; Irish
Council of the European Movement; Irish
Commission for Justice and Peace (Chairman,
1985–86).

Joe Behan (FF)

Home Address
55 Richmond Park, Bray, Co Wicklow
Constituency Office
Unit 17, Parklands Office Park, Bray,
Co Wicklow
Telephone
Office (01) 276 0804;
Email joebehan@eircom.net
Birth Place/Date
Dublin. 30 July 1959
Married
Agnes Browne. 2 daughters, 1 son
Education
St Brendan's CBS College, Bray; Carysfort
College of Education, Blackrock, Co Dublin
(BEd)
Occupation
Public representative. Formerly school
principal

Joe Behan is a new deputy.

He was elected to Wicklow County Council in
1991 and in all subsequent elections.
Cathaoirleach of Wicklow County Council and
of Mid-East Regional Authority 2006–07.
Elected to Bray UDC in 1985 and in all
subsequent elections.

Liz McManus (Lab)

Home Address
1 Martello Terrace, Bray, Co Wicklow
Constituency Office
2 Belton House, Castle Street, Bray
Telephone
Constituency office (01) 276 0583;
Fax (01) 276 0584
Birth Place/Date
Montreal, Canada. March 1947
Married
John McManus. 3 sons, 1 daughter
Education
Holy Child Convent, Killiney, Co Dublin;
University College, Dublin (BArch)
Occupation
Public representative. Writer. Formerly
architect

Liz McManus was elected Deputy Leader of
the Labour Party in 2002 and was appointed
party spokesperson on Communications,
Energy and Natural Resources in September
2007. She was party spokesperson for Health
and Children in the 29th Dáil.

First elected to the Dáil in 1992, she was the
first woman to be elected to the Dáil for
Democratic Left. Before the parties merged,
she was Democratic Left spokesperson on
Health and Children; Justice, Equality and Law
Reform; Arts, Heritage, Gaeltacht and the
Islands.

She was Minister of State at the Department
of the Environment, with special responsibility
for Housing and Urban Renewal, 1994–97.
Democratic Left spokesperson on Agriculture
and Food, Equality and Law Reform and
Health 1993–94. Chairperson, Task Force on
the Needs of the Travelling Community 1993.

Liz McManus won the Hennessy/New Irish
Writing Award, the Listowel Award and the
Irish PEN Award for her fiction. In 1990 she
published her first novel, *Acts of Subversion*,
which was nominated for the Aer Lingus/*Irish
Times* Award for new writing.

Billy Timmins (FG)

Home Address
Sruhaun, Baltinglass, Co Wicklow
Constituency Office
Weaver Square, Baltinglass
Telephone
Constituency office (059) 648 1016;
Mobile 087 815 9090
Birth Place/Date
Baltinglass. 1 October 1959
Married
Madeleine Hyland. 2 sons, 3 daughters
Education
Patrician College, Ballyfin, Co Laois; University
College, Galway (BA, Diploma in Public
Relations, Marketing and Advertising)
Occupation
Full-time public representative. Formerly army
officer who served with the United Nations in
Lebanon and Cyprus

Billy Timmins was first elected to the Dáil in
1997, winning the seat previously held by his
father, Godfrey Timmins. He was appointed
Fine Gael spokesperson on Foreign Affairs in
September 2007.

He was party spokesperson on Defence
2004–07, and Agriculture and Food 2002–04.
Party spokesperson on Defence —
Peacekeeping and Humanitarian Relief
1997–2000; Housing 2000–01; Deputy
spokesperson, Justice and Defence 2001–02.

Member, National Economic and Social Forum
2000–02. Member, Wicklow County Council
1999–2004. Won Leinster and All-Ireland club
championship medals in 1990. Hobbies are
sports, reading, hill-walking and history.

Andrew Doyle (FG)

Home Address
Lickeen, Roundwood, Co Wicklow
Constituency Office
2A, The Lower Mall, Wicklow Town,
Co Wicklow
Telephone
Home (0404) 45404; *Office* (0404) 66622;
Fax (0404) 66670; *Mobile* 086 837 0088;
Website www.andrewdoyle.ie
Birth Place/Date
Dublin. 2 July 1960
Married
Ann Smith. 3 sons, 1 daughter
Education
Trooperstown and Rathdrum National
Schools; De La Salle, Wicklow Town;
Rockwell Agriculture College Farm
Apprenticeship Scheme, Farm Management
Diploma
Occupation
Full-time public representative and farmer

Andrew Doyle is a new member of the Dáil.

He was a member of Wicklow County
Council, representing East Wicklow Electoral
Area, from 1999 until his election to the Dáil.
Cathaoirleach of Wicklow County Council,
2005–06.

Member of Wicklow Uplands Council,
Wicklow Working Together and Rathdrum
Community Resources Committee (Acorn).
Member of HSE Regional Health Farm.

Wicklow

	1st Count	2nd Count Transfer of **McKenna, Newell, Ó Síocháin, Tallon** Votes	3rd Count Transfer of **Cawley** Votes	4th Count Transfer of **Doran** Votes
Seats 5 Quota 10,821				
BEHAN, Joe (FF)	9,431	(+242) 9,673	(+283) 9,956	(+267) 10,223
BRADY, John (SF)	3,234	(+71) 3,305	(+78) 3,383	(+168) 3,551
CAWLEY, Evelyn (Ind)	2,246	(+141) 2,387		
de BURCA, Deirdre (GP)	4,790	(+193) 4,983	(+723) 5,706	(+128) 5,834
DORAN, Pat (Ind)	2,841	(+52) 2,893	(+116) 3,009	
DOYLE, Andrew (FG)	6,961	(+109) 7,070	(+209) 7,279	(+235) 7,514
FITZGERALD, Pat (FF)	5,029	(+120) 5,149	(+44) 5,193	(+368) 5,561
KELLY, Nicky (Lab)	3,857	(+44) 3,901	(+34) 3,935	(+362) 4,297
McKENNA, Carmel (Ind)	365			
McMANUS, Liz* (Lab)	6,751	(+123) 6,874	(+482) 7,356	(+188) 7,544
NEWELL, Norman (Ind)	79			
Ó SÍOCHÁIN, Donal (PD)	903			
ROCHE, Dick* (FF)	10,246	(+227) 10,473	(+201) 10,674	(+422) 11,096
TALLON, Jim (Ind)	120			
TIMMINS, Billy* (FG)	8,072	(+105) 8,177	(+132) 8,309	(+664) 8,973
NON-TRANSFERABLE		40	85	207

Wicklow

5th Count	6th Count	7th Count	8th Count	9th Count
Transfer of **Brady** Votes	Transfer of **Kelly** Votes	Transfer of **Roche** Surplus	Transfer of **de Burca** Votes	Transfer of **McManus** Surplus
(+669) 10,892				
(+896) 6,730	*(+401)* 7,131	*(+13)* 7,144		
(+266) 7,780	*(+451)* 8,231	*(+19)* 8,250	*(+1,035)* 9,285	*(+917)* 10,202
(+183) 5,744	*(+1,383)* 7,127	*(+144)* 7,271	*(+500)* 7,771	*(+245)* 8,016
(+405) 4,702				
(+486) 8,030	*(+1,619)* 9,649	*(+29)* 9,678	*(+3,440)* 13,118	
(+184) 9,157	*(+447)* 9,604	*(+70)* 9,674	*(+757)* 10,431	*(+857)* 11,288
462	401		1,412	278

Summary of Returns (Dáil General Election 2007)

	Fianna Fáil			Fine Gael			Labour		
	No. of 1st prefer-ences	% of 1st prefer-ences	% of increase/ decrease	No. of 1st prefer-ences	% of 1st prefer-ences	% of increase/ decrease	No. of 1st prefer-ences	% of 1st prefer-ences	% of increase/ decrease
Carlow–Kilkenny	32,272	47.70%	-2.50%	20,031	29.61%	7.73%	6,324	9.35%	-3.81%
Cavan–Monaghan	24,851	37.77%	2.83%	20,528	31.20%	6.03%	796	1.21%	0.32%
Clare	24,824	44.03%	-1.36%	19,854	35.21%	9.75%	892	1.58%	-1.87%
Cork East	20,431	37.97%	-3.34%	16,602	30.85%	1.76%	11,249	20.91%	-0.07%
Cork North-Central	15,136	35.74%	-5.74%	11,674	27.57%	7.18%	5,221	12.33%	0.56%
Cork North-West	24,732	53.05%	2.99%	17,913	38.42%	-3.66%	2,288	4.91%	-1.97%
Cork South-Central	26,154	44.28%	-4.29%	16,782	28.41%	9.01%	5,466	9.25%	3.31%
Cork South-West	18,093	42.57%	3.10%	15,299	36.00%	3.67%	4,095	9.64%	0.51%
Donegal North-East	19,374	50.26%	0.87%	8,711	22.60%	1.59%	703	1.82%	-0.99%
Donegal South-West	20,136	50.53%	8.44%	9,167	23.00%	-2.42%	1,111	2.79%	-0.24%
Dublin Central	15,398	44.45%	4.88%	3,302	9.53%	-1.52%	4,353	12.57%	0.39%
Dublin Mid-West	12,321	33.00%	0.94%	4,480	12.00%	0.49%	4,075	10.91%	1.91%
Dublin North	22,998	42.09%	3.85%	7,667	14.03%	2.22%	5,256	9.62%	-4.85%
Dublin North-Central	16,029	44.02%	-6.03%	9,303	25.55%	8.54%	2,649	7.27%	-3.22%
Dublin North-East	13,864	39.69%	-0.42%	8,012	22.94%	7.58%	5,294	15.16%	-1.07%
Dublin North-West	15,124	48.84%	1.31%	3,083	9.96%	2.00%	6,286	20.30%	3.51%
Dublin South	25,298	41.33%	4.69%	16,686	27.26%	7.48%	6,384	10.43%	0.94%
Dublin South-Central	15,725	33.08%	-1.24%	6,838	14.39%	-2.55%	10,041	21.13%	1.41%
Dublin South-East	9,720	28.72%	1.69%	6,311	18.65%	2.58%	5,636	16.65%	4.22%
Dublin South-West	16,355	39.27%	0.59%	8,346	20.04%	7.39%	8,325	19.99%	0.19%
Dublin West	12,726	37.45%	2.82%	6,928	20.39%	8.07%	5,799	17.06%	4.36%
Dún Laoghaire	20,471	34.87%	4.58%	13,832	23.56%	8.51%	9,392	16.00%	-6.68%
Galway East	22,137	39.68%	-7.10%	21,832	39.13%	7.61%	1,747	3.13%	3.13%
Galway West	20,468	37.15%	-4.18%	11,235	20.39%	3.49%	6,086	11.05%	0.51%
Kerry North	12,304	31.30%	1.15%	12,697	32.30%	10.21%	4,287	10.90%	-11.49%
Kerry South	15,868	40.65%	-3.98%	9,795	25.09%	7.43%	5,263	13.48%	-1.00%
Kildare North	17,851	39.50%	-3.71%	9,590	21.22%	3.68%	7,882	17.44%	-3.94%
Kildare South	17,425	50.37%	3.94%	5,939	17.17%	-0.59%	7,154	20.68%	2.16%
Laois–Offaly	40,307	56.38%	5.08%	19,560	27.36%	4.34%	1,703	2.38%	-0.15%
Limerick East	24,042	48.69%	8.75%	12,601	25.52%	-2.32%	5,098	10.33%	1.07%
Limerick West	19,097	47.23%	-6.20%	16,153	39.95%	-1.70%	2,277	5.63%	5.63%
Longford–Westmeath	22,599	41.15%		16,999	30.95%		9,692	17.65%	
Louth	23,181	42.14%	-1.44%	16,159	29.37%	9.14%	2,739	4.98%	-1.71%
Mayo	17,459	24.46%	-15.52%	38,426	53.83%	16.24%	831	1.16%	1.16%
Meath East	18,735	43.56%		11,129	25.88%		5,136	11.94%	
Meath West	20,874	51.59%		11,745	29.03%		1,634	4.04%	
Roscommon–South Leitrim	17,897	38.84%		18,031	39.13%		832	1.81%	
Sligo–North Leitrim	16,360	40.97%		15,684	39.27%		1,555	3.89%	
Tipperary North	15,245	34.31%	-8.35%	7,061	15.89%	0.98%	4,561	10.27%	-3.25%
Tipperary South	18,004	46.42%	7.91%	8,200	21.14%	-3.39%	3,400	8.77%	-0.38%
Waterford	23,025	46.49%	0.15%	13,552	27.36%	5.88%	5,610	11.33%	-2.03%
Wexford	28,949	42.19%	2.10%	21,658	31.56%	5.83%	9,445	13.77%	0.53%
Wicklow	24,706	38.05%	6.80%	15,033	23.15%	7.20%	10,608	16.34%	-13.27%
Regional Totals									
Connacht–Ulster	158,682	38.47%	-2.77%	143,614	34.82%	7.37%	13,661	3.31%	0.54%
Dublin	196,029	38.75%	1.62%	94,788	18.74%	4.28%	73,490	14.53%	-0.37%
Rest of Leinster	246,899	45.23%	1.41%	147,843	27.08%	4.87%	62,317	11.42%	-2.28%
Munster	256,955	42.71%	-0.60%	178,183	29.62%	3.92%	59,707	9.92%	-0.80%
Total	**858,565**	**41.56%**	**0.08%**	**564,428**	**27.32%**	**4.84%**	**209,175**	**10.13%**	**-0.65%**

Summary of Returns (Dáil General Election 2007)

Progressive Democrats			Green Party			Sinn Féin			Others		
No. of 1st prefer-ences	% of 1st prefer-ences	% of increase/ decrease	No. of 1st prefer-ences	% of 1st prefer-ences	% of increase/ decrease	No. of 1st prefer-ences	% of 1st prefer-ences	% of increase/ decrease	No. of 1st prefer-ences	% of 1st prefer-ences	% of increase/ decrease
1,073	1.59%	1.59%	5,386	7.96%	-0.19%	2,568	3.80%	0.38%	0	0.00%	-3.20%
0	0.00%	-1.83%	2,382	3.62%	1.84%	13,162	20.01%	2.49%	4,068	6.18%	-11.68%
810	1.44%	1.44%	2,858	5.07%	-0.76%	1,929	3.42%	3.42%	5,218	9.25%	-10.62%
0	0.00%	0.00%	1,572	2.92%	0.44%	3,672	6.82%	1.09%	282	0.52%	0.12%
0	0.00%	-6.92%	1,503	3.55%	0.99%	3,456	8.16%	1.83%	5,357	12.65%	2.10%
0	0.00%	0.00%	1,687	3.62%	3.62%	0	0.00%	0.00%	0	0.00%	-0.99%
1,596	2.70%	2.70%	4,945	8.37%	-0.59%	3,020	5.11%	1.38%	1,105	1.87%	-11.51%
0	0.00%	0.00%	2,860	6.73%	6.73%	2,150	5.06%	-0.80%	0	0.00%	-13.20%
0	0.00%	0.00%	520	1.35%	1.35%	6,733	17.47%	7.53%	2,504	6.50%	-10.35%
0	0.00%	0.00%	589	1.48%	1.48%	8,462	21.23%	10.49%	388	0.97%	-17.75%
193	0.56%	0.56%	1,995	5.76%	1.45%	3,182	9.19%	-5.42%	6,216	17.95%	-0.33%
4,663	12.49%	-7.56%	4,043	10.83%	-1.50%	3,462	9.27%	2.75%	4,295	11.50%	2.98%
1,395	2.55%	2.55%	9,107	16.67%	0.07%	1,454	2.66%	-0.41%	6,764	12.38%	-3.43%
0	0.00%	0.00%	1,891	5.19%	-0.49%	1,375	3.78%	-1.96%	5,169	14.19%	3.16%
749	2.14%	-2.01%	2,349	6.73%	1.08%	4,661	13.34%	3.10%	0	0.00%	-8.24%
0	0.00%	0.00%	853	2.75%	0.43%	4,873	15.74%	-2.54%	745	2.41%	-4.71%
4,045	6.61%	-8.39%	6,768	11.06%	1.61%	1,843	3.01%	-0.92%	180	0.29%	-5.41%
912	1.92%	-1.21%	2,756	5.80%	0.58%	4,825	10.15%	-2.55%	6,434	13.54%	5.57%
4,450	13.15%	-5.64%	4,685	13.84%	-2.39%	1,599	4.72%	-2.67%	1,441	4.26%	2.20%
0	0.00%	0.00%	1,546	3.71%	0.57%	5,066	12.16%	-8.12%	2,014	4.84%	-0.61%
553	1.63%	-6.28%	1,286	3.78%	1.29%	1,624	4.78%	-3.24%	5,066	14.91%	-7.02%
3,959	6.74%	-6.62%	4,534	7.72%	-1.60%	1,292	2.20%	-1.82%	5,233	8.91%	3.64%
3,321	5.95%	5.95%	1,057	1.89%	-0.17%	1,789	3.21%	-0.49%	3,911	7.01%	-8.93%
8,868	16.10%	3.58%	3,026	5.49%	1.06%	1,629	2.96%	-2.66%	3,784	6.87%	-1.80%
0	0.00%	0.00%	747	1.90%	1.90%	8,030	20.43%	-3.82%	1,248	3.17%	2.05%
0	0.00%	0.00%	738	1.89%	1.89%	1,375	3.52%	3.52%	5,993	15.35%	-7.87%
983	2.18%	-9.71%	2,215	4.90%	-1.08%	1,103	2.44%	2.44%	5,567	12.32%	12.32%
1,513	4.37%	-7.54%	2,136	6.18%	2.47%	0	0.00%	0.00%	424	1.23%	-0.45%
4,233	5.92%	-8.45%	812	1.14%	0.31%	3,656	5.11%	1.00%	1,220	1.71%	-2.13%
3,354	6.79%	-2.98%	1,296	2.62%	0.79%	2,081	4.21%	4.21%	903	1.83%	-9.53%
1,935	4.79%	4.79%	969	2.40%	-0.26%	0	0.00%	0.00%	0	0.00%	-2.26%
2,298	4.18%		960	1.75%		2,136	3.89%		232	0.42%	
0	0.00%	0.00%	4,172	7.58%	3.43%	8,274	15.04%	0.09%	489	0.89%	-9.51%
296	0.41%	-1.03%	580	0.81%	-0.24%	3,608	5.05%	1.77%	10,186	14.27%	-2.37%
957	2.23%		1,330	3.09%		1,695	3.94%		4,025	9.36%	
0	0.00%		1,011	2.50%		4,567	11.29%		633	1.56%	
0	0.00%		836	1.81%		3,876	8.41%		4,605	9.99%	
0	0.00%		1,209	3.03%		4,684	11.73%		442	1.11%	
634	1.43%	-2.10%	495	1.11%	1.11%	1,672	3.76%	3.76%	14,763	33.23%	7.84%
541	1.39%	1.39%	591	1.52%	1.52%	1,198	3.09%	-0.21%	6,848	17.66%	-6.85%
0	0.00%	-4.59%	1,049	2.12%	-0.80%	3,327	6.72%	0.37%	2,965	5.99%	1.02%
2,162	3.15%	3.15%	802	1.17%	1.17%	5,068	7.39%	-0.83%	532	0.78%	-11.94%
903	1.39%	1.39%	4,790	7.38%	1.50%	3,234	4.98%	2.18%	5,651	8.70%	-5.81%
12,485	3.03%	-0.25%	10,199	2.47%	1.10%	43,943	10.65%	2.64%	29,888	7.25%	-8.64%
20,919	4.14%	-2.96%	41,813	8.27%	0.23%	35,256	6.97%	-1.94%	43,557	8.61%	-0.87%
14,122	2.59%	-1.16%	23,614	4.33%	0.74%	32,301	5.92%	0.26%	18,773	3.44%	-3.83%
8,870	1.47%	-0.60%	21,310	3.54%	1.15%	31,910	5.30%	1.11%	44,682	7.43%	-4.17%
56,396	**2.73%**	**-1.23%**	**96,936**	**4.69%**	**0.85%**	**143,410**	**6.94%**	**0.43%**	**136,900**	**6.63%**	**-4.32%**

Statistics

The 30th Dáil has 166 deputies, the same as the previous Dáil. Of these 117 were outgoing members of the 29th Dáil, including Shane McEntee, elected at a by-election in 2005. 11 were previous members of the House and 38 were new deputies.

New Deputies

Andrews, Chris (FF)
Aylward, Bobby (FF)
Bannon, James (FG)
Behan, Joe (FF)
Brady, Áine (Kitt) (FF)
Brady, Cyprian (FF)
Byrne, Catherine (FG)
Byrne, Thomas (FF)
Calleary, Dara (FF)
Carey, Joe (FG)
Collins, Niall (FF)
Conlon, Margaret (FF)
Connick, Seán (FF)
Coonan, Noel (FG)
Creighton, Lucinda (FG)
D'Arcy, Michael (FG)
Dooley, Timmy (FF)
Doyle, Andrew (FG)
Feighan, Frank (FG)
Fitzpatrick, Michael (FF)
Flanagan, Terence (FG)
Kennedy, Michael (FF)
Lynch, Ciarán (Lab)
McGrath, Mattie (FF)
McGrath, Michael (FF)
McHugh, Joe (FG)
Mansergh, Martin (FF)
O'Brien, Daragh (FF)
O'Donnell, Kieran (FG)
O'Mahoney, John (FG)
O'Sullivan, Christy (FF)
Reilly, James (FG)
Scanlon, Eamon (FF)
Sheahan, Tom (FG)
Sherlock, Seán (Lab)
Tuffy, Joanna (Lab)
Vardakar, Leo (FG)
White, Mary (GP)

Ex-TDs Re-elected

Barrett, Seán (FG)
Burke, Ulick (FG)
Clune, Deirdre (FG)
Creed, Michael (FG)
Flanagan, Charles (FG)
Hayes, Brian (FG)
Kenneally, Brendan (FF)
Kitt, Michael (FF)
O'Rourke, Mary (FF)
Shatter, Alan (FG)
Sheehan, P.J. (FG)

Leading Vote-Getters

The leading vote-getter in the 2007 election was Brian Cowen who won 19,102 votes in the five-seat constituency of Laois–Offaly. However, in terms of percentage of a quota, the leading vote-getter by far was Willie O'Dea in the five-seat Limerick East, with 2.32 quotas. His closest rival was the outgoing Taoiseach, Bertie Ahern, who won 1.84 quotas in the four-seater Dublin Central.

The top ten by votes won were:

Top Ten	Votes
Brian Cowen (FF)	**19,102**
Laois–Offaly	
Willie O'Dea (FF)	**19,082**
Limerick East	
Brendan Smith (FF)	**15,548**
Cavan–Monaghan	
Enda Kenny (FG)	**14,717**
Mayo	
Séamus Brennan (FF)	**13,373**

Dublin South	
Caoimhghín Ó Caoláin (SF)	**13,162**
Cavan–Monaghan	
Michael Lowry (Ind)	**12,919**
Tipperary North	
John Browne (FF)	**12,768**
Wexford	
Bertie Ahern (FF)	**12,734**
Dublin Central	
Jimmy Deenihan (FG)	**12,697**
Kerry North	

The top ten in terms of multiple of quota were:

Top Ten	Quotas
Willie O'Dea (FF)	**2.32**
Limerick East	
Bertie Ahern (FF)	**1.84**
Dublin Central	
Brian Cowen (FF)	**1.60**
Laois–Offaly	
Brian Lenihan (FF)	**1.31**
Dublin West	
Seamus Brennan (FF)	**1.31**
Dublin South	
Jimmy Deenihan (FG)	**1.29**
Kerry North	
Enda Kenny (FG)	**1.24**
Mayo	
Áine Brady (FF)	**1.24**
Kildare North	
Mary Hanafin (FF)	**1.21**
Dún Laoghaire	
Noel Dempsey (FF)	**1.19**
Meath West	

Believe it or not...

The Dáil candidate who polled most first-preference votes but failed to be elected was Joe O'Reilly (FG) who got 9,550 votes on the first count in Cavan–Monaghan. He had 11,238 votes on the final count but lost out to Margaret Conlon of Fianna Fáil. He was subsequently elected to the Seanad.

By contrast, the candidate who was elected with the lowest first-preference total was Cyprian Brady who won 939 votes on the first count in Dublin Central. He was elected on the eighth count with the help of Bertie Ahern's surplus. Mr Brady was an outgoing Senator.

Women Deputies

There were 22 women elected in 2007, precisely the same number as were elected in 2002.

Election	No. of Women Elected
2007	22
2002	22
1997	20
1992	20
1989	13
1987	14
Nov 1982	14
Feb 1982	8
1981	11
1977	5
1973	4
1969	3

Women Elected 2007

TD	Party	Constituency
Brady, Áine	FF	Kildare North
Burton, Joan	Lab	Dublin West
Byrne, Catherine	FG	Dublin South-Central
Clune, Deirdre	FG	Cork South-Central
Conlon, Margaret	FF	Cavan–Monaghan
Coughlan, Mary	FF	Donegal South-West
Creighton, Lucinda	FG	Dublin South-East
Enright, Olwyn	FG	Laois–Offaly
Flynn, Beverley	Ind	Mayo
Hanafin, Mary	FF	Dún Laoghaire
Harney, Mary	PD	Dublin Mid-West
Hoctor, Máire	FF	Tipperary North
Lynch, Kathleen	Lab	Cork North-Central
McManus, Liz	Lab	Wicklow
Mitchell, Olivia	FG	Dublin South
O'Rourke, Mary	FF	Longford–Westmeath
O'Sullivan, Jan	Lab	Limerick East
Shortall, Róisín	Lab	Dublin North-West
Tuffy, Joanna	Lab	Dublin Mid-West
Upton, Mary	Lab	Dublin South-Central
Wallace, Mary	FF	Meath East
White, Mary	GP	Carlow–Kilkenny

Lost Seats

A total of 30 TDs lost their seats in the 2007 election. 12 were Fianna Fáil, 6 PDs, 2 Fine Gael, 1 Labour, 1 Green, 1 Sinn Féin and 7 Independents. Those who lost were:

TD	Party	Constituency
Boyle, Dan	GP	Cork South-Central
Brady, Martin	FF	Dublin North-East
Breen, James	Ind	Clare
Callanan, Joe	FF	Galway East
Callely, Ivor	FF	Dublin North-Central
Carty, John	FF	Mayo
Cassidy, Donie	FF	Longford–Westmeath
Connolly, Paudge	Ind	Cavan–Monaghan
Cowley, Dr Jerry	Ind	Mayo
Crowe, Seán	SF	Dublin South-West
Dennehy, John	FF	Cork South-Central
Ellis, John	FF	Roscommon–South Leitrim
Healy, Seamus	Ind	Tipperary South

Higgins, Joe	Soc P	Dublin West
Keaveney, Cecelia	FF	Donegal North-East
McDowell, Michael	PD	Dublin South-East
McHugh, Paddy	Ind	Galway East
Moynihan, Donal	FF	Cork North-West
Moynihan Cronin, Breda	Lab	Kerry South
Murphy, Catherine	Ind	Kildare North
Murphy, Gerard	FG	Cork North-West
O'Donnell, Liz	PD	Dublin South
O'Donovan, Denis	FF	Cork South-West
O'Malley, Fiona	PD	Dún Laoghaire
O'Malley, Tim	PD	Limerick East
Parlon, Tom	PD	Laois–Offaly
Sexton, Mae	PD	Longford–Westmeath
Smith, Michael	FF	Tipperary North
Twomey, Dr Liam	FG	Wexford
Wilkinson, Ollie	FF	Waterford

Defeated Deputies

A number of prominent politicians lost their seats in the 2007 election, among them the Tánaiste, Michael McDowell. The outgoing Minister for the Office of Public Works, Tom Parlon, was another leading member of the PDs to lose his seat. In all, six of the party's eight TDs were defeated. The most prominent of the 12 Fianna Fáil TDs to lose his seat was the former Minister, Michael Smith. The leader of the Socialist Party and its sole TD, Joe Higgins, was also defeated, as was leading Green Party deputy, Dan Boyle. Catherine Murphy, who won her seat in the Kildare North by-election of 2005, was one of seven Independents to lose out.

Resignations

Two deputies resigned during the 29th Dáil. Charlie McCreevy (FF), Kildare North, left to become Ireland's EU Commissioner. John Bruton (FG), Meath, resigned to take up the position of EU Ambassador to the United States.

Retiring Deputies

Nineteen outgoing deputies did not seek re-election in 2007. They were:

TD	Party	Constituency
Aylward, Liam	FF	Carlow-Kilkenny
Collins, Michael	FF	Limerick West
Davern, Noel	FF	Tipperary South
Dempsey, Tony	FF	Wexford
de Valera, Síle	FF	Clare
Fitzpatrick, Dermot	FF	Dublin Central
Fox, Mildred	Ind	Wicklow
Glennon, Jim	FF	Dublin North
Harkin, Marian	Ind	Sligo–Leitrim
Jacob, Joe	FF	Wicklow
McGrath, Paul	FG	Westmeath
Mitchell, Gay	FG	Dublin South-Central

Pattison, Séamus	Lab	Carlow–Kilkenny
Ryan, Eoin	FF	Dublin South-East
Ryan Seán	Lab	Dublin North
Sherlock, Joe	Lab	Cork East
Wallace, Dan	FF	Cork North-Central
Walsh, Joe	FF	Cork South-West
Wright, G.V.	FF	Dublin North

Dáil Service

The longest-serving deputy in the 30th Dáil is the Fine Gael Leader, Enda Kenny, who was elected at a by-election in 1975, caused by the death of his father, Henry. The Taoiseach, Bertie Ahern, was elected two years later in 1977. Jim O'Keeffe (FG, Cork South-West), Rory O'Hanlon (FF, Cavan–Monaghan), Ruairí Quinn (Lab, Dublin South-East) and Michael Woods (FF, Dublin North-East) were also first elected in 1977.

Occupation of Deputies

Almost all Dáil deputies describe themselves as 'full-time public representatives'. The following list details the occupations in which TDs were engaged before they were elected. As in the last Dáil, teachers were the largest single group.

Education	38
National Teachers	*14*
Second-Level Teachers	*18*
University Lecturers	*3*
Career Guidance	*2*
Pre-School	*1*
Business	22
Lawyers	16
Solicitors	*10*
Barristers	*6*
Clerical and Technical	15
Farmers	14
Accountants	10
Auctioneers	6
Publicans	6
Science and Engineering	5
Doctors	5
Nurses	3
Public Servants	4
Architects	3
Journalists	2
Trade unionists	2
Butcher	1
Army	1

Changed Seats

For the 2007 general election the number of Dáil constituencies was increased by the Constituencies Commission, by one, to 43. Five new constituencies were created, two existing constituencies gained an extra seat and two lost a seat. In the 34 previously existing constituencies, party strengths changed in 22 and remained unchanged in 12.

Changed seats in 22 existing constituencies were:

Carlow–Kilkenny	GP gain from Lab
Cavan–Monaghan	FF gain from Ind
Clare	FG gain from FF
Cork South-Central	FG and Lab gain from FF and GP
Cork South-West	FG gain from FF
Donegal North-East	FG gain from FF
Dublin North	FG gain from Lab
Dublin North-East	FG gain from FF
Dublin South	FG gain from PD
Dublin South-East	FG gain from PD
Dublin South-West	FG gain from SF
Dublin West	FG gain from Socialist
Dún Laoghaire	FG gain from PD
Galway East	FG gain from Ind
Kerry South	FG gain from Lab
Laois–Offaly	FG gain from PD
Limerick East	FG gain from PD
Mayo	FG gain from Ind
Tipperary North	FG gain from FF
Tipperary South	FF gain from Ind
Wexford	FG gain from Ind
Wicklow	FG gain from Ind

Fine Gael also gained seats in the new constituencies of Longford–Westmeath and Roscommon–South Leitrim where the PDs and Fianna Fáil lost seats respectively. Fianna Fáil lost seats in two constituencies where the number of seats was reduced, Dublin North-Central and Cork North-Central, while the party gained seats in two constituencies where the number of seats was increased, Kildare North and Meath East. Labour gained a seat in Dublin Mid-West where the number of seats was increased.

Families

Family political dynasties are a feature of Irish politics. It may not be all that surprising that the de Valera family is still represented in Dáil Éireann, almost 90 years after the First Dáil elected Eamon de Valera as its President, but the number of children, grandchildren and relatives of past TDs in the 30th Dáil is remarkable.

Some families, like the de Valeras, have been in the Dáil for three generations. Others have been more recent arrivals, while others have skipped the generations to throw up politicians in the 21st century.

The most spectacular example of a family dynasty in the 30th Dáil is surely the Kitts, with two brothers and a sister, Micheál, Tom and Áine, all elected for different constituencies. Their father was a TD for East Galway, who won his first election in 1948 and died in 1975 while still a Dáil deputy. He was succeeded as a TD for Galway East by

Michael, while Tom has been a TD for Dublin South since 1982, and Áine was first elected in 2007. The two brothers are junior Ministers. On the night of the election count, Tom joked that there were now more Kitts than PDs in the Dáil.

The Lenihans, with two brothers and an aunt, rival the Kitts as the biggest Dáil family. Brian Lenihan, the Minister for Justice, Conor, a Minister of State, and their aunt, Mary O'Rourke, a former Cabinet Minister and former Deputy Leader of Fianna Fáil, were all elected in May 2007.

The Taoiseach, Bertie Ahern, and his brother, Noel, a junior Minister, are another very successful political family.

There has been a member of the de Valera family in almost ever Dáil since 1918. There was a short break in the record between 1982 and 1987, but in more recent times two grandchildren of Eamon de Valera served in the Dáil and the Cabinet. The current family representative is Eamon Ó Cuív, the Minister for Community, Rural and Gaeltacht Affairs.

Seán Lemass, who succeeded Eamon de Valera as Taoiseach and Leader of Fianna Fail, is represented in the 30th Dáil by his grandson, Seán Haughey, who is also a son of the more recent Fianna Fáil Taoiseach, Charles Haughey.

Another family that goes all the way back to the first election contested by Fianna Fáil is the Blaney family from Donegal. The current deputy, Niall Blaney, is a grandson of Neal Blaney, who was elected as a TD in June 1927, in the first ever election contested by the party. His uncle, Neil Blaney, succeeded to the family seat in 1948, and was in turn succeeded by Niall's father, Harry, from 1997 to 2002.

A new TD in the 30th Dáil continuing a family tradition is Niall Collins from Limerick East, whose grandfather, James Collins, was first elected in 1948. He was succeeded by his son, Gerard, a prominent Fianna Fáil figure for almost three decades, who in turn was succeeded by his brother Michael. Niall Collins is a nephew of Gerard and Michael.

The Andrews cousins, Barry and Chris, are both sons of former TDs and their grandfather, Todd, while never elected to the Dáil, was a prominent figure in Fianna Fáil.

Dr Jimmy Devins from Sligo is an example of a family where politics skipped a generation. His grandfather, James, was a member of the Second Dáil, elected in 1920, but he was killed fighting on the republican side in the Civil War in 1922. Almost exactly 80 years later, his grandson, Jimmy, was first elected to the Dáil and was appointed a junior Minister after the election of May 2007.

Fianna Fáil is not the only party with family traditions. Fine Gael Leader Enda Kenny is the son of Henry, a TD, who was also a junior Minister. His Deputy Leader, Richard Bruton, is the brother of John, the former Taoiseach who left the Dáil in 2005 to take up a post as the European Union Ambassador to the United States.

The newly elected Fine Gael TD for Clare, Joe Carey, is the son of Donal, a former party TD and junior Minister, while Charlie Flanagan, who made a return to the Dáil in 2007, as a TD for Laois–Offaly, is the son of Oliver J. Flanagan, the flamboyant politician who was a TD for more than 40 years. The new Labour TD, Seán Sherlock, is the son of Joe, a TD who was first elected in 1982.

The Statistics
Out of 166 deputies in the 30th Dáil, 31 are the children of former deputies, 25 sons and 6 daughters. This represents an increase of six on the number of children of TDs in the last Dáil. As well as children of former TDs, three more — Eamon Ó Cuív, Jimmy Devins and Niall Collins — are grandchildren of TDs, although none of their parents was a member of the Dáil.

Relationships among Deputies
There are three sets of siblings in the 30th Dáil:

Michael Kitt (FF) Galway East
Tom Kitt (FF) Dublin South
Áine Brady (née Kitt) Kildare North

Brian Lenihan (FF) Dublin West
Conor Lenihan (FF) Dublin South-West

Bertie Ahern (FF) Dublin Central
Noel Ahern (FF) Dublin North-West

Joe McHugh (FG, Donegal North-East) and Olwyn Enright (FG, Laois–Offaly) are husband and wife.

Spoiled Votes
The dubious honour of having the highest number of spoiled votes belongs in 2007 to the five-seat constituency of Wexford, with 827. Two more five-seaters, Dublin South-Central and Cavan–Monaghan followed, with 789 and 760 respectively. There is no discernible pattern to the incidence of spoiled votes, as voters by and large made positive use of the franchise. Among the four-seaters, the smallest county — Louth — amassed an above-average 592 spoiled votes. Voters in the three-seat Dublin West were least inclined to spoil their votes — with the lowest tally of the election, 206.

By-elections to the 29th Dáil

Meath (11 March 2005)

The election was caused by the resignation of John Bruton (FG) in order to take up an appointment as European Union Ambassador to the United States. The seat was won by Shane McEntee (FG) on the fourth count.

Voting		%
Electorate	121,041	
Valid Poll	49,706	41.07
Quota	24,854	

1st Count		%
McEntee, Shane (FG)	16,964	34.13
Cassells, Shane (FF)	16,117	32.42
Reilly, Joe (SF)	6,087	12.25
Hannigan, Dominic (Lab)	5,567	11.20
Cambell, Sirena (PD)	2,679	5.39
O'Byrne, Fergal (Green)	1,590	3.20
Ó Gogáin, Liam (Ind)	702	1.41

Kildare North (11 March 2005)

The election was caused by the resignation of Charlie McCreevy (FF) who was appointed as Ireland's EU Commissioner. The seat was won by Catherine Murphy (Ind) on the fifth count.

Voting		%
Electorate	60,080	
Valid Poll	25,313	38.9
Quota	12,657	

1st Count		%
Murphy, Catherine (Ind)	5,985	23.64
Brady, Áine (FF)	6,201	24.50
Scully, Darren (FG)	4,630	18.29
MacNamara, Paddy (Lab)	4,507	17.81
Walsh, Kate (PD)	2,006	7.92
Power, J.J. (Green)	1,547	6.11
Browne, Gerry (Ind)	226	0.89
Ó Coistin, Seanán (Ind)	211	0.83

Richard Sinnott

Introduction

The Irish electoral system of proportional representation by means of the single transferable vote (PR-STV) provides the voter with opportunities for the expression of his or her political views and preferences that are unmatched under any other electoral system. Another way to put the matter is to say that PR-STV channels far more information and far more complex information about the voters' views into the political system. The key to these expanded opportunities and to the potentially information-rich processes involved is that voters can use their single transferable vote to register their preferences for all candidates and/or parties, at will and without restriction. How the voters avail of these opportunities is at least partially revealed in the complex pattern of vote transfers across the successive counts in the 43 constituencies. The purpose of this section is to trace these patterns and to identify the political behaviour and attitudes that lie beneath them.

Variables, caveats and methodology

The crucial variables in the transfer process are intra-party loyalty, party plumping and support for inter-party alliances. Intra-party loyalty manifests itself (or not) when the votes of a given party are being transferred and a candidate of the same party is still in contention and therefore available to receive transfers (these are generally referred to as 'intermediate transfers'). The extent of such loyalty has a fundamental bearing on the nomination strategies of the parties — if loyalty is low, nominating that extra candidate may not be such a good idea.

Party plumping occurs in a terminal transfer situation, i.e. when the votes of the last remaining candidate of a given party are being transferred and the ballot papers in question contain no further preferences. In this situation the vote becomes non-transferable. This can be seen as an extreme form of party loyalty or commitment.

Support for explicit or implicit inter-party alliances also manifests itself in terminal

Party Loyalty

	FF	FG	Lab	PD	GP	SF	Ind
2002	58.7	62.9	48.1	45.1		57.2	23.8
2007	67.1	63.4	43.4	29.9	61.1		20.4

Plumping

	FF	FG	Lab	PD	GP	SF	Ind
2002	52.0	30.8	15.4	7.5	14.9	20.0	21.0
2007	31.8	35.4	18.2	10.4	13.6	17.3	12.2

Inter-party Alliances

FF

	FF	FG	Lab	PD	GP	SF	Ind
2002		26.2	23.2		23.5	15.0	36.0
2007		12.8	17.1	36.9	23.8		25.8

FG

	FF	FG	Lab	PD	GP	SF	Ind
2002	19.7		47.6	35.9	31.3		21.3
2007	17.3		61.5	24.6		12.3	

Lab

	FF	FG	Lab	PD	GP	SF	Ind
2002	19.8	38.1		18.3	35.1	13.4	24.5
2007	19.4	47.3		4.5	36.8	13.2	24.3

PD

	FF	FG	Lab	PD	GP	SF	Ind
2002	34.6	28.2	24.6		11.8	3.6	13.0
2007	49.0	29.7	10.0		16.3	3.2	6.6

GP

	FF	FG	Lab	PD	GP	SF	Ind
2002	18.1	21.6	37.0	12.5		11.5	25.9
2007	11.0	29.4	41.8	5.6		16.0	21.3

SF

	FF	FG	Lab	PD	GP	SF	Ind
2002	26.6	13.8	20.9	6.7	29.0		26.0
2007	26.8	21.8	26.7	4.7	24.4		23.1

Ind

	FF	FG	Lab	PD	GP	SF	Ind
2002	26.7	27.4	18.6	9.9	20.0	15.6	
2007	25.6	30.0	21.3	8.7	19.4	14.0	

transfers, as in when the votes of an elected or eliminated candidate are being transferred and there is no candidate of the transferring party to receive further preferences. The question then is: what proportion of the transferred vote goes to the candidate(s) of the allied party?

Measuring these variables is a tricky business. The first problem is that the counting process does not reveal all the preferences involved, since the full set of votes of candidates elected on a count other than a first count and the votes of non-eliminated runners-up are not examined for further preferences. The second problem lies in the different ways in which non-transferable votes are handled in the distribution of surplus and eliminated votes. The problem, briefly, is that non-transferable votes are put to one side in the calculation of the destination of surplus transfers, with the consequence that such counts report zero non-transferable votes. The only exception to this rule is when the votes available for transfer are less than the surplus to be transferred. In such cases, a number of non-transferable votes is reported and this number is the difference between the votes that are available for transfers and the surplus to be transferred.

Surpluses that arise on the election of a candidate on a count other than the first count occasionally present a further problem of measurement and interpretation. This additional problem arises because the votes that are examined in order to determine the destination of the surplus consist of the votes in the 'last parcel received' by the elected candidate (i.e. the votes that put him or her over the quota). But this last parcel may have come from a candidate of a different party. It is important in such situations to take this into account as it can result in a very atypical distribution of votes.

This last point is worth an example. In Dublin South-East in the 2007 elections there was an intermediate Fianna Fáil transfer arising from the distribution of the surplus votes of Chris Andrews. The question is: how much of this vote transferred to his FF running mate, Jim O'Callaghan? On the face of it, the answer is: not much, or, to be precise, only 40 per cent. This looks like an instance of very poor party solidarity within Fianna Fáil until one realises that the surplus in question

had arisen from the transfer of the votes of the eliminated Sinn Féin candidate Daithí Doolan. This meant that all of the votes examined to determine the destination of the Andrews surplus had originated as first or second preferences for Sinn Féin. These are not the votes of typical Fianna Fáil voters and it is not surprising that when, as the last parcel received by Andrews, these votes were used to determine the destination of Andrews' surplus, more votes went to non-Fianna Fáil candidates than to the remaining Fianna Fáil candidate. Nor is it surprising that Labour and the Greens did particularly well in the process, obtaining 37 per cent of the transfers between them.

The third and final factor that needs to be taken into account relates to the assessment of support for inter-party alliances. Here it is essential to include only those cases where the transfer is a terminal one and where the other party to the alliance is still in the running. If this latter consideration is not taken into account, there is likely to be a substantial underestimation of support for the inter-party alliance in question.

Given these problems, the methodology of this analysis is as follows. The first step is to set aside all surplus transfers that report a zero non-transferable vote, as their inclusion distorts the calculation of non-transferability and overestimates loyalty and underestimates plumping. The second step

is to recalculate the rate of non-transferability in the case of transfers of surpluses that do report a non-transferable vote. The full rate of non-transferability in such cases is obtained by subtracting the surplus from the last parcel received. The third step is to note all cases of surplus transfers corrected in this way in which the last parcel received is from a party other than the party of the elected candidate. Because of their potentially distorting effect, these are also eliminated from the analysis. Fourthly, support for inter-party alliances is calculated only for those counts in which the allied party is still in contention (with any other party or independent candidate) and so is available to receive transferred votes. Fifthly and finally, counts involving multiple eliminations are set aside as it is not possible to identify the transferring party involved.

Intra-party loyalty

Party loyalty, as measured by the rate at which voters who have expressed a preference for a candidate of a particular party transfer their vote to another candidate of the same party, has declined in recent years. Between, say, 1961 and 1989, Fianna Fáil and Fine Gael loyalty was in the mid to high seventies, occasionally topping 80 per cent. In 2002 this was down to 59 per cent for Fianna Fáil and 63 per cent for Fine Gael. The 2007 election saw Fianna Fáil party loyalty increase to 67 per cent, restoring the

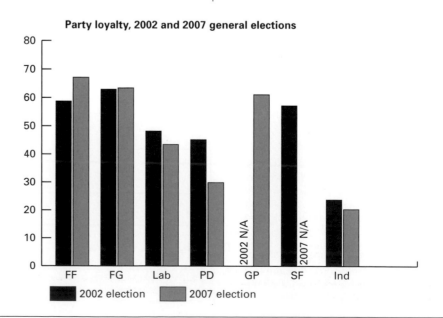

Party loyalty, 2002 and 2007 general elections

slight lead in this regard traditionally enjoyed by Fianna Fáil (FG loyalty in 2007 was 64 per cent).

For Labour in 2007, however, party loyalty was down to 43 per cent (from 48 per cent in 2002 and very substantially down on the in excess of 60 per cent Labour loyalty found in the 1960s and 1970s). However, it should be noted that the measurement of Labour loyalty is subject to varying degrees of reliability because of variations in the number of constituencies in which the party fields more than one candidate.

This limitation applies even more to the smaller parties, which tend, by and large, to nominate only one candidate per constituency. This means that issues of loyalty in the transfer of votes arise only rarely. The Progressive Democrats had just two cases in 2007, both in the constituency of Galway West where they put up three candidates — the incumbent, Noel Grealish, and two others. The ensuing rate of Progressive Democrat intra-party transfers or party loyalty was pretty miserable, amounting to 34 per cent in one case and 25 per cent in the other. As it turned out, the party's leading candidate in Galway West managed to get elected. However, this was due more to the fact that he was ranked fifth in the five-seat constituency on the basis of his own first-preference votes than to the poorly transferred support of his party running mates.

The aggregate level of PD loyal transfers in 2007 (30 per cent) was down substantially on the corresponding figure of 45 per cent in 2002. One might have thought that, as the party vote declined, its continuing support would represent a more ideologically oriented core vote that would have shown more rather than less party loyalty. The fact that, in Galway West, party loyalty went down rather than up is an indication of a retreat to a personalised core vote rather than to an ideological one. This argument would also imply that the low level of Labour Party loyalty noted above reflects widespread personalised rather than ideological support for that party too.

Green Party intra-party transfers held up quite well in the one case in which the issue arose (Dublin North). The 61 per cent loyalty of Green Party supporters in that

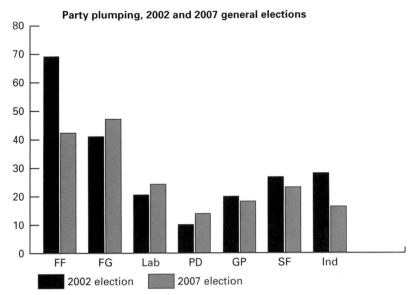

Party plumping, 2002 and 2007 general elections

Legend: 2002 election (black), 2007 election (grey)

constituency delivered 1,160 votes to party leader Trevor Sargent, giving him a very secure margin on the eighth and final count and electing him in second position. Finally, Sinn Féin loyalty cannot be assessed over time as there were no instances in 2007 in which a Sinn Féin candidate was eliminated while another Sinn Féin candidate was still in the running.

Party plumping

As we have seen, party plumping is an extreme form of party loyalty in which the voter allows his or her vote to become non-transferable rather than transfer it to another party. Historically this transfer pattern was particularly widespread among Fianna Fáil voters, who, from the mid-1950s to the mid-1970s, registered party-plumping rates in the high seventies. Fianna Fáil plumping declined to around 60 per cent in the mid-1980s. The main finding regarding party plumping in this analysis of the 2007 election is that Fianna Fáil plumping is down to 32 per cent (from 52 per cent in 2002). This is similar to the current rate of FG plumping (31 per cent in 2002 and 35 per cent in 2007) and reflects an on-going process in which Fianna Fáil is reorienting its electoral strategy in the direction of both giving and aiming to receive more transfer votes.

Supporters of the smaller parties are least likely to plump for their own party; only between one-fifth and one-sixth do so, the

rate falling to one in ten or less among Progressive Democrat supporters. If voters don't plump for a particular party, and clearly most voters now don't, the question is: which parties transfer to which?

Inter-party alliances

Let's start with the explicit pre-election alliance that was clearly in place for the 2007 election — that between Fine Gael and Labour. Fine Gael voters certainly endorsed the pact, 62 per cent of them transferring to Labour when the opportunity presented itself. This is a bit below Fine Gael endorsement of the 1973 pact but it stands up well when judged against the Fine Gael intra-party transfer rate noted earlier. It was also up substantially on the 48 per cent FG to Labour transfer in 2002.

Labour voters didn't quite reciprocate, yielding instead a transfer to Fine Gael (when FG candidates were still in contention) of 47 per cent, which was, however, a bit better than the 38 per cent figure in 2002. The problem for Labour supporters in many of these counts was the counter attraction of the Green Party. Where the Greens were in contention (though not necessarily pitched against Fine Gael), they received 37 per cent of Labour transfers. But this was not a sudden surge of Labour to the new green politics; the Labour to Green transfer in 2002 was 37 per cent.

Transfer Analysis

Inter-party alliances

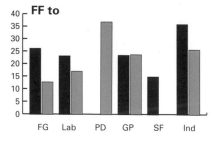

FF to

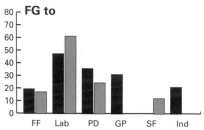

FG to

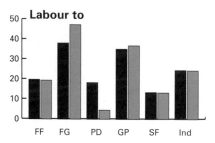

Labour to

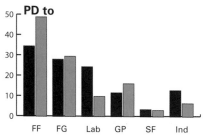

PD to

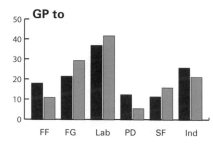

GP to

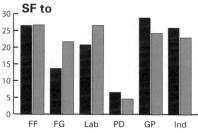

SF to

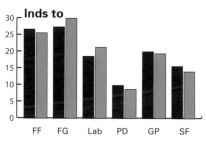

Inds to

■ 2002 election

■ 2007 election

Michael McDowell's 'One-party government — no thanks' slogan in 2002 may have kept PD to Fianna Fáil transfers relatively low (35 per cent) in that election, in which, it must be remembered, the two parties constituted the incumbent government. Whatever the explanation, the willingness of PD voters to transfer to Fianna Fáil increased substantially between the two elections (35 to 49 per cent). Some affinity between the Progressive Democrats and Fine Gael is also evident, the latter receiving 28 and 32 per cent of PD transfers in 2002 and 2007 respectively.

Fianna Fáil voters were less enthusiastic about the implicit alliance with the PDs, only 37 per cent transferring to PD candidates when that was possible. After that, the Fianna Fáil vote went in a variety of directions, the most notable features being the one-quarter going to the Greens (same as in 2002) and the fact that Fianna Fáil to Fine Gael and Fianna Fáil to Labour transfers were both down on 2002. This latter feature suggests a greater perception by Fianna Fáil voters that the 2007 election was a clear-cut contest between two blocks — themselves and the Alliance for Change.

Labour was definitely a pole of attraction for transferring Green voters (as it had also been in 2002); 37 and 42 per cent of Green votes transferred to Labour in 2002 and 2007 respectively. In the light of the pivotal role that the Greens played in the post-election formation of the FF–GP–PD government, it is striking that only 11 per cent of Green voters transferred to Fianna Fáil and that this was down from 18 per cent in 2002. And, while Green to FF transfers were down 7 points, Green to FG transfers were up 7 points (22 per cent in 2002 and 29 per cent in 2007).

With the notable exception of the PDs, all parties benefited from Sinn Féin terminal transfers and to rather similar degrees — SF transfers to parties other than the PDs ranged from 22 per cent to Fine Gael to 27 per cent to Labour and to Fianna Fáil. Sinn Féin to PD transfers were a mere 5 per cent; but then the PDs did badly from all the so-called left-wing parties — 5 per cent as we have seen from Sinn Féin, 5 from Labour and 6 from the Green Party. All of these numbers were down on 2002, perhaps in response to the PD leader's 2007 slogan of 'Left-wing government — no thanks'.

There is, in short, much to ponder in the complex evidence of the transfer patterns generated by the counting process in PR-STV. Whether looked at from the perspective of the parties or the perspective of the voters, analysing them provides a reminder of the amount of information about voters' preferences, attitudes and behaviour that the Irish electoral system manages to funnel into the political process.

The assistance of James McBride, Director of the Irish Social Science Data Archive, in preparing the data tables and graphs is gratefully acknowledged.

Richard Sinnott is Professor of Political Science in the School of Politics and International Relations at University College, Dublin

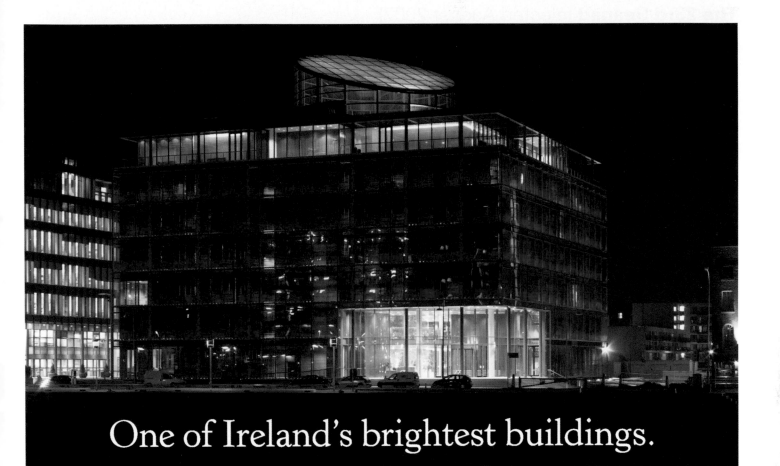

One of Ireland's brightest buildings.

Many people think of "lawyers" and "innovation" as mutually exclusive concepts.

At McCann FitzGerald, however, we see things differently.

We believe that our clients come to us for our thinking as much as for our know-how.

For example, we've not only represented many clients in disputes before the new commercial court; we're also playing a key role in drafting revised rules of procedure for all courts; and we're now working with the Courts Service on the most ambitious court project since the foundation of the State, namely, the new criminal court complex.

We've acted for Fortis in their historic joint venture with An Post; and we've worked with the Irish Bankers Federation to draft new legislation, the first of its type in Europe, enabling the issue of covered bonds.

As lawyers for the National Roads Authority, we've helped create the legal framework for the largest infrastructure programme in Ireland underpinned by a pioneering public private partnership scheme.

We've played a key role in the ground-breaking flotations of Aer Lingus and Smurfit Kappa; and we're at the forefront of private equity activity in Ireland, having acted in many of the most significant transactions of recent years, including the Statoil, SWS, Setanta and TV3 deals.

Recently, we moved from the IFSC to our new headquarters at Riverside One, a landmark building commissioned and designed to give us the infrastructure, technology and – most of all – head space we require to serve our clients over the coming years.

If you'd like to find out more about our way of thinking, please call Ronan Molony on +353 1 829 0000, or email ronan.molony@mccannfitzgerald.ie.

McCann FitzGerald

Dublin - Belfast - London - Brussels

The 23rd Seanad (elected August 2007)

Fianna Fáil	28	Green Party	2
Fine Gael	14	Sinn Fein	1
Labour	6	Others	7
Progressive Democrats	2		

	Senator	Whip	Panel/Constituency
	Bacik, Ivana	Ind	University of Dublin
	Boyle, Dan	GP	Taoiseach's nominee
*	Bradford, Paul	FG	Agricultural
	Brady, Martin	FF	Taoiseach's nominee
*	Burke, Paddy	FG	Agricultural
	Butler, Larry	FF	Industrial and Commercial
	Buttimer, Jerry	FG	Labour
*	Callanan, Peter	FF	Agricultural
	Callely, Ivor	FF	Taoiseach's nominee
	Cannon, Ciaran	PD	Taoiseach's nominee
	Carty, John	FF	Agricultural
	Cassidy, Donie	FF	Labour
	Corrigan, Maria	FF	Taoiseach's nominee
*	Coghlan, Paul	FG	Industrial and Commercial
*	Cummins, Maurice	FG	Labour
	Daly, Mark	FF	Administrative
	De Burca, Deirdre	GP	Taoiseach's nominee
	Doherty, Pearse	SF	Agricultural
	Donohoe, Paschal	FG	Administrative
	Ellis, John	FF	Taoiseach's nominee
*	Feeney, Geraldine	FF	Labour
	Fitzgerald, Frances	FG	Labour
*	Glynn, Camillus	FF	Administrative
*	Hanafin, John Gerard	FF	Labour
	Hannigan, Domnic	Lab	Industrial and Commercial
	Harris, Eoghan	Ind	Taoiseach's nominee
	Healy-Eames, Fidelma	FG	Labour
	Keaveney, Cecilia	FF	Cultural and Educational
	Kelly, Alan	Lab	Agricultural
*	Kett, Tony	FF	Administrative
*	Leyden, Terry	FF	Labour
*	MacSharry, Marc	FF	Industrial and Commercial
	McDonald, Lisa	FF	Taoiseach's nominee
*	McCarthy, Michael	Lab	Labour
	McFadden, Nicky	FG	Administrative
*	Moylan, Pat	FF	Agricultural
	Mullen, Rónán	Ind	National University of Ireland
*	Norris, David Patrick Bernard	Ind	University of Dublin
	Ó Domhnaill, Brian	FF	Taoiseach's nominee
	O'Malley, Fiona	PD	Taoiseach's nominee
*	Ó Murchú, Labhrás	FF	Cultural and Educational
*	O'Brien, Francis	FF	Agricultural
	O'Donovan, Denis	FF	Industrial and Commercial
	O'Reilly, Joe	FF	Industrial and Commercial
*	Ormonde, Ann	FF	Industrial and Commercial
*	O'Toole, Joseph John	Ind	National University of Ireland
*	Phelan, John Paul	FG	Agricultural
*	Phelan, Kieran	FF	Industrial and Commercial
	Prendergast, Phil	Lab	Labour
*	Quinn, Feargal	Ind	National University of Ireland
	Regan, Eugene	FG	Agricultural
*	Ross, Shane Peter Nathaniel	Ind	University of Dublin
	Ryan, Brendan	Lab	National University of Ireland
	Twomey, Liam	FG	Cultural and Educational
*	Walsh, Jim	FF	Agricultural
	White, Alex	Lab	Cultural and Educational
*	White, Mary M.	FF	Industrial and Commercial
*	Wilson, Diarmuid	FF	Administrative

Voting in the Seanad elections took place after the general election. The 60-member Upper House was filled by 43 senators elected by the vocational panels, six elected by the graduates of the National University of Ireland and the University of Dublin, and 11 nominated by the Taoiseach.

Of the seats on the vocational panels Fianna Fáil won 28, Fine Gael 14, Labour 6 and Sinn Féin 1. The six university members were all elected as Independents although one, Ivana Bacik, is a member of the Labour Party. Of the Taoiseach's 11, 6 take the Fianna Fáil whip and 1 is Independent, 2 are Progressive Democrats and 2 Greens.

In the list, an asterisk denotes an outgoing senator. There were 25 re-elected or re-nominated senators; 10 had lost their Dáil seats in the 2007 general election.

Tomorrow's leaders today

Excellence, Innovation and Regional Engagement

The University of Ulster is a dynamic, modern and progressive University with four campuses throughout Northern Ireland, at Coleraine, Jordanstown, Derry and Belfast, as well as Campus One, its eLearning operation.

Through our teaching and learning programmes, research and knowledge transfer, and in our work with business, industry, and the public and not-for-profit sectors, we make a significant contribution to the economic, social and cultural development of the region.

Each year, 6,500 University of Ulster graduates enter the workplace or pursue further study. We have over 127,000 graduates in 116 countries, including 11,000 in the Republic of Ireland.

If you want to learn more about the University or how we can help you, contact us on +44 (0)8 700 400 700 or email online@ulster.ac.uk.

Courses | Research | Working with Business and the Community

t. +44 (0)8 700 400 700 | online@ulster.ac.uk | www.ulster.ac.uk

Cultural and Educational Panel

Elected (5 Seats)

Alex White (Lab)	7th Count
Liam Twomey (FG)	12th Count
Cecilia Keaveney (FF)	14th Count
Labhrás Ó Murchú (FF)*	14th Count
Ann Ormonde (FF)*	15th Count

Candidates

Name	(County, Party)	Vote (1st Pref)
Nominating Bodies Sub-Panel		
Browne, Fergal	(Carlow, FG)	66
Cooney, Fintan	(Westmeath, FG)	31
Corcoran Kennedy, Marcella	(Offaly, FG)	36
Costello, Tom	(Galway, Lab)	37
Kelly, Tom	(Meath, GP)	0
Mac Eochaidh, Colm	(Dublin, FG)	45
McLaughlin, Maureen	(Donegal, Ind)	1
Merrigan, Michael	(Dublin, Ind)	10
Mooney, Paschal Canice*	(Leitrim, FF)	89
Ní Fhatharta, Connie	(Galway, FF)	45
Ó Murchú, Labhrás*	(Tipperary, FF)	128
Ormonde, Ann*	(Dublin, FF)	115
Oireachtas Sub-Panel		
Hoy, Kevin	(Dublin, FF)	1
Keaveney, Cecilia	(Donegal, FF)	131
Slowey, Terence	(Donegal, FG)	81
Twomey, Liam	(Wexford, FG)	95
White, Alex	(Dublin, Lab)	161

Alex White (Lab)

Address 1 Main Street, Rathfarnham, Dublin 14
Tel. (01) 490 3889; *Web* www.alexwhite.ie
b. 3 December 1958
m. Mary Corcoran. 2 children
Educ. Chanel College, Coolock; Trinity College, Dublin; King's Inns
Occ. Barrister. Formerly RTÉ producer
New Senator. Unsuccessful Dáil candidate for Dublin South in 2007 election. Elected to South Dublin CC 2004, Deputy Mayor, 2006–07. Producer, *The Late Late Show* 1990–94. Member, International Commission for Trade Union Rights, Irish Society for Labour Law.

Liam Twomey (FG)

Address Rosslare Medical Centre, Rosslare Strand, Co Wexford
Tel. *Office* (053) 32800; *Mobile* 086 826 7940
b. Cork. 3 April 1967
m. Elizabeth O'Sullivan. 2s
Educ. St Finbarr's, Farranferris, Cork; Trinity College, Dublin (MB, BCH, BAO, BA) MICGP; Diploma Geriatric Medicine
Occ. Public representative. Medical doctor
New Senator. Elected to Dáil in 2002 as Independent. Joined Fine Gael later, defeated in 2007 general election. Member, Irish Medical Organisation (Chairperson of Wexford Branch). PRO for Co Wexford of MICGP.

Cecilia Keaveney (FF)

Address Loreto, Moville, Co Donegal
Tel. *Office* (077) 82177; *Fax* (077) 82832
b. Derry. 27 November 1968
Educ. Carndonagh Community School,
Co Donegal; University of Ulster at
Jordanstown (BMus, MPhil)
Occ. Full-time public representative. Formerly
music teacher
New Senator. TD for Donegal North-East
1996–2007. Member, Donegal CC
1995–2003. Her father, Paddy Keaveney, was
an Independent Fianna Fáil deputy 1976–77.

Labhrás Ó Murchú (FF)

Address An Boithrín Glas, Caiseal,
Co Thiobraid Árann
Tel. (062) 61552; *Mobile* 087 252 8747
b. Cashel, Co Tipperary. 14 August 1939
m. Una Ronan
Educ. Cashel CBS
Occ. Director General, Comhaltas Ceoltóirí
Éireann
Senator since 1997. Chairman, Old Irish
Family History Foundation and of
Fondúireacht an Phiarsaigh.

Ann Ormonde (FF)

Address 2 Auburn Road, Dublin 4
Tel. (01) 260 1577; *Mobile* 087 257 2950
b. Kilmacthomas, Co Waterford
Educ. Our Lady's College, Presentation
Convent, Clonmel; UCD (MA, BComm,
HDipEd, Dip Career Guidance)
Occ. Full-time public representative. Formerly
career guidance counsellor
Senator since 1993. Member, Dublin CC,
subsequently South Dublin CC 1985.
Contested general elections between 1987
and 1997.

Agricultural Panel

Elected (11 Seats)

Pearse Doherty (SF)	1st Count
Alan Kelly (Lab)	1st Count
Pat Moylan (FF)*	14th Count
Jim Walsh (FF)*	16th Count
Francis O'Brien (FF)*	17th Count
Paddy Burke (FG)*	20th Count
Peter Callanan (FF)*	22nd Count
Paul Bradford (FG)*	23rd Count
John Paul Phelan (FG)*	23rd Count
Eugene Regan (FG)	27th Count
John Carty (FF)	27th Count

Candidates

Name	(County, Party)	Vote (1st Pref)
Nominating Bodies Sub-Panel		
Bohan, Mary	(Leitrm, FF)	30
Bradford, Paul	(Cork, FG)	54
Burke, Paddy	(Mayo, FG)	71
Byrne, Maria	(Limerick FG)	40
Callanan, Peter	(Cork, FF)	41
Coleman, Alan	(Cork, FF)	26
Colleary, Aidan	(Sligo, FF)	31
Connolly, Domnick	(Roscommon, FG)	15
Foley, Derry	(Tipperary, FG)	11
Kennedy, Roger	(Tipperary, FF)	9
Kiely, Vincent	(Limerick, FF)	22
Kyne, Seán	(Galway, Ind)	23
MacPartlin, Declan	(Wexford, Ind)	22
McGowan, Patrick	(Donegal, FF)	19
Moylan, Pat	(Offaly, FF)	73
Murphy, Eugene	(Roscommon, FF)	18
O'Brien, Francis	(Monaghan, FF)	71
Phelan, Marty	(Laois, FG)	33
Walsh, Jim	(Wexford, FF)	75
Oireachtas Sub-Panel		
Carty, John	(Mayo, FF)	47
Comiskey, Michael	(Leitrim, FG)	30
Doherty, Pearse	(Donegal, SF)	103
Hunt, Bridie	(Mayo, FF)	0
Kelly, Alan	(Tipperary, Lab)	96
O'Connor, Tomas	(Kerry, FF)	0
Phelan, John Paul	(Kilkenny, FG)	46
Regan, Eugene	(Dublin, FG)	38
Wilkinson, Ollie	(Waterford, FF)	28

Pearse Doherty (SF)

Address Margheraclogher, Derrybeg, Letterkenny, Co Donegal
Tel. *H* (074) 953 2832; *Mobile* 086 381 7747
b. Glasgow, Scotland. 6 July 1977
m. Róisín Doherty. 2s
Educ. Pobal Scoil Gaoth Dobhair; Bolton St DIT (Civil Engineering)
Occ. Public representative. Formerly civil engineer
New Senator. Member, Donegal CC for Glenties Area (2004-07). Contested General Election in Donegal South-West in 2002 and 2007 and European election in 2004.

Alan Kelly (Lab)

Address Castletown, Portroe, Nenagh, Co Tipperary
Tel. 087 679 2859
b. 13 July 1975
m. Regina O'Connor
Educ. Nenagh CBS; University College, Cork (BA Hons: M.Phil Hons Political History); Boston College (Certificate in Political Leadership); University College, Dublin (MBS in eCommerce)
Occ. eBusiness Co-ordinator/Manager with Bord Fáilte/Fáilte Ireland
New Senator. Founder of Jim Kemmy Branch of Labour Party in UCC 1995; Chairperson, Labour Youth 2000; member, General Council 2001;

Director, Tom Johnson Summer School 2001–02. Author, *A Political History of County Tipperary 1916–1997*. Winner of numerous hurling, Gaelic football and rugby medals.

Pat Moylan (FF)

Address Harbour Road, Banagher, Co Offaly
Tel. *H* (0509) 51113; *Fax* (0509) 51858; *Mobile* 087 257 4476
b. Banagher. 12 September 1946
m. Mary Dunne. 3s, 1d
Educ. Banagher Vocational School
Occ. Public representative. Farmer
Member of the Seanad since 1997 when elected on Agricultural panel, Taoiseach's nominee 2002–07. Member, Offaly CC 1975–2003; Chairperson 1991–92, 1992–93.

Jim Walsh (FF)

Address Mountgarrett Castle, New Ross, Co Wexford
Tel. *H* (051) 421 771; *Mobile* 086 600 8155
b. May 1947
m. Marie Furlong. 1s 2d
Educ. New Ross CBS
Occ. Former company director, farmer
Senator since 1997. Member, Wexford CC 1979–2003 (Chairperson, 1992–93); member, New Ross UDC 1974–2003; Chairperson 8 times

Francis O'Brien (FF)

Address Corwillian, Latton, Castleblayney, Co Monaghan
Tel. *H* (042) 974 1152; *Mobile* 086 383 1055
b. Ballybay, Co Monaghan. 7 April 1943
m. Gertrude Smith. 3s 1d
Educ. Drumfreehan National School, Latton, Co Monaghan
Occ. Public representative. Farmer
Senator since 1989. Member, Monaghan CC 1979–2003 (Chairperson, 1986–87); East Border Region Committee from 1987 (Chair, 1991–92).

Paddy Burke (FG)

Address Knockaphunta, Westport Road, Castlebar, Co Mayo
Tel. *H* (094) 902 2568
b. Castlebar. 15 January 1955
m. Dolores Barrett
Educ. Ballinafad College, Castlebar; Rockwell Agricultural College, Co Tipperary; Franciscan Brothers Agricultural College, Mount Bellew, Co Galway
Occ. Public representative. Self-employed
Senator since 1993. Leas-Chathaoirleach of last Seanad, September 2002–2007. Member, Mayo CC 1993–2003. Member, Mayo–Galway Regional Development Organisation.

Peter Callanan (FF)

Address Ballymountain, Innishannon, Co Cork
Tel. *H* (021) 477 5192; *Mobile* 086 824 4770
b. Clonakilty, Co Cork
m. Sheila Harrington. 4s 2d
Educ. Mount Mellary College, Co Waterford
Occ. Farmer
Senator since 1997. Member, Cork CC 1979–2003 (Vice-Chairperson, 1989–90). Member, local farming and sporting organisations.

Paul Bradford (FG)

Address Mourne Abbey, Mallow, Co Cork
Constituency Office Church View, Sandfield, Mallow
Tel. *H* (022) 29375; *O* (022) 42181; *Web* www.paulbradford.ie
b. Mallow. December 1963
Educ. Patrician Academy, Mallow
Occ. Public representative. Farmer
Senator since 2002 and previously 1987–89; TD 1989–2002. Contested Cork-East Dáil constituency in 2007 and 2002. FG spokesperson on Foreign Affairs in last Seanad. Chairperson of the Oireachtas Sub-Committee on Human Rights in last Dáil and Seanad.

Agricultural Panel

John Paul Phelan (FG)

Address Smithstown, Tullogher, Mullinavat, Co Kilkenny
Tel. *O* (056) 779 3210; *Fax* (056) 779 3211; *Mobile* 087 805 2088
b. Waterford. 27 September 1978
Educ. Good Counsel College, New Ross, Co Wexford; Waterford Institute of Technology (BBS)
Occ. Full-time public representative
Elected to Seanad 2002 as youngest senator. Member, Kilkenny CC 1999–2003. Seanad spokesman on Finance and member, Joint Oireachtas Committee on Finance and the Public Service during last Dáil and Seanad.

Eugene Regan (FG)

Address Brighton Lodge, Brighton Avenue, Monkstown, Co Dublin
Tel. *H* (01) 280 9417; *O* 086 818 6733; *Mobile* 087 243 2704;
Email eugeneregansc@eircom.net
b. Meath. March 1952
m. Kista Bang. 2d
Educ. University College Dublin (BA, M.Econ); Vrije Universiteit, Brussels, Belgium (Masters in International Law); King's Inns, Dublin (Barrister-at-Law); Irish Management Institute Dublin (Dip Applied Finance)

Occ. Senior Counsel
New Senator. Member, Cabinet, EU Commissioner Peter Sutherland, 1985–88; stagiaire EEC Commissioner Patrick Hillery's office 1974–75; economist IFA, 1975–76; Director, IFA Brussels office 1976–79. Barrister 1995–2005, SC 2005. Elected Dún Laoghaire-Rathdown CC 2004 (Cathaoirleach, 2006–07).

John Carty (FF)

Address Carrowmore, Knock, Co Mayo
Constituency Office Ballyhaunis Road, Claremorris, Co Mayo
Tel. *H* (094) 938 8149; *O* (094) 937 2707; *Mobile* 087 298 2661;
Web www.johncarty.ie
b. Knock. 12 August 1950
m. Kathleen Regan. 6s, 2d
Educ. St Patrick's College, Ballyhaunis, Co Mayo; Warrenstown Agricultural College, Co Meath; St Patrick's College, Maynooth (Diploma in Local History)
Occ. Public representative. Formerly Agricultural Officer. Farmer

New Senator. Member of the Dáil for Mayo 2002–07. Member, Joint Oireachtas Committee on Social and Family Affairs (Party Whip) and Joint Oireachtas Committee on Agriculture and Food in 29th Dáil. Member, British–Irish Inter-Parliamentary Body 2002–07. Member, Mayo CC 1999–03.

Labour Panel

Elected (11 Seats)

Geraldine Feeney (FF)*	9th Count
Donie Cassidy (FF)	13th Count
John Hanafin (FF)*	14th Count
Terry Leyden (FF)*	15th Count
Phil Prendergast (Lab)	17th Count
Michael McCarthy (Lab)*	18th Count
Jerry Buttimer (FG)	20th Count
Frances Fitzgerald (FG)	21st Count
Fidelma Healy Eames (FG)	22nd Count
Maurice Cummins (FG)*	23rd Count
Ned O'Sullivan (FF)	23rd Count

Candidates

Name	(County, Party)	Vote (1st Pref)

Nominating Bodies Sub-Panel

Name	(County, Party)	Vote
Cassells, Shane	(Meath, FF)	42
Cuddihy, Paul	(Kilkenny, FG)	21
Cummins, Maurice	(Waterford, FG)	62
Daly, Pat	(Clare, FF)	30
Feeney, Geraldine	(Sligo, FF)	80
Hanafin, John	(Tipperary, FF)	75
Harty, Mary	(Limerick, FG)	25
Leyden, Terry	(Roscommon, FF)	57
McCarthy, Michael	(Cork, Lab)	58
McGinley, Kieran Jack	(Dublin, Ind)	1
O'Donovan, Patrick	(Limerick, FG)	47
O'Reilly, Michael	(Dublin, Ind)	29
O'Sullivan, Ned	(Kerry, FF)	41
Ridge, Katie	(Kildare, FG)	34

Oireachtas Sub-Panel

Name	(County, Party)	Vote
Brady, Martin	(Dublin, FF)	35
Buttimer, Jerry	(Cork, FG)	61
Byrne, Eric	(Dublin, Lab)	48
Cassidy, Donie	(Westmeath, FF)	66
Connolly, Paudge	(Monaghan, Ind)	19
Daly, Jim	(Cork, FG)	14
Fitzgerald, Frances	(Dublin, FG)	54
Healy Eames, Fidelma	(Galway, FG)	48
Lydon, Don	(Dublin, FF)	39
Murnane O'Connor, Jennifer	(Carlow, FF)	25
Prendergast, Phil	(Tipperary, Lab)	65

Geraldine Feeney (FF)

Address 'Ard Caoin', Ballinode, Sligo
Tel. *H* (071) 914 5690; *Mobile* 087 230 6944
b. Tullamore, Co Offaly. 9 September 1957
m. Widowed. 2s, 2d
Educ. Sacred Heart School, Tullamore; UCG
Occ. Public representative. Public relations consultant
Senator since 2002. Member, Oireachtas Joint Committee on Health and Children, in last Seanad. Chairperson, Fianna Fáil Social and Family Affairs Policy Committee. Member, Fianna Fáil national executive. Member, the Medical Council.

Donie Cassidy (FF)

Address Castlepollard, Co Westmeath
Tel. *H* (044) 966 2777; *Mobile* 087 250 7817
b. Castlepollard. 15 September 1945
m. Anne Geraghty. 4s
Occ. Public representative. Businessman
Senator from 1982 to 2002 when he was elected to Dáil for Westmeath constituency but lost seat in 2007 general election. Leader of the Seanad 1997–2002 and from 2007. Member, Joint House Services Committee; Committee of Procedure and Privileges. Member, Westmeath CC 1985–2003 (Chairperson, 1989–90).

Labour Panel

John Hanafin (FF)

Address 10 Rosemount, Clongour, Thurles, Co Tipperary
Tel. *H* (0504) 31560; *Mobile* 087 233 4935
b. Thurles. 27 September 1960
m. Linda Cummins. 2s, 1d
Educ. CBS Thurles; Cistercian College, Roscrea; UCD (BA History and Geography); Marketing Institute of Ireland (Certificate in Marketing); Institute of Public Administration, Dublin
Occ. Public representative. Auctioneer and valuer
Senator since 2002. Member, North Tipperary CC 1998–2003. Brother of Mary Hanafin, TD for Dún Laoghaire since 1997 and Minister for Education and Science since 2004. Son of Des Hanafin, Senator 1969–92 and 1997–2002.

Terry Leyden (FF)

Address Castlecoote, Co Roscommon
Tel. *H* (0903) 26422; *Mobile* 087 797 8922
b. Roscommon. 1 October 1945
m. Mary Margaret O'Connor. 3d, 1s
Educ. Roscommon CBS and Vocational School; NUI Galway (Dip, Politics, Sociology and Economics)
Occ. Public representative. Formerly architectural designer
Senator since 2002 and previously in 1992. TD from 1977 to 1992. Minister of State, Department of Post and Telegraphs and the Department of Transport 1982; Department of

Health. Minister for Trade and Marketing 1989–92. Member, Roscommon CC 1974–2003.

Phil Prendergast (Lab)

Address 6 Marlfield Road, Clonmel, Co Tipperary
Tel *H* (052) 24380; *Mobile* 086 855 5472
b. 1960
m. Ray Prendergast. 2s
Educ. Dip. in Prefessional Development
Occ. Nurse, midwife
New Senator. Unsuccessful candidate in Tipperary South in 2007 general election. Member, Clonmel Corporation 1994–2007 and Tipperary South Riding CC 1999–2007; Mayor of Clonmel, 2003–04. Former member, Workers' and Unemployed Action Group.

Michael McCarthy (Lab)

Address 47 Castle Street, Dunmanway, Co Cork
Tel. *O* (023) 54726; *Mobile* 087 648 1004; *Web* www.michaelmccarthy.ie
b. Bantry, Co Cork. 15 November 1976
m. Nollagh McCarthy
Educ. Coláiste Chairbe, Dunmanway
Occ. Public representative. Formerly pharmaceutical company employee
Senator since 2002. Contested Cork South

Dáil constituency in 2002, 2007. Member, Joint Oireachtas Committee on Agriculture and Food and Joint Committee on Environment and Local Government 2002–2007. Member, Cork CC 1999–2003.

Jerry Buttimer (FG)

Address 25 Benvoirlich Estate, Bishopstown, Cork
Tel. *H* (021) 454 1923; *Mobile* 086 235 6892
b. Cork. March 1967
Educ. Maynooth College; UCC
Occ. Public representative. Secondary teacher and Director of adult education
New senator. Contested Dáil election in Cork South Central in 2007. Former youth and development officer, Cork County GAA Board; member, Croke Park's marketing committee; chairman, Bishopstown GAA club. Member, Cork City Council 2004–07.

Frances Fitzgerald (FG)

Address 116 Georgian Village, Castleknock, Dublin 15
Tel. *Mobile* 087 257 9026
b.Croom, Co Limerick. August 1950
m. Michael Fitzgerald. 3s
Educ. Sion Hill, Blackrock, Co. Dublin; UCD; London School of Economics (BSocSc; MSc in Social Administration and Social Work)

Occ. Public representative. Formerly social worker
New Senator. Former Dáil TD for Dublin South East 1992–2002; contested Dublin Mid-West in 2007 general election. Member, Fine Gael front bench for 8 years up to 2002. Chairperson, Council for the Status of Women 1989–92. Appointed Fine Gael leader in the Seanad in September 2007.

Fidelma Healy-Eames (FG)

Address Maree, Oranmore, Co Galway
Tel. *H* (091) 792 017
b. 14 July 1962
m. Michael Eames. 1s, 1d
Educ. Carysfort College, Blackrock, Co Dublin; Western Connecticut State University; NUI Galway (B.Ed, MSc, PhD)
Occ. Businesswoman. Formerly primary teacher, lecturer
New Senator. Unsuccessful candidate in Galway West in 2002, 2007 general elections. Member, Galway CC 2004–07. Member, GMIT Governing Body; Western Rail Committee; Galway Arts Centre Board; Director Galway Airport.

Maurice Cummins (FG)

Address 34 Ursuline Court, Waterford
Tel. *H* (051) 855 486
b. Waterford. 25 February 1953
m. Anne O'Shea. 1s, 1d
Educ. De La Salle, Newtown, Waterford
Occ. Public representative. Formerly claims manager
Senator since 2002. Fine Gael Whip, Spokesperson on Justice and Law Reform in last Seanad. Member of Joint Committee of Justice, Equality, Defence and Women's Rights, Joint House Services Committee, Seanad Committee on Procedures and Privileges 2002–07. Mayor of Waterford, 1995–96.

Ned O'Sullivan (FF)

Address Cahirdown, Listowel, Co Kerry
Tel. *H* (068) 21831; *Mobile* 087 245 9290
b. Listowel. 25 November 1950
m. Madeleine Murphy. 3 children
Educ. St Patrick's College of Education, Dublin; UCD
Occ. Public representative, draper. Formerly primary teacher
New Senator. Member, Kerry CC 1991–2007 and Listowel Town Council 1985–2007. Member Fianna Fáil National Executive 1995–99. Director Shannon Foynes Port Company; Chairman, North Kerry Patients' Action Group.

Industrial and Commercial Panel

Elected (9 Seats)

Dominic Hannigan (Lab)	1st Count
Marc MacSharry (FF)*	8th Count
Paul Coghlan (FG)	26th Count
Denis O'Donovan (FF)	30th Count
Mary White (FF)*	32nd Count
Larry Butler (FF)	32nd Count
Kieran Phelan (FF *	32nd Count
Paudie Coffey (FG)	35th Count
Joe O'Reilly (FG)	36th Count

Candidates

Name	(County, Party)	Vote (1st Pref)
Nominating Bodies Sub-Panel		
Bailey, John	(Dublin, FG)	9
Breen, Gerry	(Dublin, FG)	22
Bridgett, Gerry	(Kidare, FF)	8
Butler, Larry	(Dublin, FF)	51
Butler, Seamus	(Longford, FF)	10
Cahill, Michael	(Kerry, FF)	39
Coghlan, Paul	(Kerry, FG)	52
Collins, Thomas	(Mayo, FG)	12
Crowe, John	(Clare, FG)	25
Daly, James	(Laois, FG)	16
Dolan, Hugh	(Galway, FF)	17
Finnegan, Edwin	(Dublin, FF)	9
Harrington, Noel	(Cork, FG)	22
Henry, Imelda	(Sligo, FG)	25
Kilbride, Frank	(Longford, FG)	31
MacSharry, Marc	(Sligo, FF)	106
McGloin, Enda	(Leitrim, FG)	21
McHugh, Tom	(Galway, FG)	19
Millington, Gordon Stopford	(Antrim, Ind)	2
Moriarty, Luke	(Dublin, FF)	6
Murphy, Kevin	(Cork, FG)	10
O'Domhnaill, Brian	(Donegal, FF)	21
O'Donoghue, Seamus	(Laois, FG)	22
O'Meara, Pat	(Tipperary, FF)	47
Phelan, Kieran	(Laois, FF)	53
Smyth, Michael	(Monaghan, Ind)	17
Terry, Sheila	(Dublin, FG)	35
Walsh, Dermot	(Dublin, Ind)	1
White, Mary	(Dublin, FF)	53
Oireachtas Sub-Panel		
Callely, Ivor	(Dublin, FF)	13
Coffey, Paudie	(Waterford, FG)	25
Hannigan, Dominic	(Meath, Lab)	109
Hayes, William	(Dublin, FF)	0
Hoade, Mary	(Galway, FF)	40
O'Donovan, Denis	(Cork, FF)	70
O'Reilly, Joe	(Cavan, FG)	36
Scully, Diarmuid	(Limerick, FG)	13

Dominic Hannigan (Lab)

Address 68 Lagavooran Manor, Drogheda, Co Louth
Office Labour Party Advice Centre, Burrows Hall, Golf Links Road, Bettystown, Co Meath
Tel. *O* (041) 988 6307; *Mobile* 087 641 8960; *Web* www.dominichannigan.com
b. 1 July 1965
Educ. UCD (Engineering degree); City University, London (Masters in Transport); University of London (Masters in Finance)
Occ. Public representative. Formerly engineer, planner with Camden Council, London New senator. Unsuccessful candidate in Meath East in 2007 general election. Elected, Meath CC for East Meath area, 2004.

Marc MacSharry (FF)

Address Fatima, Pearse Road, Sligo
Tel. *Mobile* 087 267 4764
b. Dublin. 12 July 1973
m. Marie Murphy. 1s, 1d
Educ. St John's Marist Brothers, Sligo; Castleknock College, Dublin
Occ. Chief Executive, Sligo Chamber of Commerce
First elected to Senate 2002. Party spokesperson on Marine and Natural Resources in last Seanad. Son of Ray MacSharry, TD Sligo–Leitrim 1969–88, Cabinet Minister March–December 1982, 1987–88; MEP 1984–87; EU Commissioner 1988–93.

Paul Coghlan (FG)

Address Ballydowney, Killarney, Co Kerry
Office 95 New Street, Killarney
Tel. *H* (064) 31733; *O* (064) 31892
b. Killarney. June 1944
m. Peggy O'Shea. 2s, 2d
Educ. St Brendan's College, Killarney; De La Salle College, Waterford
Occ. Public representative, auctioneer, businessman
First elected to Seanad 1997. FG spokesperson on Enterprise, Trade and Employment in last Seanad. Former member, Kerry CC, Killarney UDC. Former President Killarney Chamber of Commerce; founding director, Radio Kerry; trustee and former Chairman of Muckross House. Member, Institute of Bankers in Ireland; the Life Insurance Association; and Institute of Professional Auctioneers and Valuers.

Denis O'Donovan (FF)

Address Montrose House, Slip, Bantry, Co Cork
Tel. *H* (027) 51541; *Mobile* 087 254 3806
b. Bantry. 23 July 1955
m. Mary Murphy. 3s, 1d
Educ. Bantry Secondary School; Carrignavar Secondary College; University College, Cork (BCL)
Occ. Public representative. Solicitor

Lost his seat in Cork South-West in 2007 Dáil election. Senator previously 1997–2002, Taoiseach's nominee, 1989–93. Chairman, Joint Oireachtas Committee on Article 35.4.1 of the Constitution and Section 39 of the Courts of Justice Act 1924 during last Dáil. Member, Cork CC 1985–2003 (Chairman, 1989–90).

Mary White (FF)

Address 6 Wyckham Park Road, Dundrum, Dublin 16
Tel. *M* 086 256 0533;
Web www.senatormarywhite.ie
b. Dundalk. 7 October 1944
m. Padraic White. 1d
Educ. Holy Family Convent, Droichead Nua, Co Kildare; Bolton Street College of Technology; UCD (BA Econ/Pol)
Occ. Entrepreneur. Co-Founder Lir Chocolates
Senator since 2002. Member, Fianna Fáil National Executive 1993–98 and from 2006. Chairwoman, Presidents Award – Gaisce, 1999–2001.

Larry Butler, (FF)

Address: 3 Whitehall Mews, Westminster Road, Foxrock, Dublin 18
Tel. (01) 289 6320, *Mobile* 086 855 0905
B. Graiguenamanagh, Co Carlow

m. Kathleen McNicholas. 2s, 2d
Occ. Full-time public representative. Previously builder
First-term in Senate for long-serving Dún Laoghaire–Rathdown councillor, first elected in 1991, and latterly FF leader on council. Unsuccessful Seanad candidate in 2002. Peace Commissioner. Nominated by the Electrical Industries Federation of Ireland.

Kieran Phelan (FF)

Address Raheen Upper, Donaghamore, Portlaoise, Co Laois
Tel. *H* (0505) 46562; *Mobile* 087 287 6088
b. Rathdowney, Co Laois. 19 November 1949
m. Mary Clancy. 4d, 1s
Educ. CBS Roscrea; Multyfarnham, Co Westmeath (Diploma in Agriculture)
Occ. Farmer and auctioneer
Member of Seanad since 2002. Party spokesperson on Arts, Sport and Tourism in last Seanad. Member, Laois CC 1991–2003 (Chairperson, 1998–99).

Paudie Coffey (FG)

Address Mount Bolton, Portlaw, Co Waterford
Tel *H* (051) 387 295
b. Waterford. 15 May 1969
m. Suzanne McAleenan. 1d, 1s

Educ. St Declan's Community College, Kilmacthomas; Waterford RTC (National Craft Certificate, City & Guilds Electrical Engineering); UCD (Certificate in Health & Safety at Work)
Occ. ESB official, former electrician
New Senator. Contested 2007 Dáil election for Waterford. Member, Waterford CC 1999–2007, former Deputy Mayor of Co Waterford. Former selector/trainer of Waterford U/21 hurling team.

Joe O'Reilly (FG)

Address 2 The Willows, Chapel Road, Bailieborough, Co Cavan
Office 11 Rossa Place, Cavan
Tel. *H* (042) 966 6580;
Web www.joeoreilly.com
b. Cavan. April 1955
m. Mary Tully. 3s
Educ. St Aidan's Comprehensive School, Cootehill; UCD; St Patrick's College, Drumcondra
Occ. Public representative, publican, primary teacher
Previously a senator 1989–92. Unsuccessful Dáil candidate for Cavan–Monaghan in 2007 election. Member, Cavan CC 1985–2007, former Chairperson.

Administrative Panel

Elected (7 Seats)

Nicky McFadden (FG)	2nd Count
Brendan Ryan (Lab)	7th Count
Diarmuid Wilson (FF)*	9th Count
Mark Daly (FF)	10th Count
Camillus Glynn (FF)*	13th Count
Tony Kett (FF)*	13th Count
Paschal Donohoe (FG)	13th Count

Candidates

Name	(County, Party)	Vote (1st Pref)
Nominating Bodies Sub-Panel		
Buckley, Molly	(Offaly, FG)	40
Corrigan, Maria	(Dublin, FF)	43
Daly, Mark	(Kerry, FF)	120
Glynn, Camillus	(Westmeath, FF)	75
Kett, Tony	(Dublin, FF)	88
McVitty, Peter	(Cavan, FG)	32
Murphy, Gerard	(Cork, FG)	57
O'Dowd, Michael	(Louth, FG)	16
Ormond, Peter	(Offaly, FF)	28
Oireachtas Sub-Panel		
Callanan, Joe	(Galway, FF)	49
Donohoe, Paschal	(Dublin, FG)	64
Fleming, Tom	(Kerry, FF)	38
McFadden, Nicky	(Westmeath, FG)	132
Mulherin, Michelle	(Mayo, FG)	44
Ryan, Brendan	(Dublin, Lab)	129
Wilson, Diarmuid	(Cavan, FF)	115

Nicky McFadden (FG)

Address 9 Arcadia Crescent, Athlone, Co Westmeath
Tel. *H* (090) 647 8004; *Mobile* 087 677 1267; *Email* nicky.mcfadden@gmail.com
b. Athlone, 6 December 1962
m. 2d
Educ. St Joseph's College Summerhill, Athlone; Athlone Institute of Technology (Diploma in Legal Studies)
Occ. Full-time public representative. Formerly medical secretary and ESB employee.
New Senator. Elected to Athlone Town Council, 1999; co-opted to father's seat on Westmeath CC 2003, elected 2004. Member, governing body of Athlone IT; Chairperson, board of management, Athlone Community College; President, Athlone Guide Dogs Association; Director, Athlone Regional Sports Centre, Athlone e-com and Athlone Community Task Force. Received almost 6,000 votes in 2007 general election.

Brendan Ryan (Lab)

Address Baltrasna, Skerries, Co Dublin
Tel. (01) 849 0265;
Email bren@brendan-ryan.ie
Web www.brendan-ryan.ie
b. Portrane, Co Dublin. 15 February 1953
m. Margie Monks. 3d

Educ. DIT, UCD, DCU (BSc, MSc — food science, MBA)
Occ. Operations manager
New Senator. Unsuccessful Dáil candidate for Dublin North for seat formerly held by his older brother, Sean Ryan (TD 1989–97 and 1998–2007; Senator 1997–98). Representative on Fingal Community Forum; member and Treasurer of Skerries Community Association; Secretary, Hills and District Residents' Association; member, Skerries Community Centre Board of Management.

Diarmuid Wilson (FF)

Address 46 Carrickfern, Keadue Lane, Cavan
Tel. (049) 436 2256; *Mobile* 087 232 2959
b. Cavan, 20 November 1965
m. Marion Kelly. 1s 1d
Educ. Cavan Vocational School; St Patrick's College, Maynooth; Brunel University, London
Occ. Youth worker
Member of Seanad since 2002. Member, Cavan CC 1999–2003.

Mark Daly (FF)

Address 34 Henry Street, Kenmare, Co Kerry
Tel. 086 8032612
b. Cork. 12 March 1973
Educ. Holy Cross College, Kenmare; DIT Bolton St; University of Greenwich
Occ. Public representative

New Senator. Former special assistant to MEP Brian Crowley. Former reality TV cast member and property programme presenter.

Camillus Glynn (FF)

Address 8 Newbrook Road, Clonmore, Mullingar, Co Westmeath
Tel. *H* (044) 934 7151; *Mobile* 087 812 2997
b. Grehanstown, Killucan, Co Westmeath. 4 October 1941
m. Margaret Fallon. 2s, 2d
Educ. St Mary's CBS, Mullingar; St Loman's Nursing School
Occ. Public representative. Formerly psychiatric nurse, substance abuse therapist
Senator since 1997. Party spokesperson on Health and Children, in last Seanad. Member, Westmeath CC 1979–2003 (Chairman, 1988–89, 1993–94).

Tony Kett (FF)

Address 54 Whitethorn Road, Artane, Dublin 5
Tel. *H* (01) 831 8821; *Mobile* 087 237 1615
b. Ballinasloe, Co Galway. June 1951
m. Noreen Kilkenny. 1s, 2d
Educ. St Joseph's College, Garbally, Ballinasloe; College of Commerce, Rathmines
Occ. Administrator, Central Remedial Clinic, Dublin

Senator since 1997. Member, Dublin City Council 1988–2003; originally co-opted in 1988 to replace Bertie Ahern when he became Minister for Labour.

Paschal Donohoe (FG)

Address 86 Shandon Park, Phibsborough, Dublin 7
Tel. *Mobile* 087 281 6868;
Email paschal.donohoe@gmail.com
b. Dublin. 19 September 1974
m. Justine Davey. 1s
Educ. St Declan's CBS Cabra; Trinity College, Dublin (Economics and Politics)
Occ. Public representative. Sales manager
New Senator. Unsuccessful candidate in Dublin Central in 2007 general election. Elected, Dublin City Council for Cabra/Glasnevin electoral area, 2004.

Nominated (11 Seats)

Martin Brady (FF)

Dan Boyle (GP)

Ivor Callely (FF)

Ciarán Cannon (PD)

Maria Corrigan (FF)

Deirdre de Burca (GP)

John Ellis (FF)

Eoghan Harris (Ind)

Lisa McDonald (FF)

Brian Ó Domhnaill (FF)

Fiona O'Malley (PD)

Martin Brady (FF)

Address 37 Grangemore Drive, Dublin 13
Tel. H (01) 848 4509
b. Virginia, Co Cavan. 7 May 1947
m. Veronica Brady. 3d
Educ. Franciscan Brothers College, Clara, Co Offaly
Occ. Public representative. Formerly Telecom Éireann executive
New Senator. TD for Dublin North-East 1997–2007 when he lost his seat in general election. Member Joint Committees on Heritage and the Irish Language, Family, Community and Social Affairs, Public Enterprise and Transport in last Dáil. Member Dublin City Council 1991–2003.

Dan Boyle (GP)

Address 45 Capwell Avenue, Turner's Cross, Cork
Office 99 Douglas Street, Cork
Tel. H (021) 496 5663; O (021) 470 4238;
Mobile 087 277 2701;
Web www.danboyle.ie
b. Chicago, USA. 14 August 1962
m. Bláithín Hurley. 1d
Educ. Coláiste Chríost Rí; Cork Institute of Technology (Diploma in Child/Community Care)
Occ. Public representative. Formerly community youth worker

New Senator. TD for Cork South-Central 2002–07. Member Green Party negotiating team for present coalition Government. GP Whip and Finance spokesperson in 29th Dáil. Member, Cork City Council 1991–2002. Former Vice-President, National Youth Council of Ireland; member, the National Economic and Social Council 1998–2002 and Public Transport Partnership Forum 1999–2002. Member, National Council of Friends of the Earth and former Director.

Ivor Callely (FF)

Address Lansdale House, 7 St Lawrence Road, Clontarf, Dublin 3
Office 191 Howth Road, Killester, Dublin 3
Tel. H (01) 833 0350: O (01) 833 4331
b. Dublin. 6 May 1958
m. Jennifer Foley. 2s, 1d
Educ. St Paul's College, Raheny, Dublin; Fairview College, Dublin (Diplomas in Business Studies, Accountancy and Sales and Marketing)
Occ. Public representative. Formerly medical representative, Minister of State
New Senator. TD for Dublin North-Central 1989–2007 when defeated after constituency revision. Minister of State at Department of Health and Children, with responsibility for Services for Older People, 2002–05. Resigned over having had house painted for free, in early 1990s, by large building company. Chairman, Joint Oireachtas Committee on Enterprise and Small Business 1997–2002. Member, Dublin City Council and Eastern Health Board 1985–2002.

Taoiseach's Nominees

Ciarán Cannon (PD)

Address Carrabane, Athenry, Co Galway
Tel *H* (091) 847 668; *Mobile* 087 228 3377
b. Galway. 19 September 1965
m. Niamh Lawless. 1 child
Educ. Presentation College, Athenry, Co Galway
Occ. Public representative. Formerly chief executive of charitable organisation
New Senator. Contested 2007 general election in Galway East. Member, Galway CC for Loughrea area 2004–07.

Maria Corrigan (FF)

Address 22 Orby Drive, The Gallops, Leopardstown, Dublin 18
Tel. *H* (01) 294 2201; *M* 086 607 8139;
Web www.mariacorrigan.com
b. Dublin. 9 May 1968
m. Single
Educ. University College Dublin (Bachelors and masters degrees in psychology)
Occ. Psychologist
New Senator. Contested Dublin South in 2002 and 2007 general elections. Member Dún Laoghaire/Rathdown CC 1999–2007. Member, Psychological Society of Ireland; National Advisory Committee on Drugs. Former member, Combat Poverty Agency; Higher Education Authority.

Deirdre de Burca (GP)

Address Apt 2, 6 Eglington Road, Bray, Co Wicklow
Tel *Mobile* 086 806 1450;
Web www.deirdredeburca.com
b. Cork. 15 October 1963
m. Single
Educ. Cabinteely Community School, Co Dublin; Carysfort Teacher Training College, Blackrock, Co Dublin; UCD
Occ. Public representative. Formerly psychologist, primary school teacher
New Senator. Member Wicklow CC 1999–2007, Bray Town Council 2004–07. Contested Wicklow constituency in 2007 general election. Member, An Taisce; Wicklow Planning Alliance; Foundation for Sustainable Economics (Feasta); Sustainable Communities Ireland; and Peace and Neutrality Alliance (PANA).

John Ellis (FF)

Address Fenagh, Ballinamore, Co Leitrim
Tel. *H* (071) 964 4252; *Mobile* 087 259 4978
b. Fenagh. 2 May 1952
m. Patricia Donnelly. 2s, 1d
Educ. St Felim's College, Ballinamore, Co Leitrim
Occ. Public representative. Farmer
Previously a Senator 1977–81 and 1983–87 and TD for Sligo–Leitrim 1981–82 and 1987–2007 when he lost seat after constituency revision. Chairman Oireachtas Transport Committee in last Dáil and previously Chairman Oireachtas Committee on Agriculture, Food and the Marine; former member, Education and Science committees, and Public Accounts Committee. Member, Leitrim CC 1974–2003 (Chairperson, 1986–87). Member, Midland and Western Livestock Improvement Society.

Eoghan Harris (Ind)

Address Escalonia, Baltimore, Co Cork
Tel. *H* (028) 20107; *Mobile* 087 782 5854;
Email eoghanpharris@hotmail.com
b. Cork. 13 March 1943
m. Divorced. 2d
Educ. Presentation Brothers College; UCC
Occ. Writer, lecturer and commentator. Formerly TV producer
New Senator. Lectures on screenwriting at Centre for Film Studies, UCD, and National Film School (DLIADT) at Dún Laoghaire; weekly columnist in *Sunday Independent*. Former producer of RTÉ current affairs programmes, *Seven Days*, and *Féach*; screenwriter, *Sharpe* series for Carlton Television; producer documentaries on Des O'Malley and Det Garda Jerry McCabe for Praxis Pictures. Theatre credits include *The Ballad of Jim Larkin* (Gaiety Theatre 1981); *The Pope's Gig* (Edinburgh Festival 1984); *Souper Sullivan* (Abbey Theatre 1985). Political polemics include *Television and Terrorism* (1987), *The Necessity of Social Democracy* (1989), as well as the blueprint for Mary Robinson's successful campaign for the Presidency.

Lisa McDonald (FF)

Address 35 Heathfield, Clonard, Wexford
Office 68 South Main Street, Wexford.
Tel. *Mobile* 087 918 4034
b. Wexford. 9 July 1974
m. Richard Simpson. 1s
Educ. Presentation Secondary School,
Wexford; UCD; Incorporated Law Society of
Ireland
Occ. Solicitor
New Senator. Contested 2007 general
election in Wexford. Member, Wexford CC
2004–07. Former Ógra representative on
Fianna Fáil National Executive and National
Youth Committee. Member of Committee of
15, Fianna Fáil National Executive until 2004.

Brian Ó Domhnaill (FF)

Address Main Street, Gortahork, Co Donegal
Tel. *H* (074) 913 5292; *O* (074) 916 5466;
Mobile 086 821 8084
b. Letterkenny, Co Donegal.18 October 1977
m. Single
Educ. Falcarragh Community School,
Falcarragh, Co Donegal; University of Ulster
(BSc hons)
Occ. Public representative. Formerly teacher
New Senator. Member Donegal CC 2004–07.
Elected to Údarás na Gaeltachta 1999.

Fiona O'Malley (PD)

Address Seaspray, Sandycove Avenue East,
Dún Laoghaire, Co Dublin
Tel. *Mobile* 086 608 6888
b. Limerick. 19 January 1968
m. Single
Educ. Laurel Hill, Limerick; Trinity College,
Dublin (BA French and the History of Western
Art and Architecture); City University, London
(MA Museum and Gallery Management)
Occ. Public representative. Formerly arts
administrator
New Senator. TD for Dún Laoghaire from
2002 until lost seat in 2007. Member Dún
Laoghaire–Rathdown CC 1999–2003.
Daughter of Desmond O'Malley, founder of
the Progressive Democrats, TD for Limerick
East 1968–2002; Minister for Justice, Industry
and Commerce, and Trade, Commerce and
Tourism in various governments from 1970 to
1992.

University of Dublin

Elected (3 Seats)

Shane Ross (Ind)*	1st Count
David Norris (Ind)*	1st Count
Ivana Bacik (Ind)	10th Count

Electorate	48,880
Total Poll	16,977
Spoiled Votes	60
Valid Poll	16,917
Quota	4,230

First Count

Bacik, Ivana	2,794
Conway, shay	214
Douglas, Stephen	183
Efobi, Ike	201
Gueret, Maurice	1,155
Hutchinson, Edgar D.	330
McDonagh, Rosaleen	684
Martin, David	223
Norris, David	5,240
O'Connor, Seán	514
Ross, Shane	5,379

Shane Ross (Ind)

Address Glenbrook, Enniskerry, Co Wicklow
Tel. *H* (01) 211 6692; *W* (01) 618 3014
b. Dublin. 11 July 1949
m. Ruth Buchanan. 1s, 1d
Educ. Rugby School, TCD, BA (Mod)
Occ. Business editor *Sunday Independent*. Formerly stockbroker. Longest-serving senator–since 1981. Chairman, SVM Global Investment Trust; Vice President, Trinity College Historical Society; President, Trinity Business Alumni. Son of John Ross, Dublin University Senator 1961–65.

David Norris (Ind)

Address 18 North Great George's Street, Dublin 1
Tel. (01) 618 0314
b. Leopoldville, Belgian Congo. July 1944
Educ. St Andrew's College, High School, Dublin; TCD, BA (Mod) MA.
Occ. Formerly university lecturer
Senator since 1987; member, Amnesty International; Royal Zoological Society of Ireland; Irish Equity; National Union of Journalists; Irish Federation of University Lecturers. Founding Chairman of North Great George's Street Preservation Society, James Joyce Centre, Campaign for Homosexual Law Reform.

Ivana Bacik (Ind)

Address Portobello, Dublin 8
Tel. *W* (01) 817 2932
B. London, England. 25 May 1968
m. Co-habiting with partner Alan Saul. 1 d
Educ. Cloughduv National School, Cloughduv, Co Cork; Alexandra College, Milltown, Dublin 6; Trinity College, Dublin; London School of Economics; Inns of Court, School of Law, London
Occ. Reid Professor of Criminal Law, Criminology and Penology at TCD; barrister. President of TCD Students' Union (1989–90), campaigned to provide information on abortion. Contested Seanad elections in 1997 and 2002, and European parliament election in 2004. Although member of the Labour Party, sitting as an Independent member of the Seanad.

Co-author of *Abortion and the Law, Towards a Culture of Human Rights in Ireland*, and *Crime and Poverty in Ireland* and contributor to *Criminal Justice in Ireland* (O'Mahony, ed, 2002).

National University of Ireland

Elected (3 Seats)

Joe O'Toole (Ind)*	21st Count
Feargal Quinn (Ind)*	21st Count
Rónán Mullen (Ind)	21st Count

Electorate:

Valid Poll	35,989
Quota	8,998

First Count

Bresnihan, Valerie	3,282
Brodbin, Shane	220
Connolly, Mark	120
Crawley, Liam	814
Garavan, Mark	951
Healy, Paddy	1,393
Hillery, John	1,734
Hogan, Martin	683
Kennedy, John	1,305
Lowe, Martina	596
MacCarthaigh, Daithi	1,005
Monaghan, O.	327
Mullen, Rónán	4,661
O'Callaghan, Bernie	305
Ó Gógáin, Liam	174
O'Shea Farren, Linda	563
O'Sullivan, Bernadine	2,395
O'Toole, Joe	5,412
Philips, Susan	706
Price, Brendan	1,289
Quinn, Feargal	3,863
Ryan, Brendan	3,283
O'Sullivan, Daniel K.	372

Joe O'Toole (Ind)

Address Thornton, Kilsallaghan, Co Dublin
Tel. *H* (01) 835 1338, *W* (01) 618 3786;
Email joe@joeotoole.net
b. Dingle, Co Kerry. July 1947
m. Joan Lynam. 2s, 3d
Educ. CBS Dingle, St Patrick's Teacher
Training College, Dublin; Maynooth College;
UCD (BA, HDipED)
Occ. Primary teacher, principal teacher and
trade union official. Gen Sec, INTO
1991–2002; President, ICTU 2001–03; Vice-
Chair, Personal Injuries Assessment Board.
Board member, Irish Auditing and
Accountancy Supervisory Authority, GAA
National Management Committee. Senator
since 1987.

Feargal Quinn (Ind)

Address Sutton Cross, Dublin 13,
Tel. *O* (01) 618 3222, *Mobile* 087 686 5215
b. Dublin. 1936
m. Denise Prendergast. 3s, 2d.
Educ. Newbridge College, Kildare; UCD
(BComm)
Occ. Founder and President, Superquinn
Chairman, EuroCommerce; adjunct professor,
NUI Galway; former Chairman, An Post; Irish
Management Institute; finance committee of
Dublin Archdiocese; President, Marketing
Institute of Ireland. Senator since 1993. Three

honorary doctorates and Papal Knighthood in
1994.

Rónán Mullen (Ind)

Address Ahascragh, Ballinasloe, Co Galway
Tel. (01) 676 9807, (01) 618 3000;
Email ronan@ronanmullen.ie
b. Ballinasloe, Co Galway. 13 October 1970
m. single
Educ. Kilglass National School; Holy Rosary
College, Mountbellew, Co Galway; NUI
Galway (BA 1991); King's Inns (Barrister at
Law, 2003)
Occ. Columnist (*Irish Daily Mail*), Lecturer
(Institute of Technology, Blanchardstown) and
Barrister
New Senator, independent, with emphasis on
promoting respect for life, family-friendly
social policies, a quality educational system
and global solidarity. Former communications
office Dublin Catholic Archdiocese. President
of UCG Students Union 1991–92; winner, *Irish
Times* Debates (King's Inns Team) 2000.

General Elections 1923–2007 (Party Seats and % of First-Preference Votes)

Year of Election	Total Seats	Fianna Fáil (Anti-Treaty in 1923)		Fine Gael (Cumann na nGaedheal to 1933)		Labour		Farmers		National League		Centre Party (later merged with Fine Gael)		Other Parties** and Independents	
		Seats	% Votes	Seats	% Votes	Seats	% Votes	Seats	% Votes	Seats	% Votes	Seats	% Votes	Seats	% Votes
1923	153	44	27.6	63	38.9	14	12.4	15	10.6					17	10.5
June 1927	153	44	26.1	47†	27.5	22	13.8	11	8.9	8	7.3			21	16.4
Sept 1927	153	57	35.2	62†	38.7	13	9.5	6	6.4	2	1.3			13	8.9
1932	153	72	44.5	57†	35.3	7	7.7	4	2.1					13	10.4
1933	153	77†	49.7	48	30.5	8	5.7					11	9.1	9	5
1937	138	69†	45.2	48	34.8	13	10.3							8	9.7
1938	138	77†	51.9	45	33.3	9	10.0							7	4.8

		Fianna Fáil		Fine Gael		Labour		Clann na Talmhan		Clann na Poblachta		National Progressive Democrats		Other Parties** and Independents	
1943	138	67†	41.9	32	23.1	17	15.7	14	10.3					8	9
1944	138	76†	48.9	30	20.5	12††	11.5	11	10.8					9	8.3
1948	147	68†	41.9	31	19.8	19††	11.3	7	5.3	10	13.2			12	8.5
1951	147	69†	46.3	40	25.7	16	11.4	6	2.9	2	4.1			14	9.6
1954	147	65	43.4	50	32.0	19†	12.0	5	3.1	3	3.8			5	5.7
1957	147	78	48.3	40	26.6	12†	9.1	3	2.4	1	1.7			13	11.9
1961	144	70	43.8	47	32.0	16†	11.6	2	1.5	1	1.2	2	1	6	8.9
1965	144	72	47.8	47	33.9	22†	15.4							3	2.9
1969	144	75†	45.7	50	34.1	18	17.0							1	3.2
1973	144	69†	46.2	54	35.1	19	13.7							2	5
1977	148	84	50.6	43	30.5	17†	11.6							4	7.3

		Fianna Fáil		Fine Gael		Labour		Progressive Democrats		Green Party		SFWP / WP / Democratic Left*		Other Parties** and Independents	
1981	166	78	45.3	65	36.5	15	9.9					1	1.7	7	6.6
Feb 1982	166	81†	47.3	63	37.3	15	9.1					3	2.2	4	4.1
Nov 1982	166	75	45.2	70	39.2	16	9.4					2	3.1	3	3.1
1987	166	81	44.2	51†	27.1	12	6.4	14	11.9			4	3.8	4	6.6
1989	166	77	44.2	55	29.3	15	9.5	6	5.5	1	1.5	7	5	5	5
1992	166	68	39.1	45	24.5	33	19.3	10	4.7	1	1.4	4	2.8	5	8.2
1997	166	77	39.3	54	28.0	17	10.4	4	4.7	2	2.8	4	2.5	8	12.3

		Fianna Fáil		Fine Gael		Labour		Progressive Democrats		Green Party		Sinn Féin		Other Parties** and Independents	
2002	166	81	41.5	31	22.5	21†	10.8	8	4.0	6	3.8	5	6.5	14	10.9
2007	166	78†	41.6	51	27.3	20	10.1	2	2.7	5	4.7	4	6.9	5	6.7

* Sinn Féin the Workers' Party became The Workers' Party in 1982, then Democratic Left split off in 1992, and later merged with Labour, in 1999.

** Other parties

	June 1927	Sinn Féin 5
	1957	Sinn Féin 4
	1981	SLP 1
	1987	DSP 1
	1989	DSP 1
	1997	Sinn Féin 1, Socialist Party 1
	2002	Socialist Party 1

† includes outgoing Ceann Comhairle returned without contest

†† In 1943 Labour divided into Labour and National Labour and re-merged in 1950

Constitutional Referenda 1937–2007

Date	Subject	Electorate	Total Poll	%	Spoiled Votes	%	Total Valid Poll	%	Yes Votes	%	No Votes	%	% of Elect. Yes	% of Elect. No
1/7/37	Plebiscite	1,775,055	1,346,207	75.8	134,157	10.0	1,212,050	68.3	685,105	56.5	526,945	43.5	38.6	29.7
17/6/59	Straight Vote	1,678,450	979,531	58.4	39,220	4.0	940,311	56.0	453,322	48.2	486,989	51.8	27.0	29.0
16/10/68	Formation of Dáil Consts	1,717,389	1,129,477	65.8	48,489	4.3	1,080,988	62.9	424,185	39.2	656,803	60.8	24.7	38.2
16/10/68	Straight Vote	1,717,389	1,129,606	65.8	48,212	4.3	1,081,394	63.0	423,496	39.2	657,898	60.8	24.7	38.3
10/5/72	EEC Membership	1,783,604	1,264,278	70.9	10,497	0.8	1,253,781	70.3	1,041,890	83.1	211,891	16.9	58.4	11.9
7/12/72	Voting Age	1,783,604	903,439	50.7	47,089	5.2	856,350	48.0	724,836	84.6	131,514	15.4	40.6	7.4
7/12/72	Position of RC Church	1,783,604	903,669	50.7	49,326	5.5	854,343	47.9	721,003	84.4	133,340	15.6	40.4	7.5
5/7/79	Adoption	2,179,466	623,476	28.6	15,517	2.5	607,959	27.9	601,694	99.0	6,265	1.0	27.6	0.3
5/7/79	Seanad University Seats	2,179,466	622,646	28.6	24,562	3.9	598,084	27.4	552,600	92.4	45,484	7.6	25.4	2.1
7/9/83	Protection of Unborn	2,358,651	1,265,994	53.7	8,625	0.7	1,257,369	53.3	841,233	66.9	416,136	33.1	35.7	17.6
14/6/84	Voting for Non-citizens	2,399,257	1,138,895	47.5	40,162	3.5	1,098,733	45.8	828,483	75.4	270,250	24.6	34.5	11.3
26/6/86	Divorce	2,436,836	1,482,644	60.8	8,522	0.6	1,474,122	60.5	538,279	36.5	935,843	63.5	22.1	38.4
24/5/87	Single European Act	2,461,790	1,085,304	44.1	4,904	0.5	1,080,400	43.9	755,423	69.9	324,977	30.1	30.7	13.2
18/6/92	Maastricht Treaty	2,542,840	1,457,219	57.3	7,488	0.5	1,449,731	57.0	1,001,076	69.1	448,655	30.9	39.4	17.6
25/11/92	Right to Life	2,542,841	1,733,309	68.2	81,835	4.7	1,651,474	64.9	572,177	34.6	1,079,297	65.4	22.5	42.4
25/11/92	Travel	2,542,841	1,733,821	68.2	74,454	4.3	1,659,367	65.3	1,035,308	62.4	624,059	37.6	40.7	24.5
25/11/92	Information	2,542,841	1,732,433	68.1	74,494	4.3	1,657,939	65.2	992,833	59.9	665,106	40.1	39.0	26.2
24/11/95	Divorce	2,628,834	1,633,942	62.2	5,372	0.3	1,628,570	62.0	818,842	50.3	809,728	49.7	31.1	30.8
28/11/96	Bail	2,659,895	777,586	29.2	2,878	0.4	774,708	29.1	579,740	74.8	194,968	25.2	21.8	7.3
30/10/97	Cabinet Confidentiality	2,688,316	1,268,043	47.2	66,091	5.2	1,201,952	44.71	632,777	52.6	569,175	47.4	23.5	21.2
22/5/98	Amsterdam Treaty	2,747,088	1,543,930	56.2	33,228	2.2	1,510,702	55.0	932,632	61.7	578,070	38.3	33.9	21.0
22/5/98	Northern Ireland	2,747,088	1,545,395	56.3	17,064	1.1	1,528,331	55.6	1,442,583	94.4	85,748	5.6	52.5	3.1
11/6/99	Local Govt	2,791,415	1,425,881	51.1	109,066	7.6	1,316,815	47.2	1,024,850	77.8	291,965	22.2	36.7	10.5
7/6/01	Death penalty	2,867,960	997,885	34.8	14,480	1.5	983,405	34.3	610,455	62.1	372,950	37.9	21.3	13.0
7/6/01	Int. Criminal Court	2,867,960	997,565	34.8	17,819	1.8	979,746	34.2	628,695	64.2	350,963	35.8	21.9	12.2
7/6/01	Nice Treaty 1	2,867,960	997,826	34.8	14,887	1.5	982,939	34.3	453,461	46.1	529,478	53.9	15.8	18.5
6/3/02	Abortion	2,923,918	1,254,175	42.9	6,649	0.5	1,247,526	42.7	618,485	49.6	629,041	50.4	21.2	21.5
19/10/02	Nice Treaty 2	2,923,918	1,446,588	49.5	5,384*	0.4	1,441,204	49.3	906,317	63.0	534,887	37.0	31.0	18.3
11/06/04	Citizenship	3,041,688	1,823,434	60.0	20,219	1.1	1,803,215	59.0	1,427,520	79.2	375,695	20.8	49.6	12.4

*Spoilt votes reduced due to use of electronic voting in seven constituencies.

Opposition Spokespersons

FINE GAEL FRONT BENCH
(Appointed September, 2007)

Finance & Deputy Leader Richard Bruton TD
Agriculture, Fisheries and Food Michael Creed TD
Arts, Sport and Tourism Olivia Mitchell TD
Children Alan Shatter TD
Communications, Energy and Natural Resources Simon Coveney TD
Community, Rural & Gaeltacht Affairs Michael Ring TD
Defence Jimmy Deenihan TD
Education and Science Brian Hayes TD

Enterprise, Trade and Employment Leo Varadkar TD
Environment, Heritage and Local Government Philip Hogan TD
Foreign Affairs Billy Timmins TD
Health James Reilly TD
Immigration and Integration Denis Naughten TD
Justice, Equality and Law Reform Charles Flanagan TD
Social and Family Affairs Olwyn Enright TD
Transport and the Marine Fergus O'Dowd TD
Chief Whip Paul Kehoe TD
Leader in the Seanad Sen. Frances Fitzgerald

LABOUR PARTY FRONT BENCH
(Appointed September, 2007)

Agriculture and Food Seán Sherlock TD
Arts, Sport and Tourism Mary Upton TD
Communications, Energy and Natural Resources Liz McManus TD
Community and Rural Affairs Jack Wall TD
Constitutional Matters and Law Reform Brendan Howlin TD
Defence and the Irish language Brian O'Shea TD
Disability Issues and Equality Kathleen Lynch TD
Education and Science Ruairí Quinn TD
Enterprise, Trade and Employment Willie Penrose TD
Environment and Heritage Joanna Tuffy TD
Europe and Human Rights Joe Costello TD
Finance Joan Burton TD

Foreign Affairs Michael D. Higgins TD
Health Jan O'Sullivan TD
Housing and Local Government Ciarán Lynch TD
Justice Pat Rabbitte TD
Social and Family Affairs Róisín Shortall TD
Transport Tommy Broughan TD
Chief Whip Emmet Stagg TD
Assistant Whip Brian O'Shea TD
Commuter Issues Sen. Dominic Hannigan
Consumer Affairs Sen. Brendan Ryan
Tourism Sen. Alan Kelly
Older People Sen. Phil Prendergast
Marine Sen. Michael McCarthy
Children Sen. Alex White

Political Parties: Headquarters

Fianna Fáil
Áras de Valera
65/66 Lower Mount Street
Dublin 2
Tel: (01) 676 1551
Fax: (01) 678 5690
Email: info@fiannafail.ie
Website: www.fiannafail.ie
General Secretary: Sean Dorgan

Fine Gael
51 Upper Mount Street
Dublin 2
Tel: (01) 619 8444
Fax: (01) 662 5046
Email: finegael@finegael.com
Website: www.finegael.com
General Secretary: Tom Curran

The Labour Party
17 Ely Place
Dublin 2
Tel: (01) 678 4700
Fax: (01) 661 2640
Email: head_office@labour.ie
Website: www.labour.ie
General Secretary: Mike Allen

Progressive Democrats
25 South Frederick Street
Dublin 2
Tel: (01) 679 4399

Fax: (01) 679 4757
Email: info@progressivedemocrats.ie
Website: www.progressivedemocrats.ie
General Secretary: John Higgins

The Green Party/Comhaontas Glas
5A Upper Fownes Street
Dublin 2
Tel: (01) 679 0012
Fax: (01) 679 7168
Email: info@greenparty.ie
Website: www.greenparty.ie
General Secretary: vacant

Sinn Féin
44 Parnell Square
Dublin 1
Tel: (01) 872 6100
Fax: (01) 878 3595
Email: sfadmin@eircom.net
Website: www.Sinnfein.ie
National Organiser: Olive Sloane

The Workers' Party
23 Hill Street
Dublin 1
Tel: (01) 874 0716
Fax: (01) 874 8702
Email: wpi@indigo.ie
Website: www.Workers-party.org
General Secretary: John Lowry

The Socialist Party
141 Thomas Street
Dublin 8
Tel: (01) 677 2592
Email: info@socialistparty.net
Website: www.socialistparty.net
General Secretary: Kevin McLoughlin

Comhar Criostaí/The Christian Solidarity Party
73 Deerpark Road
Mount Merrion
Co. Dublin
Tel/Fax: (01) 288 0051
General Secretary: Oisín Ó Searchóid

The Socialist Workers' Party
105 O'Hogan Road
Ballyfermot
Dublin 10
Chairman: Kieran Allen

The Communist Party of Ireland
James Connolly House
7 Bloom Lane
Lower Ormond Quay
Dublin 2
Tel: (01) 874 7981
Email: cpi@eircom.net
Website: www.communistpartyofireland.ie
General Secretary: Eugene McCartan

The TV debate

The European Parliament

The 6th direct elections to the European Parliament were held on 11 June 2004 in Ireland. With the expansion of the European Union in Eastern Europe, the Treaty of Nice provided that the newly elected parliament had 732 seats compared to 626 in the previous parliament.

The Treaty and expansion of the parliament led to re-adjustments in the seats allocated to all member states, resulting in the loss of two seats for Ireland, down from 15 to 13. The Treaty provided that Ireland would have 12 seats once the EU expanded to 27 members, as it did in 2007. Pending the accession of Romania and Bulgaria in 2007, however, their seats were allocated to existing members for the 2004 elections, giving Ireland 13 seats.

The Constituency Commission re-drew the constituencies for the election in the light of this fact. Its main changes involved the loss of one seat each in the old Leinster and Munster constituencies, which were renamed East and South respectively. County Clare was moved from the Munster constituency into the old Connacht–Ulster constituency, which was re-named North-West. Dublin remained the only four-seat constituency, while each of the others had three seats.

The Commission's recommendations provided for a national average of one MEP per 301,323 people, based on population figures from 2002. The greatest number of people per MEP was 332,446 in the South constituency, and the least was 271,429 in the North-West. The population number per MEP for Dublin was 280,705, and for the East constituency it was 327,586.

In the European Parliament, Fianna Fáil MEPs belong to the Union for Europe of the Nations Group; Fine Gael to the European People's Party (Christian Democrats) and European Democrats Group; Labour to the Socialist Group; Sinn Féin to the Confederal Group of the European United Left — Nordic Green Left; Independent Marian Harkin to the Alliance of Liberals and Democrats for Europe; and Independent Kathy Sinnott to the Independence/Democracy Group. In Northern Ireland, the Ulster Unionist Party MEP belongs to the European People's Party (Christian Democrats) and European Democrats Group.

The ending of the dual mandate means that people can no longer sit in both the Dáil and the European Parliament. Three of the MEPs elected in 2004 contested the general election in 2007 — Simon Coveney (FG), Mary Lou McDonald (SF) and Mairead McGuinness (FG). Simon Coveney was elected to the Dáil and had to step down from the European Parliament; his place was taken by Colm Burke, the first replacement on the Fine Gael list for the South constituency.

After that change, the replacement lists for MEPs was as follows:

Dublin
Fianna Fáil: Royston Brady, Pat Carey, Seán Haughey, Michael Mulcahy, Ann Ormond.
Fine Gael: Colm MacEochaidh, Gavin Doyle, Olga Barry, Katherine Meenan.
Labour: Ivana Bacik, Kevin Baneham, Nap Keeling, Rebecca Moynihan.
Sinn Féin: Killian Forde, Robbie Smyth.

East
Fianna Fáil: Seamus Kirk, Donie Cassidy, John Browne, Gerry Bridgett, Tony Dempsey.
Fine Gael: Michael O'Dowd, Paul McGrath, Martin McDonald.

South
Fianna Fáil: Gerard Collins, Michael Ahern, Billy Kelleher, Tom Fleming, Marie Hoctor.
Fine Gael: Kevin Murphy, Peter Kelly.
Kathy Sinnott List: Siobháin Daly, Denny O'Connor, Ger South.

North-West
Fianna Fáil: Dr James McDaid, Michael Kitt, Anthony P. Vesey, Patrick McGowan, Bernie O'Callaghan.
Fine Gael: Madeleine Taylor-Quinn, Jimmy McClearn, Seán McKiernan, Ciaran Twomey.
Marian Harkin List: Paudge Connolly, James Breen.

Liam Aylward (East)

Fianna Fáil member. Born in Knockmoylon, Mullinavat, Co Kilkenny, 27 September 1952. Laboratory technician. Member of Dáil for Carlow–Kilkenny (1977–2007). Minister of State at the Department of Forestry (1988–89), Department of Energy (1989–92), Department of Education (1992–94), and Department of Agriculture (2002–04). Elected to EP 2004. Committees: Environment, Public Health and Food Safety; Agriculture and Rural Development, Delegation to the ACP–EU Joint Parliamentary Assembly

Colm Burke (South)

Fine Gael member. Born in Dripsey, Co Cork, 15 January.1957. BCL from UCC. Solicitor. Replacement for Simon Coveney who was elected to the EP in 2004 and to the Dáil in the 2007 general election. Member of Cork City Council (1995–2007); Lord Mayor of Cork (2003–04). Committees: Foreign Affairs; Delegation for Relations with the United States.

The European Parliament

Brian Crowley (South)

Fianna Fáil member. Born 4 March 1964. Diploma in Law from UCC. Senator 1993–94. Member of Council of State (1997–2004). Elected to EP 1994 and all subsequent elections. Leader of Fianna Fáil group in EP. President of Union for Europe of the Nations Group in EP. Committees: Conference of Presidents; Constitutional Affairs; Delegation for Relations with the United States.

Proinsias De Rossa (Dublin)

Labour Party member. Born in Dublin, 15 May 1940. Member of Dáil (1982–2002). Former leader of the Workers' Party and Democratic Left. Minister for Social Welfare (1994–97). Member of European Parliament (1989–92 and since 1999). Rapporteur for EP's report on future of European Social Model (2006). Member of the European Convention on the Future of Europe (2002–03) and Labour Party Delegation to the National Forum on Europe. Committees: Employment and Social Affairs and Petitions; Delegation for Relations with the Palestinian Legislative Council; Temporary Committees into the crisis of the Equitable Life Assurance Society, and on the alleged use of European countries by the CIA for the transport and illegal detention of prisoners.

Avril Doyle (East)

Fine Gael member. Born in Dublin, 18 April 1949. BSc from UCD. Former Mayor of Wexford. Minister of State, Department of Finance (1982–87 and 1995–97); Department of Transport, Energy and Communications (1995–97). Member of Dáil (1982–89 and 1992–97) and of the Seanad (1989–92 and 1997–2002). First elected to EP 1999. Leader of the Irish Delegation in the EPP–ED Group. Vice-Chair of the European Parliament Delegation for Relations with the Gulf States, including Yemen; member of Delegation for Relations with China. Committees: Vice-Chair, Fisheries; member, Environment and Public Health; Industry, Research and Energy.

Marian Harkin (North-West)

Independent member. Born in Sligo, 26 November 1953. BSc from University College Dublin. Secondary teacher. Elected to Dáil as Independent for Sligo–Leitrim 2002. Member of Council of the West. Elected to EP 2004 on second attempt. Committees: Petitions; Regional Development; Delegation for Relations with Canada. Substitute Employment and Social Affairs, Education and Culture, Delegation for Relations with the United States

Jim Higgins (North-West)

Fine Gael member. Born in Ballyhaunis, Co Mayo, 4 May 1945. Post-primary teacher. BA from University College Galway. Member of Dáil (1987–2002). Senator (1981, Taoiseach's nominee; 1983–87, 2002–07). Minister of State at Department of Finance (1995), at Department of Taoiseach and Government Chief Whip (1995–97). Committees: Regional Development; Delegation for Relations with Canada.

Mary Lou McDonald (Dublin)

Sinn Féin member. Born in Dublin, 1 May 1969. BA (Mod) from TCD; MA from University of Limerick. Sinn Féin Political Strategy Coordinator (2002–04). Member of Sinn Féin Árd-Chomhairle since 2001. Member of EP since 2004. Unsuccessful candidate in 2007 general election. Committees: Employment and Social Affairs; Delegation for Relations with Switzerland, Iceland and Norway and to the European Economic Area (EEA).

The European Parliament

Mairead McGuinness (East)

Fine Gael member. Born in Drogheda, 13 June 1959. BAgrSc (Econ) UCD. Radio and television broadcaster and agricultural journalist. Former chairperson, Guild of Agricultural Journalists. First elected to EP 2004; unsuccessful candidate in 2007 general election. Committees: Chairwoman, Committee of Inquiry into the crisis of the Equitable Life Assurance Society; member Agriculture and Rural Development; Petitions

Gay Mitchell (Dublin)

Fine Gael member. Born in Dublin, 30 December 1951. MSocSc from Queens's University Belfast. Chartered secretary and administrator. Member of Dáil (1981–2007). Chairman of Committee of Public Accounts (1987–93). Chairman of Oireachtas European Affairs Committee (2002–04). Lord Mayor of Dublin (1992–93). Minister of State at Departments of Taoiseach and Foreign Affairs with responsibility for European Affairs 1994–97. Elected to EP 2004. Committees: Development; Economic and Monetary Affairs; Petitions; Vice-Chairman, EU Delegation to the ACP-EU Joint Parliamentary Assembly.

Seán Ó Neachtain (North-West)

Fianna Fáil member. Born in An Spidéal, Co Galway, 22 May 1947. BA, HDipEd from University College Galway. Former secondary teacher. Member of Galway County Council (1991–2002). Member of the West Regional Authority (1992–2002). Member of the Border, Midland and Western Regional Assembly (2000–02). Member of Údarás na Gaeltachta (1979–91, 1999–2002); Chairman (1991–96). Member of Committee of the Regions (1994–2002); Chairman of European Alliance Political Group (1998–2002); Vice-Chairman, Commission for Education and Culture (2002). Vice-President, Atlantic Arc Commission (1991–96). Replaced Pat the Cope Gallagher EP 2002 when latter appointed Minister of State. Elected to EP 2004. Committees: Delegation for Relations with Canada; Conference of Delegation Chairmen; Transport and Tourism; Fisheries; Temporary Committee of Inquiry into the Crisis of the Equitable Life Assurance Society.

Eoin Ryan (Dublin)

Fianna Fáil member. Born in Dublin, 24 February 1953. Member of Dáil (1992–2007). Senator (1989–92, Taoiseach's nominee). Minister of State for Local Development and National Drugs Strategy (2000–02). Elected to EP 2004. Committees: Economic and Monetary Affairs; Petitions; Temporary Committee on the alleged use of European countries by the CIA for the transport and illegal detention of prisoners; Delegation for Relations with the countries of South Asia and the South Asia Association for Regional Cooperation (SAARC)

Kathy Sinnott (South)

Independent member. Born in Chicago, 29 September 1950. Dual Irish/US citizen. Married with nine children. Founder/secretary, Association for Severely and Profoundly Mentally Handicapped (1983–97). Honorary PhD from St Mary-of-the-Woods College, Indiana, USA (2005). First elected EP 2004. Committees: Vice-Chair, Petitions; member, Environment; Employment and Social Affairs.

Elected

Jim Allister (DUP)[1]
Bairbre de Brún (SF)
Jim Nicholson (UUP)*

	Number	%
Electorate	1,072,669	
Total Poll	554,744	51.72
Spoiled Votes	5,467	0.98
Valid Poll	49,277	51.21
Seats	3	
Quota	137,320	
Candidates	7	

Voting by Party

1st Pref	Number	%	% 1999
DUP	175,761	32.00	28.4
Sinn Féin	144,541	26.31	17.3
UUP	91,164	16.60	17.6
SDLP	87,559	15.94	28.1
GP	4,810	0.88	
Others	45,442	8.27	

	Quotas	Seats
DUP	1.28	1
SF	1.05	1
UUP	0.66	1
SDLP	0.64	0

[1] Jim Allister later resigned from the Democratic Unionist Party.

Jim Allister

Independent member. Born in Crossgar, Co Down, 2 April 1953. LLB (Hons) from Queen's University Belfast (1975). Barrister-at-Law (1976). QC (2001). First elected to EP as DUP member 2004; resigned from party March 2007 in protest at its decision to enter Northern Ireland Executive with Sinn Féin. Member of Newtownabbey Borough Council (1985–87). Chief Whip of DUP group in Northern Ireland Assembly (1982–86). Member of secretariat of Non-Attached Group in EP as assistant to Dr Ian Paisley MEP (1980–82). Committees: Fisheries; Constitutional Affairs; Delegation to the ACP–EU Joint Parliamentary Assembly.

Bairbre de Brún

Sinn Féin member. Born in Dublin, 10 January 1954. Teacher, community worker (1976–97). Member of Assembly for West Belfast (1998–2004). Minister of Health, Social Services and Public Safety, Northern Ireland Executive (1999–2000 and 2000–02). Head of International Department, Sinn Féin (1994). Party negotiator since 1997. Committees: Regional Development; Delegation for Relations with the United States.

Jim Nicholson

Ulster Unionist member. Born in Armagh, 29 January 1945. Farmer and full-time politician. Vice-president of the Ulster Unionist Council. Mayor of Armagh (1996). Member of the Northern Ireland Assembly (1982–86). Member of the House of Commons (1983–85). First elected to EP 1989. Chairman of the Delegation for Relations with Australia and New Zealand (1997–2002). Chairman of the Delegation for Relations with the United States (2002–04). Committees: Quaestors; Regional Development; Fisheries. Member Delegation for Relations with Australia and New Zealand and Delegation for Relations with South Asia.

The European Parliament

An election to the European Parliament was held on 11 June 2004. The Republic of Ireland results are summarised on this page and details of the counts in each of the constituencies are given on the following pages.

Dublin

Elected

Gay Mitchell (FG)
Eoin Ryan (FF)
Proinsias De Rossa (Lab)*
Mary Lou McDonald (SF)

	Number	%
Electorate	821,723	
Total Poll	435,136	52.95
Spoiled Votes	13,239	3.04
Valid Poll	421,897	51.34
Seats	4	
Quota	84,380	
Candidates	12	

Voting by Party

1st Pref	Number	%	% 1999
Fianna Fáil	97,950	23.22	24.67
Fine Gael	90,749	21.51	30.09
Labour	95,051	22.53	15.90
Sinn Féin	60,395	14.32	5.85
Green Party	40,445	9.59	12.70
Socialist Party	23,218	5.50	3.78
Christian Solidarity Party	5,352	1.27	3.36
Others	8,737	2.07	2.49

	Quotas	Seats
FF	1.16	1
FG	1.08	1
Lab	1.13	1
SF	0.72	1

East

Elected

Mairead McGuinness (FG)
Liam Aylward (FF)
Avril Doyle (FG)*

	Number	%
Electorate	822,221	
Total Poll	471,895	57.39
Spoiled Votes	18,717	3.97
Valid Poll	453,178	55.12
Seats	3	
Quota	113,295	
Candidates	13	

Voting by Party

1st Pref	Number	%	% 1999
Fianna Fáil	113,660	25.08	34.24
Fine Gael	183,760	40.55	34.06
Labour	59,158	13.05	11.13
Sinn Féin	39,356	8.68	5.85
Green Party	25,576	5.64	13.78
Others	31,668	6.99	0.93

	Quotas	Seats
FF	1.00	1
FG	1.62	2
Lab	0.52	
SF	0.35	
GP	0.23	
Others	0.28	

North-West

Elected

Seán Ó Neachtain (FF)
Marian Harkin (Ind)
Jim Higgins (FG)

	Number	%
Electorate	688,804	
Total Poll	435,910	63.29
Spoiled Votes	14,487	3.32
Valid Poll	421,423	61.18
Seats	3	
Quota	105,356	
Candidates	9	

Voting by Party

1st Pref	Number	%	% 1999
Fianna Fáil	114,224	27.10	35.6
Fine Gael	100,966	23.96	19.9
Labour	13,948	3.31	3.3
Sinn Féin	65,321	15.50	6.4
Green Party	0	0.00	0
Others	126,964	30.13	34.8

	Quotas	Seats
FF	1.08	1
FG	0.96	1
Lab	0.13	
SF	0.62	
GP	0.00	
Others	1.21	1

South

Elected

Brian Crowley (FF)*
Simon Coveney (FG)
Kathy Sinnott (Ind)

	Number	%
Electorate	810,277	
Total Poll	498,394	61.51
Spoiled Votes	14,124	2.83
Valid Poll	484,270	59.77
Seats	3	
Quota	121,068	
Candidates	10	

Voting by Party

1st Pref	Number	%	% 1999
Fianna Fáil	198,670	41.02	52.9
Fine Gael	118,937	24.56	17.27
Labour	19,975	4.12	6.3
Sinn Féin	32,643	6.74	6.48
Green Party	10,896	2.25	2.29
Others	103,149	21.30	14.76

	Quotas	Seats
FF	1.64	1
FG	0.98	1
Lab	0.16	
SF	0.27	
GP	0.09	
Others	0.85	1

Seats 4
Quota 84,380

	1st Count	2nd Count	3rd Count	4th Count	5th Count	6th Count
	Number of Votes	Transfer of **Mitchell** Surplus	Transfer of **Price, Prendeville, Doonan, Despard** Votes	Transfer of **Higgins** Votes	Transfer of **Brady** Votes	Transfer of **Bacik** Votes
BACIK, Ivana (Lab)	40,707	*+996* 41,703	*+921* 42,624	*+2,789* 45,413	*+2,107* 47,520	-47,520
BRADY, Royston (FF)	36,269	*+324* 36,593	*+830* 37,423	*+901* 38,324	-38,324	
DE ROSSA, Proinsias (Lab)	54,344	*+1,899* 56,243	*+1,223* 57,466	*+4,958* 62,424	*+4,146* 66,570	*+29,524* 96,094
DESPARD, Barry (CSP)	5,352	5,443	*+91*	-5,443		
DOONAN, Paul (Ind)			*+33* 1,853	1,886	-1,886	
HIGGINS, Joe (SP)			*+242* 23,218	*+1,081* 23,460	24,541	-24,541
McDONALD, Mary Lou (SF)	60,395	*+294* 60,689	*+1,341* 62,030	*+6,325* 68,355	*+3,798* 72,153	*+4,390* 76,543
McKENNA, Patricia (GP)	40,445	*+1,061* 41,506	*+3,178* 44,684	*+4,417* 49,101	*+2,791* 51,892	*+7,651* 59,543
MITCHELL, Gay (FG)	90,749	*-6,369* 84,380				
PRENDEVILLE, Tom (Ind)			*+53* 2,071	2,124	-2,124	
PRICE, Brendan (Ind)	4,813	*+118* 4,931	-4,931			
RYAN, Eoin (FF)	61,681	*+1,258* 62,939	*+1,937* 64,876	*+1,047* 65,923	*+19,887* 85,810	
Non-transferable papers not effective		*+3873* 3,873	*+4,104* 7,977	*+5,595* 13,572	*+5,955* 19,527	
TOTAL	421,897	421,897	421,897	421,897	421,897	421,897

East

Seats 3 Quota 113,295	1st Count	2nd Count	3rd Count	4th Count	5th Count	6th Count	7th Count
	Number of Votes	Transfer of **McGuinness** Surplus	Transfer of **Ó Coistín, Dubsky, Neal, Ó Gógáin** Votes	Transfer of **Barrett, Reid** Votes	Transfer of **White** Votes	Transfer of **Dwyer** Votes	Transfer of **Kirk**
AYLWARD, Liam (FF)	68,206	+65 68,271	+485 68,756	+1,979 70,735	+2,482 73,217	+4,909 78,126	+32,632 110,758
BARRETT, Justin (IND)			+22 10,997	+1,004 11,019	12,023	-12,023	
CASSELLS, Peter (Lab)	59,158	+106 59,264	+967 60,231	+2,888 63,119	+7,390 70,509	+9,392 79,901	+4,080 83,981
DOYLE, Avril (FG)	69,511	+545 70,056	+1,103 71,159	+3,270 74,429	+6,094 80,523	+5,697 86,220	+4,826 91,046
DUBSKY, Eoin (Ind)	1,955	+5 1,960	-1,960				
DWYER, John (SF)	39,356	+30 39,386	+872 40,258	+2,763 43,021	+3,526 46,547	-46,547	
KIRK, Seamus (FF)	45,454	+60 45,514	+659 46,173	+1,696 47,869	+1,760 49,629	+4,304 53,933	-53,933
McGUINNESS, Mairead (FG)	114,249	-954 113,295					
NEAL, Joe (Ind)	1,487	+5 1,492	-1,492				
Ó COISTÍN, Seanán (Ind)	3,130	+11 3,141	-3,141				
Ó GÓGÁIN, Liam (Ind)	3,407	+11 3,418	-3,418				
REID, Clifford T. (Ind)	10,692	+26 10,718	+1,314 12,032	-12,032			
WHITE, Mary (GP)	25,576	+68 25,644	+1,449 27,093	+3,344 30,437	-30,437		
Non-transferable papers not effective	+2,158	+8,115 2,158	+9,185 10,273	+22,245 19,458	+12,395 41,703	54,098	
TOTAL	453,178	453,178	453,178	453,178	453,178	453,178	453,178

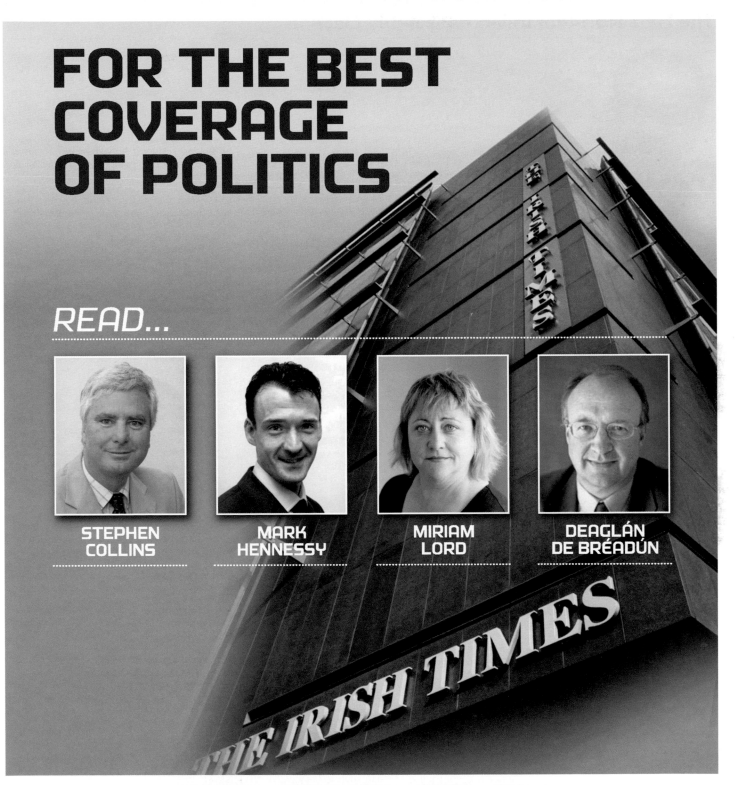

FOR THE BEST
COVERAGE
OF POLITICS

READ...

STEPHEN
COLLINS

MARK
HENNESSY

MIRIAM
LORD

DEAGLÁN
DE BRÉADÚN

THE IRISH TIMES

The 2007 Northern Ireland Assembly Election

Gerry Moriarty

The March 2007 Northern Ireland Assembly election was a remarkable moment in modern British–Irish history when anxious guarded optimism could be translated into an astonishing political pact between the bitterest of enemies — Ian Paisley and Gerry Adams — if they could just mind their mouths and hold their nerve.

The election took place with the conditions for a power-sharing agreement in place. After years and years of interminable, frustrating, stop-start political process there was a chance that the North could emerge from a grim past into a difficult but hopeful future: the IRA war was over, the IRA had decommissioned, Sinn Féin had signed up to policing, the St Andrews Agreement blueprint for devolution was spread out on the table awaiting implementation.

A political miracle really was possible. But there were dark forces swirling about that could dash this opportunity for agreement. Elections are times when politicians can be at their most atavistic and tribal. The challenge was to ensure that nothing was said or done during the election that would shatter the opportunity to transform Northern Ireland. There was no shortage of would-be wreckers.

This was a curious election. The fact was, particularly on the unionist side, people weren't quite sure what they were voting for. A deal or no deal? Hard to tell. As far as Gerry Adams, Sir Reg Empey and Mark Durkan — the leaders respectively of Sinn Féin, the Ulster Unionist Party and the SDLP — were concerned, the election was to re-float devolution. The Northern Executive had capsized more than four years earlier, in October 2002, on the rock of the alleged IRA spy ring at Stormont, and now was the time to salvage the vessel.

So, while we know now that devolution was the ultimate outcome, at the time of the campaign, running from February to polling

day on 7 March, it was far from certain that a deal would be possible. And that was primarily down to Ian Paisley, and the ambiguous, all-things-to-all-people strategy he felt forced to employ during the election.

We knew — because senior DUP, Dublin and London sources told us so — that Dr Paisley did indeed want to see the Northern Executive and Assembly restored after the election. We detected, too, a psychological alteration in Dr Paisley after the St Andrews Agreement. We recalled that Friday, 13 October, at St Andrews, when Bertie Ahern presented the DUP leader with a wooden bowl carved from a fallen walnut tree that had stood on the site of the Battle of the Boyne.

That made an impression on Dr Paisley. But what made an impression on the rest of us was his reaction when he said that he hoped that that day would mark the start of a better future for his children and grandchildren and all the people of Ireland, not just the people of Northern Ireland, and indeed not just the unionist people of the North.

He was up for a deal for certain, but would his party and his outside unionist opponents allow him to forge such an historic accommodation with his republican rivals? As the campaign kicked off, there were three factions in the DUP: those who were ready for government; those who would agree to devolution but, like St Augustine, not just yet, dear Lord; and those who would rather wander in the political wilderness than exercise power with Martin McGuinness.

Furthermore, the UK Unionist Party leader, Robert McCartney, was becoming something of a rallying figure for unionist refuseniks. Even in Dr Paisley's backyard of Ballymena, DUP councillors were abandoning the party and the Doc. Hard words were being spoken. This was a splintering of support, rather than the dreaded split, but early in the campaign we wondered would it snowball.

So Dr Paisley had to tread carefully, mindful that unionist opposition to a deal inside and outside the DUP must not be allowed to reach critical mass. Just as republicans stretched out the peace process almost beyond its endurance to ensure relative Sinn Féin and IRA unity, so were Dr Paisley and his key strategist, Peter Robinson, going to play a self-serving game to hold their party together.

During the campaign the stock line was that the prospects of a deal rested solely with Sinn Féin delivering on its commitments. As the campaign rumbled on, we asked again and again whether devolution was possible by the deadline of 26 March, set by the then Northern Secretary, Peter Hain. 'You are not

asking the question of the right person,' was Dr Paisley's standard response. 'You should be asking IRA/Sinn Féin.' But there were no demands for 'sackcloth and ashes' surrender and repentance: he seemed to realise that he must curb his tongue.

It was all down to 'delivery, delivery, delivery,' added North Belfast MP Nigel Dodds, one of the DUP senior sceptics whom Dr Paisley dare not lose from his party. Paisley, with his huge, bombastic, confident personality, had always run a tight ship, but nonetheless there were mutinous mutterings, principally from MEP Jim Allister, who was not even standing and later resigned from the party, but also from the likes of MPs Gregory Campbell and William McCrea, and party chairman Lord (Maurice) Morrow.

Yet, there was an equal underlying sense that Paisley was tuned into the political zeitgeist, that he realised what many in his party did not, that the people were ahead of such politicians and were ready for an agreement. 'We are heartily sick of perpetual political process; do the deal, give our head peace,' was the message.

One of the most telling examples of that general shift in attitude occurred during a canvass with successful DUP candidate Jimmy Spratt in the unionist/loyalist Rathmore Estate in South Belfast early in the campaign. Spratt and a local woman engaged in what was a very Irish circular exchange, where the true message was not explicitly expressed but was implicitly understood.

'As long as you're all working together; isn't that what's important?' the woman repeatedly said to him.

'Absolutely,' Spratt agreed, pointing to his record with other unionists and 'constitutional' nationalists. But what the woman was referring to was working with Sinn Féin. Her message too was simple: get on with it. And Spratt knew it full well.

On the same canvass, Victor Gourley told Spratt that he was certain of his number one vote because he was a good man. But should the DUP enter government with Sinn Féin? *The Irish Times* asked tentatively, expecting a negative response. 'Of course; aren't they elected?' said Mr Gourley.

On that canvass and on virtually every other walkabout, there was no talk of constitutional issues: they just did not register with the public. Whatever about the politicians, the people who would put them into power seemed to feel that these matters, subject of murder and mayhem for so many awful years, were settled.

As the campaign progressed towards polling day, that point was filtering through to the DUP candidates, who subtly, barely discernibly, moderated their message and tone accordingly, to reflect the developing positive public mood.

In the end, Dr Paisley was given a powerful mandate to do the deal. The DUP won 36 seats, up six from the Assembly poll of 2003, double the take of the Ulster Unionists, now firmly vanquished by Dr Paisley — albeit crushed by a policy brazenly stolen from David Trimble and John Hume, but, hey, that's politics. All the Doc's enemies were routed: Robert McCartney fought six seats and didn't make an impact in one, not even in his own North Down constituency where he lost his seat. It was a similar abject tale for the other dissident unionists who challenged him.

Who won on the nationalist battlefront was less critical as both Sinn Féin and the SDLP were ready and willing to share power, just waiting for Dr Paisley. But Gerry Adams was anxious to maintain and extend his primacy over the SDLP. Sinn Féin, too, with its all-Ireland ambitions, was keen that a good result in the election (together with the subsequent power-sharing deal) would provide the bounce for a successful general election in the Republic. (It didn't, but that's a story told elsewhere in this book.)

A number of de-selections had created some disaffection in the Sinn Féin camp, while the SDLP believed that it had a real chance of winning a second and additional seat in Newry and Armagh from Sinn Féin, and perhaps a seat or two extra elsewhere. Moreover, up to a dozen republican dissidents were standing against Sinn Féin, creating minor SDLP optimism that the Sinn Féin percentage vote would suffer.

But, similar to the fate of the unionist rejectionists, the republican purists failed utterly to make an impression. Just as the mood for a deal was with the DUP, so was it with Sinn Féin, which increased its seats from 24 to 28. The SDLP, despite initial hopes, was very disappointed, taking only 16 seats, down two, which meant that it could have only one minister in the Northern Executive.

The Alliance Party made history with the election in South Belfast of Anna Lo, the first Chinese politician to gain a seat to a legislative body in Britain or Ireland. Against the odds, it also won seven seats, up one from the previous election.

The Greens also made a breakthrough in Northern Ireland, with the election of Brian Wilson in North Down. Dawn Purvis retained the Progressive Unionist Party's Belfast East seat won by the late David Ervine. Hospitals candidate Dr Kieran Deeny held his seat in West Tyrone.

When all the votes were counted, we had the makings of a government. Thus was the scene set for those mind-boggling pictures of Ian Paisley and Gerry Adams sitting virtually side-by-side at Stormont on 26 March, and for the ultimate Miracle at Stormont on 8 May, when devolution was restored. It's still hard to credit but it required the Assembly election to make it happen.

Gerry Moriarty is the Northern Editor of *The Irish Times*

Members of the Northern Ireland Executive

Devolution was restored to the Northern Ireland Assembly on 8 May 2007 following the election of a four-party executive of 12 ministers.

First Minister

Ian Paisley, (DUP)
Democratic Unionist Party MP and MLA for North Antrim. Now 81, he concludes a mercurial career as a firebrand politician and preacher by doing what appeared almost unthinkable — sharing power with Sinn Féin. Expected to hand over in the next year or so (most likely to Peter Robinson or, less likely, to Nigel Dodds) and must use the time to prove that the DUP and Sinn Féin can actually work together to make devolution work.

Deputy First Minister

Martin McGuinness, (SF)
Sinn Féin MP for Mid-Ulster, the party's chief negotiator, and former IRA leader. As education minister in the 1998–2003 Assembly, he made his mark by abolishing the controversial 11-plus primary to secondary school transfer exam, to the annoyance of unionist politicians. Achieving a successful working relationship with Dr Paisley is the real test of his personal and political skills.

Agriculture and Rural Development

Michelle Gildernew (SF)
Sinn Féin MP and MLA for Fermanagh and South Tyrone, who overcame her pre-election gaffe about not reporting armed republican dissidents. To the fore in dealing with the dangers posed by the summer 2007 foot-and-mouth scare in England.

Culture, Arts and Leisure

Edwin Poots (DUP)
Democratic Unionist Party MLA for Lagan Valley. Must prove that the DUP, with its perceived anti-fun religious fundamentalist influences, is not a party of philistinism. Sinn Féin will have a difficult time persuading the hard-working Mr Poots to push the Irish-language Act through the Assembly.

Education

Caitriona Ruane (SF)
Sinn Féin MLA for South Down, who is targeting Eddie McGrady's Westminster seat. She will push Irish-language Act, and must also try to find an accommodation with unionism over what will replace the 11-plus exam. Former spokeswoman for the Colombia Three.

Employment and Learning

Sir Reg Empey (UUP)
Ulster Unionist Party leader, MLA for East Belfast. Took more junior of the party's two departments so that he could concentrate on the challenging task of revitalising the party after disastrous Assembly election. Post will suit him as he had similar jobs-promotion portfolio in first Assembly and also on Belfast City Council.

Enterprise, Trade and Investment

Nigel Dodds (DUP)
Democratic Unionist Party MP and MLA for North Belfast. Former successful social development minister, now charged with stimulating the North's tired economy. A hardliner, who came onside with Dr Paisley at the last moment, he holds a brief that will involve him in considerable North–South activity.

Environment

Arlene Foster (DUP)
Democratic Unionist Party MLA for Fermanagh and South Tyrone. A solicitor, she — with Jeffrey Donaldson — was a headline-grabbing defector from the Ulster Unionist Party to the DUP. Believed to have — probably minor — ambitions to take Michelle Gildernew's Westminster seat in the constituency.

Finance and Personnel

Peter Robinson (DUP)
Democratic Unionist Party deputy leader, MP and MLA for East Belfast and the party's chief strategist. He controls the purse strings and must ensure that the departments of nationalist, as well as unionist, ministers are seen to be properly and fairly funded.

Health, Social Services and Public Safety

Michael McGimpsey (UUP)
Ulster Unionist Party MLA for South Belfast, and surprise choice for portfolio, ahead of deputy leader Danny Kennedy and North Down MLA Alan McFarland. Former Assembly minister who will need all his experience to manage this big-budget but tough department.

Regional Development

Conor Murphy (SF)
Sinn Féin MP and MLA for Newry and Armagh, and former IRA prisoner. Rapidly promoted in recent years through the party to stand alongside Adams, McGuinness and Kelly as one of the key republican players.

Social Development

Margaret Ritchie (SDLP)
Social Democratic and Labour Party MLA for South Down, the SDLP's only minister and also a prospect to replace Eddie McGrady as MP for the constituency. Has hugely difficult task of trying to achieve affordable housing in Northern Ireland.

Junior ministers

In the office of the First and Deputy First Ministers

Ian Paisley Jr, DUP MLA, and Gerry Kelly, Sinn Féin MLA.

Gerry Kelly, Sinn Féin MLA for North Belfast, former IRA prisoner, must ensure that Dr Paisley does not steal a march on Martin McGuinness.

Northern Ireland Assembly results

Antrim East

Electorate	56,666
Turnout	30,293
Spoiled Votes	254
Total Valid Poll	30,039
Percentage Turnout	53.46
Quota	4,292
Candidates	14

Count	1
*Sammy Wilson (DUP)	6,755
*George Dawson (DUP)(1)	4,167
*Sean Neeson (All)	3,114
*Roy Beggs (UUP)	3,076
*David Hilditch (DUP)	2,732
*Ken Robinson (UUP)	1,881
Danny O'Connor (SDLP)	1,769
Stewart Dickson (All)	1,624
Mark Dunn (UUP)	1,617
Oliver McMullan (SF)	1,168
Tom Robinson (UKU)	731
Mark Bailey (Green)	612
John Anderson (Ind)	398
Tim Lewis (C)	395

(1) George Dawson died on 7 May 2007 and was replaced by Alastair Ian Ross, whose appointment was notified by the Chief Electoral Officer with effect from 14 May 2007.
* Elected in 2003

Antrim North

Electorate	72,814
Turnout	44,655
Spoiled Votes	324
Total Valid Poll	44,331
Percentage Turnout	61.33
Quota	6,334
Candidates	13

Count	1
*Ian Paisley (DUP)	7,716
Daithi McKay (SF)	7,065
*Ian Paisley Jnr (DUP)	6,106
*Mervyn Storey (DUP)	5,171
+Robert Coulter (UUP)	5,047
Declan O'Loan (SDLP)	3,281
Deirdre Nelson (DUP)	2,740
Orla Black (SDLP)	2,129
Lyle Cubitt (UKU)	1,848
Robert Swann (UUP)	1,281
Jayne Dunlop (All)	1,254
Paul McGlinchey (Ind Rep)	383
James Gregg (Ind)	310

* Elected in 2003
+ Elected in 2003 from another constituency

Antrim South

Electorate	65,654
Turnout	38,481
Spoiled Votes	306
Total Valid Poll	38,175
Percentage Turnout	58.61
Quota	5,455
Candidates	14

Count	1
+Mitchel McLaughlin (SF)	6,313
+William McCrea (DUP)	6,023
*David Ford (All)	5,007
*David Burnside (UUP)	4,507
Trevor Clarke (DUP)	4,302
Mel Lucas (DUP)	2,840
*Thomas Burns (SDLP)	2,721
Danny Kinahan (UUP)	2,391
Noreen McClelland (SDLP)	1,526
Stephen Nicholl (UUP)	927
+Robert McCartney (UKU)	893
Pete Whitcroft (Green)	507
Stephen O'Brien (C)	129
Marcella Delaney (WP)	89

* Elected in 2003
+ Elected in 2003 from another constituency

Belfast East

Electorate	49,757
Turnout	29,631
Spoiled Votes	0
Total Valid Poll	29,631
Percentage Turnout	59.55
Quota	4,234
Candidates	15

Count	1
*Peter Robinson (DUP)	5,635
*Naomi Long (All)	5,585
*Reg Empey (UUP)	4,139
Wallace Browne (DUP)	3,185
Dawn Purvis (PUP)	3,045
*Robin Newton (DUP)	2,335
*Michael Copeland (UUP)	1,557
Niall Ó Donnghaile (SF)	1,055
Jim Rodgers (UUP)	820
Mary Muldoon (SDLP)	816
Steve Agnew (Green)	653
Glyn Chambers (C)	427
Thomas Black (Soc)	225
Joe Bell (WP)	107
Rainbow George (MPH)	47

* Elected in 2003

Belfast North

Electorate	49,372
Turnout	30,067
Spoiled Votes	352
Total Valid Poll	29,715
Percentage Turnout	60.9
Quota	4,246
Candidates	14

Count	1
*Nigel Dodds (DUP)	6,973
*Gerry Kelly (SF)	5,414
Caral Ní Chuilin (SF)	3,680
*Fred Cobain (UUP)	2,498
*Nelson McCausland (DUP)	2,462
*Alban Maginness (SDLP)	2,212
Pat Convery (SDLP)	1,868
William Humphrey (DUP)	1,673
Raymond McCord (Ind)	1,320
Peter Emerson (Green)	590
Tommy McCullough (All)	486
+Robert McCartney (UKU)	360
John Lavery (WP)	139
Rainbow George (MPH)	40

* Elected in 2003
+ Elected in 2003 from another constituency

Belfast South

Electorate	48,923
Turnout	30,533
Spoiled Votes	189
Total Valid Poll	30,344
Percentage Turnout	62.41
Quota	4,336
Candidates	18

Count	1
Jimmy Spratt (DUP)	4,762
*Alasdair McDonnell (SDLP)	4,379
*Alex Maskey (SF)	3,996
Anna Lo (All)	3,829
*Carmel Hanna (SDLP)	3,748
*Michael McGimpsey (UUP)	2,647
Christopher Stalford (DUP)	2,035
*Esmond Birnie (UUP)	1,804
Bob Stoker (UUP)	1,122
Brenda Cooke (Green)	737
Andrew Park (PUP)	410
David Hoey (UKU)	298
Jim Barbour (Soc)	248
Paddy Lynn (WP)	123
Roger Lomas (C)	108
Rainbow George (MPH)	66
Charles Smyth (Capitalism)	22
Geoffrey Wilson (Ind)	10

* Elected in 2003

Belfast West

Electorate	50,792
Turnout	34,238
Spoiled Votes	448
Total Valid Poll	33,790
Percentage Turnout	67.41
Quota	4,828
Candidates	14

Count	1
*Gerry Adams (SF)	6,029
++Sue Ramsey (SF)	4,715
Paul Maskey (SF)	4,368
Jennifer McCann (SF)	4,265
*Fra McCann (SF)	4,254
*Diane Dodds (DUP)	3,661
*Alex Attwood (SDLP)	3,036
Margaret Walsh (SDLP)	1,074
Seán Mitchell (People)	774
Louis West (UUP)	558
John Lowry (WP)	434
Geraldine Taylor (Rep SF)	427
Dan McGuinness (All)	127
Rainbow George (MPH)	68

* Elected in 2003
++ Appointed to 2003–07 Assembly to fill a vacancy

North Down

Electorate	57,525
Turnout	30,930
Spoiled Votes	223
Total Valid Poll	30,707
Percentage Turnout	53.77
Quota	4,388
Candidates	16

Count	1
*Alex Easton (DUP)	4,946
*Peter Weir (DUP)	3,376
Stephen Farry (All)	3,131
*Leslie Cree (UUP)	2,937
Brian Wilson (Green)	2,839
*Alan McFarland (UUP)	2,245
Alan Graham (DUP)	2,147
Marion Smith (UUP)	2,098
*Robert McCartney (UKU)	1,806
Brian Rowan (Ind)	1,194
Alan Chambers (Ind)	1,129
Liam Logan (SDLP)	1,115
James Leslie (C)	864
Deaglan Page (SF)	390
Elaine Martin (PUP)	367
Chris Carter (Ind)	123

* Elected in 2003

South Down

Electorate	71,704
Turnout	46,623
Spoiled Votes	513
Total Valid Poll	46,110
Percentage Turnout	65.02
Quota	6,588
Candidates	16

Count	1
*Caitriona Ruane (SF)	6,334
*Margaret Ritchie (SDLP)	5,838
*P.J. Bradley (SDLP)	5,652
*Jim Wells (DUP)	5,542
*Willie Clarke (SF)	5,138
John McCallister (UUP)	4,447
Michael Carr (SDLP)	2,972
Eamonn McConvey (SF)	2,662
William Burns (DUP)	2,611
Ciaran Mussen (Green)	1,622
Henry Reilly (UKIP)	1,229
David Griffin (All)	691
Martin Cunningham (Ind)	434
Nelson Wharton (UKU)	424
Peter Bowles (C)	391
Malachi Curran (Lab)	123

* Elected in 2003

Fermanagh and South Tyrone

Electorate	65,826
Turnout	46,845
Spoiled Votes	403
Total Valid Poll	46,442
Percentage Turnout	71.16
Quota	6,636
Candidates	13

Count	1
*Arlene Foster (DUP)	7,138
*Michelle Gildernew (SF)	7,026
*Tom Elliott (UUP)	6,603
Gerry McHugh (SF)	5,103
Sean Lynch (SF)	4,704
*Maurice Morrow (DUP)	4,700
Tommy Gallagher (SDLP)	4,440
Kenny Donaldson (UUP)	2,531
Vincent Currie (SDLP)	2,043
Gerry McGeough (Ind Rep)	814
Allan Leonard (All)	521
Michael McManus (Rep SF)	431
+Robert McCartney (UKU)	388

* Elected in 2003
+ Elected in 2003 from another constituency

Foyle

Electorate	64,889
Turnout	41,455
Spoiled Votes	419
Total Valid Poll	41,036
Percentage Turnout	63.89
Quota	5,863
Candidates	14

Count	1
*William Hay (DUP)	6,960
*Mark Durkan (SDLP)	6,401
Martina Anderson (SF)	5,414
*Raymond McCartney (SF)	4,321
*Pat Ramsey (SDLP)	3,242
Lynn Fleming (SF)	2,914
*Mary Bradley (SDLP)	2,891
Helen Quigley (SDLP)	2,648
Eamonn McCann (Soc Env)	2,045
Peggy O'Hara (Ind Rep)	1,789
Peter Munce (UUP)	1,755
Adele Corry (Green)	359
Yvonne Boyle (All)	224
Willie Frazer (Ind U)	73

* Elected in 2003

Lagan Valley

Electorate	70,101
Turnout	42,058
Spoiled Votes	236
Total Valid Poll	41,822
Percentage Turnout	60
Quota	5,976
Candidates	14

Count	1
*Jeffrey Donaldson (DUP)	9,793
Paul Butler (SF)	5,098
Basil McCrea (UUP)	4,031
Trevor Lunn (All)	3,765
Jonathan Craig (DUP)	3,471
*Edwin Poots (DUP)	3,457
Paul Givan (DUP)	3,377
++Marietta Farrell (SDLP)	2,839
*Billy Bell (UUP)	2,599
Ronnie Crawford (UUP)	1,147
Michael Rogan (Green)	922
+Robert McCartney (UKU)	853
Neil Johnston (C)	387
John Magee (WP)	83

* Elected in 2003
+ Elected in 2003 from another constituency
++ Appointed to 2003–07 Assembly to fill a vacancy

Northern Ireland Assembly results

Londonderry East

Electorate	56,104
Turnout	34,180
Spoiled Votes	258
Total Valid Poll	33,922
Percentage Turnout	60.92
Quota	4,847
Candidates	15

Count	1
*Gregory Campbell (DUP)	**6,845**
*Francie Brolly (SF)	**4,476**
*George Robinson (DUP)	**3,991**
*David McClarty (UUP)	**2,875**
Adrian McQuillan (DUP)	**2,650**
*John Dallat (SDLP)	**2,638**
Billy Leonard (SF)	2,321
*Norman Hillis (UUP)	2,054
Orla Beattie (SDLP)	1,797
Barney Fitzpatrick (All)	1,401
Edwin Stevenson (UUP)	1,338
Leslie Cubitt (UKU)	549
Phillippe Moison (Green)	521
Michael McGonigle (Rep SF)	393
Victor Christie (Ind)	73

* Elected in 2003

Newry and Armagh

Electorate	70,823
Turnout	50,165
Spoiled Votes	546
Total Valid Poll	49,619
Percentage Turnout	70.83
Quota	7,089
Candidates	12

Count	1
*Conor Murphy (SF)	**7,437**
Cathal Boylan (SF)	**7,105**
*Danny Kennedy (UUP)	**6,517**
William Irwin (DUP)	**6,418**
Mickey Brady (SF)	**6,337**
*Dominic Bradley (SDLP)	**5,318**
Sharon Haughey (SDLP)	4,500
*Paul Berry (Ind U)	2,317
*Davy Hyland (Ind Rep)	2,188
Willie Frazer (Ind U)	605
Arthur Morgan (Green)	599
Máire Hendron (All)	278

* Elected in 2003

Strangford

Electorate	66,648
Turnout	36,340
Spoiled Votes	321
Total Valid Poll	36,019
Percentage Turnout	54.53
Quota	5,147
Candidates	15

Count	1
*Iris Robinson (DUP)	**5,917**
*Jim Shannon (DUP)	**4,788**
*Kieran McCarthy (All)	**4,085**
Simon Hamilton (DUP)	**3,889**
*David McNarry (UUP)	**3,709**
Michelle McIlveen (DUP)	**3,468**
Joe Boyle (SDLP)	3,068
Angus Carson (UUP)	2,128
Dermot Kennedy (SF)	1,089
*George Ennis (UKU)	872
Stephanie Sim (Green)	868
Michael Henderson (UUP)	675
David Gregg (Ind)	650
Bob Little (C)	508
Cedric Wilson (Ind U)	305

* Elected in 2003

Tyrone West

Electorate	58,367
Turnout	41,839
Spoiled Votes	385
Total Valid Poll	41,454
Percentage Turnout	71.68
Quota	5,923
Candidates	12

Count	1
*Barry McElduff (SF)	**6,971**
*Pat Doherty (SF)	**6,709**
Clare McGill (SF)	**4,757**
*Tom Buchanan (DUP)	**4,625**
Allan Bresland (DUP)	**4,244**
*Kieran Deeny (Ind)	**3,776**
*Derek Hussey (UUP)	3,686
Josephine Deehan (SDLP)	2,689
*Eugene McMenamin (SDLP)	2,272
Seamus Shiels (SDLP)	1,057
Joe O'Neill (Rep SF)	448
+Robert McCartney (UKU)	220

* Elected in 2003
+ Elected in 2003 from another constituency

Mid Ulster

Electorate	61,223
Turnout	44,728
Spoiled Votes	451
Total Valid Poll	44,277
Percentage Turnout	73.06
Quota	6,326
Candidates	12

Count	1
*Martin McGuinness (SF)	**8,065**
Ian McCrea (DUP)	**7,608**
*Francie Molloy (SF)	**6,597**
Michelle O'Neill (SF)	**6,432**
*Patsy McGlone (SDLP)	**4,976**
*Billy Armstrong (UUP)	**4,781**
Kate Lagan (SDLP)	2,759
Walter Millar (UKU)	1,210
Ann Forde (DUP)	1,021
Brendan McLaughlin (Rep SF)	437
Margaret Marshall (All)	221
Harry Hutchinson (Ind)	170

* Elected in 2003

Upper Bann

Electorate	70,716
Turnout	43,235
Spoiled Votes	353
Total Valid Poll	42,882
Percentage Turnout	61.14
Quota	6,127
Candidates	16

Count	1
*John O'Dowd (SF)	**7,733**
*David Simpson (DUP)	**6,828**
*Samuel Gardiner (UUP)	**5,135**
*Dolores Kelly (SDLP)	**4,689**
*Stephen Moutray (DUP)	**3,663**
Dessie Ward (SF)	3,118
Jnr McCrum (DUP)	2,975
George Savage (UUP)	**2,167**
Arnold Hatch (UUP)	1,815
David Calvert (ND)	1,332
Helen Corry (Green)	1,156
Sheila McQuaid (All)	798
Pat McAleenan (SDLP)	761
Barry Toman (Rep SF)	386
David Fry (C)	248
Suzanne Peeples (Ind)	78

* Elected in 2003

Proposed Heuston Gateway

Proposed New Market Square

Dublin
An Economic Success

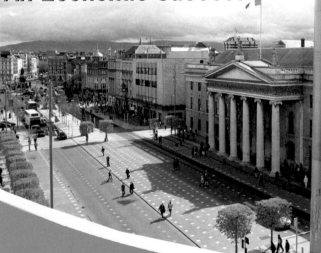

- Attracting **Inward Investment**
- **Promoting** Inner City Living
- Securing **Economic Development** for the City
- Facilitating **Development**
- Working in **partnership** with **key agencies**

For further information contact:
Economic Development Unit, Dublin City Council,
Block 4, Floor 3, Civic Offices, Dublin 8.
Email edu@dublincity.ie
Tel 01 222 0100 Fax 01 222 2278

Dublin City
Baile Átha Cliath

Index

Index

Advertisers